C000261141

"It is stunning . . . he ran great
identities and suffering extrac
strength of the book is that he
humourless campaigning and m;
than a travel book, yet as enter.
Sunday Express

"Monbiot is fascinating about the forest, the birds, the plants and,
above all, the people. His descriptions of the various tribes and
their beliefs are both erudite and affecting in their warmth. He is
also extremely funny. . . . Running through this book is, of course,
the self-portrait. And very charming it is. Monbiot is a man one
would be proud to travel with. Perhaps it's that which makes it a
good travel book"—*Sunday Telegraph*

"Their adventures in Irian read like *Raiders of the Lost Ark* as they
tricked their way past Indonesian police, army and spies, hacked
their way over unmapped mountains and forests, and lived with
tribes who were often paralysed with trauma. But although the
book reflects Monbiot's experiences and personal feelings, it avoids
the tacky journalese of many other investigative authors. The result
is astonishing: part travelogue, part anthropology and the rest well-
researched political journalism"—*New Scientist*

"A cross between Redmond O'Hanlon and John Pilger: outlandish tropical fauna and well-served outrage . . . Monbiot himself is honest, engaging and modest, and there aren't too many
writers like that left"—*Sunday Correspondent*

"This is no frivolous jaunt . . . Monbiot gallantly risks his own life
and that of his friend Adrian to bring back his disturbing
report"—*Mail on Sunday*

"George Monbiot's fresh, often amusing account offsets the young
author's wonder at the untouched natural beauty of the place with
his horror at the systematic genocide being waged against its
ancient tribal culture"—*Sunday Telegraph*

"A book that everyone should read"—*Norman Lewis*

POISONED ARROWS

An investigative journey to the
forbidden territories of West Papua

george monbiot

GREEN BOOKS

This edition published in 2003
by Green Books Ltd
Foxhole, Dartington
Totnes, Devon TQ9 6EB
edit@greenbooks.co.uk   www.greenbooks.co.uk

Original edition published in Great Britain
by Michael Joseph Ltd 1989

First published in paperback in 1989 by Sphere Books

Printed by MPG Books, Bodmin, Cornwall

ISBN 1 903998 27 1

George Monbiot is the author of *The Age of Consent: a manifesto for a new world order* and *Captive State: the corporate takeover of Britain*. His other books include *Amazon Watershed* and *No Man's Land*. He is a columnist for *The Guardian* and Visiting Professor of Planning at Oxford Brookes University. He has held visiting professorships or fellowships at the universities of Oxford (environmental policy), Bristol (philosophy), Keele (politics) and East London (environmental science).

LIST OF ILLUSTRATIONS

TO ADRIAN

For obvious reasons certain names and minor details in this account have been changed.

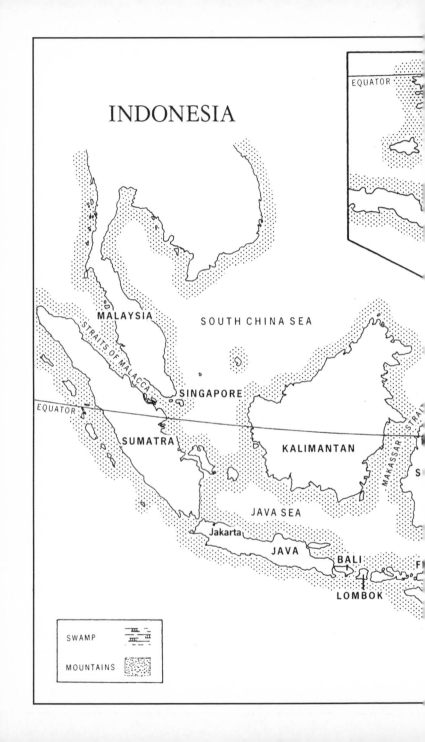

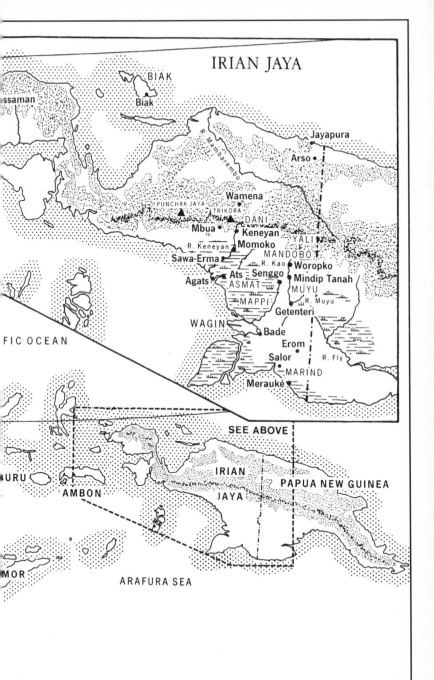

Preface to the 2003 edition

It is a measure of this book's failure that, sixteen years after I began to research it, and fourteen years after it was first published, it has lost none of its relevance. Naïve, optimistic, presumptious, I believed, in 1987, that books could change the world. Given that I haven't stopped writing, I suppose some part of me believes it still.

This is not to say that there is no point in writing, and certainly not to say that there is no point in campaigning. Indeed, it is arguable that no political change of any kind can take place today without both. But what I believed sixteen years ago was that simply by documenting and exposing oppression, and joining the campaigns against it, I would participate in an inexorable process of bringing it to an end. I underestimated the great noise of competing sources of information, the brief attention span of the media, and the obdurate will of the powerful. *Poisoned Arrows* was widely and warmly reviewed, sold well and generated a good deal of public debate. But it changed nothing and was, as a result, a failure. The battles which needed to be fought in 1987 still need to be fought today.

Soon after *Poisoned Arrows* was first published, the Berlin Wall was demolished and the Cold War came to an end. Indonesia ceased to be seen as a key Western asset in the struggle against communism. But those who imagined that this would result in the immediate liberation of its people were wrong. President Suharto, the dictator whose entire political career had been an artefact of the Cold War, remained in office until 1998. Even then, he was effectively deposed by the International Monetary Fund, whose disastrous policies had all but destroyed the Indonesian economy. Like all dictators, Suharto had sustained his power through a combination of fear and hypnosis. The people of Indonesia knew that he would never hesitate to spill their blood when they questioned his authority. Partly as a result, they had continued to believe in that authority and its persistence, almost as they might believe in a god.

The new government promised to review the status of the people of East Timor, the nation which Suharto, with the approval of the Western powers, had annexed in 1975. In 1999, the East Timorese voted, in a referendum organised by the United Nations, for independence. The Indonesian army sought, through terrorising the population with the help of the civilian militias it had armed, to prevent them from breaking away. But, after a great deal of bloodshed, the militias were driven back, and in 2001 East Timor elected its first independent government.

The people of West Papua, the territory annexed by Indonesia in 1963, and which this book mostly concerns, might have expected to be permitted to make a similar choice. There is little doubt that the indigenous people there want independence just as badly as the East Timorese did. But the major difference between East Timor and West Papua, as far as the Indonesian authorities are concerned, is that West Papua has abundant and valuable natural resources. These have been plundered since the territory was seized in 1963, and their exploitation is now the principal means by which the army units stationed there finance themselves. West Papua is regarded as a source of free wealth by senior army officers, and is considered too valuable to release.

So, while its people have asked for independence, they have instead been given something which the government calls "autonomy", but which appears to have enhanced the freedom only of the soldiers stationed there. In principle, the Papuans are permitted a measure of self-government and a share in the proceeds of the resources extracted from their land. In practice, their timber, minerals, fish, sago and land continue to be stolen, while their attempts to establish their own peaceful political organisations have been ruthlessly curtailed. In November 2001, just one month after the government announced that West Papua would be granted "special autonomy", Theys Eluay, chairman of the newly-formed Papuan Presidium Council, was abducted by soldiers and killed.

Scores of other political leaders have been imprisoned and tortured. In 2001, the Swiss journalist Oswald Iten spent 11 days in jail in West Papua, during which he watched political prisoners being beaten and kicked to death. Just as it did in East Timor, the army has established civilian militias in West Papua, composed of migrants from other islands. Among them are groups now controlled by Muslim extremist organisations of the kind believed to have been responsible for the bomb attack in Bali in 2002. Britain and the United States continue to sell arms to Indonesia, many of which are used by its soldiers in West Papua. In 2001, the US Ambassador, Robert Gelbard, revealed that his government was providing direct military assistance to the troops attacking the separatist movements there.

Since this book was first published, much of the territory has been stripped of its resources. In 2001, the environmental group Walhi predicted that West Papua's forests would be logged out by 2015. Oil palm plantations keep expanding, the Freeport mine continues to dump its waste into the rivers and the Papuans who seek to resist these operations are still being killed by the army.

The one positive development is that the transmigration programme has all but ceased to exist. In 1994, the World Bank published a review of the scheme, which confirmed the allegations made in this book. Though it has failed to compensate the people who lost their land and their livelihoods, it has been forced to stop supporting the programme. The financial crisis of 1997 and 1998 meant that the Indonesian government was also deprived of the means to fund it. Spontaneous migrants continue to arrive in West Papua, many of whom are used as cheap labour to assist the army's theft of the territory's resources. The Indonesian government has yet to announce that the transmigration programme is dead, and some Papuans fear that it might resume as the economy recovers.

At the end of the first edition there was a petition addressed to the United Nations, requesting that UN observers be sent to West Papua, and that donor nations should impose humanitarian conditions on the grants and loans they made. Many thousands of signatures were sent to the UN, which failed even to acknowledge their receipt. This time, I think it would be better if you joined one of the many campaign groups which have emerged or developed over the past 14 years. West Papuans and their supporters have not given up the fight for freedom: as the East Timor campaign showed, a demand which looks impossible during times of political stasis suddenly becomes irresistible during periods of flux. Our effort must be to sustain our campaigns until we encounter the conditions which permit their fulfilment. There is a list of the names and addresses of some of the most effective groups at the back of this book.

I have not returned to West Papua since 1988, but both Adrian and I have continued to meet exiles and visitors from the territory, and to seek to stay in touch with events there. After *Poisoned*

Arrows was published, I worked in Brazil for couple of years, then, with Adrian, in East Africa. Somehow, despite the tensions of working together, we have remained best friends. We have both continued to work as campaigning journalists. I have written several other books on human rights and government corruption. Adrian has worked on human rights and development issues all over the world. Some of his photographs can be seen at www.arbib.org.

It has been a strange experience reading *Poisoned Arrows* again. It is so long since I wrote it that I had forgotten most of what happened to us. I have caught myself asking, was that really me?, was I really there? Then a word or a phrase will suddenly lodge in my mind, and I will remember a smell, or the intermittent warmth of forest sunlight on my skin, or the steam rising from a rock by the river. Then the emotions associated with that episode return: the wonder, the horror and the intense, grinding fear, which stayed with me for months after I came home. Only then do I begin to remember what happened, and to confirm to myself that the half-formed man in this book was me.

The prose style of a 24 year-old is seldom exhilarating, but I'm glad to say that though I was an incompetent author, I did not make the mistake of attempting to overdress it. It is a plain tale, plainly told, without elegance or grace. Fortunately, the story appears to be compelling enough to carry the reader along. In quite a few places I have felt compelled to make minor alterations, where the original copy was confusing or particularly clumsy, or where a statement has subsequently turned out to be incorrect. The most significant alteration is the use of the term "West Papua" throughout the text. The first edition used the Indonesian government's name for the territory: "Irian Jaya". The Papuans who read it protested that they have never accepted that name for their land, and have never regarded themselves as "Irianese". Apart from that, I have tried to change as little as possible. I am sorry to say that it is still worth reading.

Oxford
March 2003

Chapter 1

Walisi came barefooted over the reef, waving something for us to see. We picked across to meet him, taking care not to tread on a stonefish, or one of the seasnakes that Walisi's children had insisted on finding for us. In the old man's hand was a rotten fish, impaled on a piece of cane, with a string noose dangling close to its tail. I had no notion of what he was going to do with it, as Walisi had a boundless repertoire of tricks and deliberate mystique. When he knew he'd intrigued us he turned and loped off along the dry reef platform. The yellow light of the late afternoon flattened him against the reef, a crafty, crop-headed old man, messing about with a bit of local magic until the tide came in. Beyond him the water rocked against the platform, and beyond that there was a swarm of coral islands, each like our own, with its hedge of palm trees and little haze of clouds. Walisi stopped sharply and pointed to a hole in the sand, just a finger's width across. He squatted beside it, making no effort to enlighten us, and brushed away the broken coral at the edge of the hole, opening it up until he could fit the fish inside. He shoved it down gently, until only the top of the cane and a tail of string were sticking out, and replaced the bits of coral.

Walisi winked at us, then rolled a cigarette on his thigh, spinning out the mystery. We couldn't help but play his game, staring at the hole and twitching with curiosity. He began to clap, loudly and solemnly, and as he did so the bit of cane started to tremble, minutely at first, then fiercely, juddering against the rocks. The string shot towards the hole, and Walisi stuck out a hand and grabbed it. His arm was wrenched towards the sand. He struggled to haul the string up, water spouted from the vent, and out of it burst the strangest thing I'd ever seen, thrashing and splattering in a little pool of sea water. It tried to impale Walisi's hands with sharp spikes jutting from its forearms. It looked like a lobster whose body had condensed around its shoulders and, like a boxer, it jabbed fiercely to the left and right. Walisi pushed it down by its

1

head, half-burying those hideous arms in the sand, and wound string all down the body until he'd tied it up. He held it up by the noose and said "Supper."

Walisi's mantis shrimp was just one of a host of things that I, a supposed zoologist, had never heard about before I got to Wekri Island, among the swarm of atolls north of Java. When the tide came over the reef it brought once a giant cuttlefish, perhaps a metre long, that we met among the shoals of coloured fish when we were snorkelling and, in a way, conversed with. When I wiggled my fingers it blushed deep brown with curiosity and came right up, staring into my mask with soft cowlike eyes. If I swished my hand in front of it, it'd turn yellow with fright and dart back a yard, then edge subtly towards me again, unable to keep its emotions from its skin. There were eels too, two metres long and just one or two centimetres in width, in black and white hoops; and compound anemones like lunar trees, black, velvet and suddenly inflammatory, several minutes after contact. Wekri Island, we allowed ourselves to believe, was our discovery, for its only other visitors were the two Dutch girls we'd arrived with. My old friend Adrian Arbib and myself, on a spontaneous month's holiday in Indonesia, believed we'd found what all the tourist brochures promise but never produce.

Indonesia then—in 1985—had been nothing to me but a break from England. We had tripped around Java and seen, it seems now, nothing that was not put there for us to see. After wandering through Bali and Lombok then tiring a little of the trenchant holiday trail, we moved out with the two friends we'd made in Java to see the Thousand Islands. The first of these were just an hour's sailing from Jakarta, but we paid a boatman to take us further north, until we'd passed by all the traces of tourism, and got in amongst the undiminished atolls inhabited only by fishermen. Walisi was the first man we'd met as we stumbled up the beach of Wekri Island, and he had agreed to keep us in his house for a small price. All we did for two hot weeks was swim and eat and sleep; the last above the high tide, that came in among the stilts of the house at night. I can properly say that the time I spent there held less anxiety than any other I can remember. It now seems so odd to me, so hard to understand, that Indonesia then had no associations but enchantment.

I have learnt to hate such enlightenment, that seems to make everything look dark. Things wilt when you stare at them too hard, and find out how they work, and why they've become what they are. Indonesia was gentle, happy and as simple as a picture postcard in 1985, for I blissfully knew no better: it was all sun and sealife then. Any knowledge I carried back was just in the form of some potential illumination, a fascination with the place that could one day show me that all was not as I had seen it. Indeed I would have been a cold reef-living fish if I had failed to be fascinated. Adrian and I had trodden on just four of Indonesia's fourteen thousand islands. The country whose inner provinces we had trifled with on holiday was three thousand miles wide—wider, that is, than the United States—and within it were the least-changed of all tropical places, without the faintest mark of white men or their world. Among the people of Indonesia, the fifth most numerous on earth, were cultures as far apart as any could be, from the most technologically sophisticated to colourful, quite extraordinary, tribal societies, whose members had yet to encounter metal. To spend a month in a country, yet to see just the tiniest fraction of it, can only be intriguing to someone from a place like England.

For two years the fascination that I carried back was of little use to me. Back in Britain I joined the BBC, working first on natural history radio programmes, then on current affairs for the World Service. Adrian, a professional photographer, left his dissatisfactions in England and found work in Denver, in the States. At first my jobs were stimulating, instructive, all that they should have been; but disillusionment came to me quickly. Current affairs became depressingly regular: every day there was a new programme to make, every day the work of the day before had been rendered worthless. I wanted something bigger, with an end.

The work I did was also incomplete. There were great sections of the world that seemed never to be covered, on either our news or anyone else's, and I began to feel after a bit that they suffered from their lack of coverage: there were no correctives to keep the excesses of leadership in check. Rumours, often of stories far greater than those that we actually ran, came sporadically from these black holes. I began to follow them as closely as I could, picking up stories from exiles and returning travellers, and friends in human rights and environmental groups. I was looking for something big enough to carry an entirely absorbing project, with endpoints, that would justify overturning my comfortable existence. I played with several ideas, but none of them leapt out at me.

When the story I was waiting for arrived it was not the tales of horror and destruction that first made me sit up and take notice, but the name and its associations—of sun and sealife and fascination—that came at the front of it: Indonesia. When I tuned into what I heard, over lunch with a friend campaigning for a human rights group, I realised he was talking of something quite astonishing. Over the next few weeks I followed it up with others who knew a little, and found myself piecing together a picture that, though fragmentary and unconfirmed, suggested an issue dark enough, and sweeping enough, to justify abandoning my livelihood.

At the far Pacific end of Indonesia, quite literally a continent apart from the little coral island where Walisi caught the mantis shrimp, was the remotest tropical place on earth. In West Papua, one half of the old island of New Guinea, were people who used stone tools, and fought their tribal wars with wooden-headed arrows. In the mountains the tribespeople, naked in the bitter cold, were so removed from the outside world that they had no common language with their neighbours in adjacent valleys. In the southern swamps, the world's largest and least-penetrable, there was still headhunting and cannibalism. It was the last place on earth where unknown tribes were still likely to exist. In that province, which the Indonesians called "Irian Jaya", there was said to be evolving a holocaust as horrendous as Stalin's purgings of the Soviet ethnic groups. The government of Indonesia had embarked on a scheme to wipe its tribal people out. And the method it was using was so callous, so simply destructive, that it was eliminating both the tribes themselves, and the people sent out to despatch them.

Though the people of West Papua might have appeared barbarous to western eyes, they were said by anthropologists to have evolved a social structure and a welfare system more stable and more accommodating than anything we knew in the developed world. They had lived in more or less the same way for something like fifty thousand years, and learnt to use the forests they inhabited without destroying them. They had in those forests developed a culture of extraordinary colour and complexity, distinct in every way from that of other people. They, in West Papua, and the tribal groups in the other outer islands were said, however, to be an embarrassment to the government. Their existence was an affront

4

to the country's progressive, developed view of itself, they were a focus for political discontent, and they held up the lucrative development projects the government wanted to start on their land. In West Papua especially the tribal people caused trouble for the administration. They believed they had no right to be ruled from Jakarta, as they were a different race with a different lifestyle, living on a different continent. They claimed that their country was taken over unfairly, without their consent, by Indonesia, and they backed up their claim by trying to fight, with poisoned arrows and wooden spears, the army sent by the fifth largest nation in the world. The Indonesians, the human rights campaigners said, had found a way of wiping out not just those rebels, but the lives of the whole one million tribal, racially different people that lived in those wildest lands.

In Java, two and a half thousand miles from the jungles of West Papua, there was a population crisis. Through good health care and sanitation many more children had survived than in earlier times, and now on that island the size of England there were a hundred and five million people. The farmers were running out of land and the people in the towns were short of work: the crisis in some parts threatened to become a catastrophe. That situation, so the campaigners said, was the government's excuse for eliminating its embarrassments in the distant provinces.

The Indonesian government was in the middle of a scheme to move out sixty-five million of the crowded Javanese and send them to the outer islands. While the government claimed that its purpose was the redistribution of the poor, the campaigners said that the motive had become perverted. The gigantic project, bigger in its plans than any other official migration in the world, was designed to replace those disaffected tribal people with loyal and developed Javanese. In the distant outer islands it was, quite literally, wiping them out. Their lands were being taken, their villages destroyed, and their traditions brutally suppressed. When they resisted—and whole tribal groups had—they were eliminated. Those who escaped the soldiers were pushed towards bewilderment, reputedly starvation, and eventual extinction, without resources and in an alien culture that made no room for them. Even the migrants were said to be in substantial trouble, for they found themselves dumped, by ruthless ambitions of the government, on infertile soils that couldn't support them, with no money, no contact, no means of escape, among the hostile people they'd displaced. There were, moreover, said to be substantial foreign interests involved: American, European and Australian. At that stage, however, they were not at all clear to me.

That was the version that the human rights groups told. The government, as I found out from material that ministers had written, told a very different story. It said that the migration project—or 'transmigration' as it was called—was a simple humanitarian programme. There was an enormous problem in Java. People were desperate for land and employment there, and their situation was quickly getting worse. Every year, as the population rose, there were two million more beings on that one little island, and there was simply nowhere for them to go. West Papua and the other outer islands, where the population hadn't risen for thousands of years, were almost empty by comparison. The most obvious solution to the troubles in Java was to give some of the crowded people empty lands in the outer provinces. Transmigration gave the migrants a boost, helped to relieve the pressure in Java and incidentally brought considerable benefits to the tribal people. While parts of Indonesia had been enjoying the advantages of development, the big outer islands had been left out. Transmigration brought their people roads, factories and jobs, and helped them pull out of their undeveloped ways. Nearly all the land the programme used was empty, and where local people had to be moved from their houses, they had a chance to learn the improved techniques of the migrants and become settled farmers. Transmigration, the government said, did nothing but good.

For better or worse it seemed that the Indonesian government would never achieve that extraordinary target of moving sixty-five million people. Already the project had been through a steep decline, when the country had run out of money, and the numbers of people being moved from Java had dropped to a trickle. It was a fabulously expensive project. By 1986 four million transmigrants had left Java, for places like Sumatra and Kalimantan, and they had cost the government seven billion US dollars. In 1987, however, as the economy slowly mended, it seemed that transmigration was picking up again. The government had restated its initial target, and people were predicting that perhaps twenty million or so would eventually get to move. Sumatra and Kalimantan had suffered, so the campaigners said, some of the troubles that West

Papua was beginning to face. The migrants sent there had wrecked the remarkable forests, driven out the tribal people and, in places, found themselves in terminal trouble. Now the programme was to be concentrated on West Papua, with a greater zeal and intensity than the other islands had felt. The reason for that, the campaigners said, was historical.

The Indonesian government had, it seemed, made enemies of most of the Papuan people, when it took charge of their country in 1963. West Papua, as all of Indonesia had once been, was a part of the vast Dutch maritime empire, the Dutch East Indies. When the rest of Indonesia got its independence from Holland, in 1950, the Dutch argued strongly that they should exclude West Papua (or West New Guinea as it was called then). The people there were black, curly-haired, tribal Melanesians, living two and a half thousand miles from Java, where pale, straight-haired, technologically developed Asians lived. The religion, the lifestyle, politics and history of West Papua were quite unconnected to the way things were on the other Indonesian islands, and it sat, in fact, on a different continent. West Papua, with the rest of New Guinea, was the northern edge of the Australasian continent; while the dominant islands of Indonesia were part of the South East Asian plate. It seemed to the Dutch that it was neither fair nor natural for the Papuans to be ruled from Java. So they began to prepare West Papua for independence, to coincide with the rest of New Guinea's release from colonisation. Then the whole island—the West Papuan half and the Papua New Guinea half—could form a single state, of Melanesian, largely tribal people.

The Indonesians, however, had proclaimed, before their own independence, that all the colonies that had once been a part of the Dutch East Indies should become a part of their country. Though Holland, in 1950, had managed to separate West Papua from the other islands, the Indonesians, with some powerful friends in the United Nations, after a lot of campaigning and a failed invasion, won it back in 1963.

Ever since then, some of the Papuans had shown their resentment about being ruled from Jakarta, and fought with tribal weapons to regain their independence. Whatever the Indonesians said or did, they could not convince those people that their land formed a natural part of Indonesia. The government tried to draw the Papuans into the mainstream of Indonesian life, hoping to defuse the resistance that way. It started programmes for housing the tribal people in Indonesian-style homes, getting them to wear Indonesian clothes and to take on the language and traditions of Indonesia. Some efforts at persuasion were less than sensitive, and tribal villages were bombed and napalmed, and their leaders were tortured and dropped back to their deaths from helicopters. It seemed that the various schemes did little to quell the resentment.

In transmigration, the human rights campaigners said, the government had found a new and more effective way of getting rid of the dissent in West Papua. Rather than trying to change the people there it would overwhelm them. Four million people from Java were scheduled to move into West Papua, and the one million Papuans would become a minority in their own country, and their tribal customs could be suppressed. The lands that they had fought to hold onto could be taken away from them, and the extraction of timber and minerals from the province could go ahead as had always been planned. By sending real Indonesians there West Papua could be made a real and productive part of Indonesia. The campaigners believed that before very long transmigration would mean the end of the Papuans people, as anything other than a displaced and blasted fragment of what they were before. Already, in 1987, with a hundred thousand Javanese settlers moved out there, the programme was said to be causing some terrible troubles, taking the land, the jobs and the fragile forest that the people depended on, obliterating resistance. To judge from the reports I heard it was as bloody and one-sided an affair as the Spanish conquest of South America; and those first hundred thousand transmigrants were just the trickle before the predicted flood.

The human rights campaigners in Europe said that transmigration was just one product of a government that had no qualms about eliminating its human problems. Certainly President Suharto's administration was ruthlessly intolerant of serious threats to its control. As I read more, however, I saw that it was not a blindly despotic leadership. Indonesia was not a democracy of the sort we knew in the West; but from what I could gather the government represented most of its people well. Suharto was popular in Java, and his determination to keep the opposition out of serious politics caused only mild public unhappiness. Politics, like everyday life in Java, was organised by way of a broad consensus, and there was little desire for confrontation and open debate.

Suharto had brought Indonesia out of some of the instability and economic mess that Sukarno, the first president, had got it into. He had been in power for twenty years, and the majority wanted him to stay.

For the minority, the people who disputed the way the country was run, the President's New Order system was bad news. Indonesia had, ever since its inception, been a military state, and the army and the government shared the administration. President Suharto himself was an army general and he dealt with the threats he perceived in a ruthlessly military fashion. He was, for instance, horrified by communism. Members of the Indonesian Communist Party had been in prison since it was banned by the ascending general in 1966, and some were still being shot. Though Suharto himself was a Muslim there were reports that fundamentalist Muslims, perhaps alongside other disruptive militants, were tortured or killed by soldiers. In every case his government had shown it had few qualms about the way it dealt with its fears. In transmigration, I heard, Suharto had found his way, though wasteful and astonishingly destructive, of eliminating dissent in the outer islands.

It was impossible, at that stage, to tell how true the claims of the campaigners were. I believed that much of what they said was likely to be correct, but that some of it was over the top. To deal with the situation at all fairly, though, I had to put aside those feelings, and give equal weight to the claims of both sides. If I was to go to Indonesia to see transmigration for myself I needed to be as prepared to confirm the government's view of things as that of the human rights groups. What attracted me especially to the story was that no one else I met was in any position to judge for themselves. The major groups had funded the devotion of an issue of a specialist magazine to transmigration, in which they laid down most of their claims against the government. Many of their allegations, however, as they were aware, were hard to substantiate, as few people without a vested interest had seen even a fraction of what was said to be going on. The information came mostly from Papuan refugees, returned transmigrants, the odd expatriate, scientist or tourist—sometimes a conscience-stricken development consultant—who had seen a little; Papuan rebel groups with links abroad and facts gleaned from official reports. No journalists—other than a couple of parties led around by a strict government escort—had got to the controversial places. As far as satisfactory news reporting went, West Papua was complete black hole, and anything could or could not have been happening there.

By July of 1987 I was convinced that the story, whichever version was correct, was a big one, and was crying out for someone to go in and find the truth of it. Certainly, if the campaigners were right, there were atrocities to investigate as frightful as any generated in Vietnam. As well as scenting the big issue, something that maybe I could help to put right, I found myself entirely intrigued by the place the story was set in: one half of the third largest island on earth, scarcely explored, changed only in those transmigration areas, with the most extraordinary tales of people and cultures quite unconnected to the rest of the world. For my two reasons then—my frustrations about the state of the world and my frustrations about the limitations of my job—I felt I had found the story I was looking for. Just perhaps I could find some end points, and a way out of my circular existence.

It wasn't quite as easy as that however. Both transmigration and West Papua had been left alone by journalists for good reasons. The government was jumpy about its controversies, and tended to eliminate people who saw embarrassing things. Six Australian journalists had been shot by the army in East Timor, Indonesia's other most disputed province. West Papua was reckoned to be just as dangerous for unauthorised outsiders. I knew there was no way to get in officially and see what I wanted, so my efforts to get to the story would depend on avoiding detection. The Indonesian secret service was active in West Papua, and said by some to be the most efficient network in Asia; and the army was omnipresent. It had, I saw quite coldly from my desk in London, the makings of a great story.

There were other fears, however, that were more real to me then. I would be leaving behind everything that was good about home and striking off blindly into something I didn't know. I didn't want to leave my girlfriend, I didn't like the risk of dropping my cosy job and failing to get the story. By then, though, I had followed the issue too far to want to let go. By contrast to the intrigues of West Papua I had begun to despise the repetition of my day-by-day job, and I slowly found myself planning for the trip, without having made a conscious decision to go. There was perhaps another thing that encouraged me to leave. Though by then of course I knew that everything was not beautiful and well with Indonesia, I still imagined I'd be able to see it with the eyes I'd used in 1985. I guessed that whatever my troubles, whatever the troubles of the country, I would find Indonesia enchanting. It was indeed, the more I looked at it, a truly fascinating place. I sold the idea to a publisher, and handed in my notice at the BBC.

Then, when I was really forced to think about it clearly, I realised that I couldn't go alone. I was a lousy traveller, as I had painfully found five years before, on a long journey in East Africa. I'd been homesick and lonely throughout, and saw that I had none of the confidence I needed abroad. I wanted, moreover, a photographer on the trip, as the book I would write needed illustrations, and I scarcely knew which way to point a camera. I phoned Denver in August.

"Where?" asked Adrian, with a second's delay from the States.

"Irian Jaya, it's on the end of Indonesia. It used to be half of New Guinea."

There was a heartbeat on the line and we were shouting to make ourselves heard.

"And what's going on there?"

"Transmigration. There are lots of people being moved out from Java. They say it's doing in the local people."

"OK." A pause.

"What do you mean, OK?"

"OK, I'll come."

"But, but don't you want to think about it, perhaps—"

"I'll see you in September then," shouted Adrian, and that was the end of the call.

In England Adrian and I started learning Indonesian properly—we'd got by with about three hundred words on Wekri Island—and researching more thoroughly the nature of the place and the sort of troubles we might expect. For Adrian I saw, frustrated working in the West, Indonesia was just as much a matter of escape as it was for myself. I flew to Amsterdam for a few days to meet campaigners there, and old missionaries and ex-colonials who could give me some idea of where we should go and how we ought to move around.

Adrian and I began to sketch out a loose schedule, and I found myself becoming increasingly excited. We planned, in West Papua, to meet up with those rebels, the extraordinary tribal army said to be fighting with spears and poisoned arrows, which was to me then a schoolboy dream of noble savagery. We wanted to get out on an excursion with them and see how they worked. As we read about the remotest tribal areas we realised that the people there had perhaps the most fascinating, independently developed culture on earth. They were, quite literally in places, the inhabitants of a lost other world. I was itching to get to them, and the outlandish natural environment around them. Then there were the biggest transmigration sites, areas where trouble was said to be rapidly approaching the boil, in the south of West Papua. In every case we would have to sneak around, with different guises, finding new tricks to get ourselves into places that had been absolutely sealed from the outside world. We would spend a short time in Jakarta and rural Java, then get out to where our story truly began—in the forests of West Papua—as quickly as possible. We pooled all the money we had. In October we were ready to go, and as I boarded the plane the troubles, the apparent idiocy, of my idea struck home fully for the very first time.

Chapter 2

Jakarta in 1985 had been a fascinating bustle, an amazing confusion of rich and poor people, post-revolutionary statues and pedlars whose lives would stay the same through any changes of government. Towards the end of 1987 the same scenes were immediately oppressive. As we took the bus from the airport to the capital of Indonesia I sensed the intense humidity, the intense air pollution, I heard the shouting and the motorhorns, and saw the crush of people on the pavements so tight that they had all to move in one direction, and I felt it as an overwhelming dread. The air, that had clung to the malarial swamp the town was built on, flapped like a wet cloth around my head. We checked into a cheap hotel and I lay on my bed in an immediate sweat. The fears I had held down in Europe had begun to bubble up.

Wandering out into the smog later that afternoon I realised that, in my happy way two years before, I somehow hadn't noticed the crowding in the city. Every inch of pavement, street, building and vehicle was taken up. Mopeds went by swaying about beneath as many as seven people. On the pavements and spilling out into the streets were hawkers of every sort: fruit-sellers, noodle-makers, syrup-mixers, shoe-shiners, newspaper boys and cigarette men. Through them pedestrians poured: civil servants in groups of two hundred, all in their regulation fake-batik shirts; businessmen with western spectacles and briefcases; high-ranking soldiers with neat green uniforms and red epaulettes. Faces swam out of the sea, youths trying out their six same English words—"Hello mister, where you come from?"—again and again. On the roads traffic of every kind was packed: buses with surplus passengers clinging to the doors; ministerial Mercedes with tinted windows, bicycle carts and motored scootercarts, that spun round corners like runaway sidecars.

I tried to talk to people but, in those main streets at least, there was nowhere we could comfortably stand, without being jostled, or pushed on by those streams of unidirectional pedestrians. We passed the granite obelisks of multinational banks, and run-down tiled houses crammed in above the pavements, and people living beneath corrugated iron and packing cases. Eventually we stopped and sat on a bollard beside a sewage canal, the one unoccupied strip of that part of town, and I watched the people go by. They were mostly much smaller than us, with fine slight bones and honey-coloured skins, straight hair and rather mystically beautiful looks. Even the old people looked to our eyes youthful, and almost epicene. Despite the vegetable rubbish in the streets and the filth in the canal behind us, everyone was as clean and neat as they could afford to be: even the poorest were better turned out than ourselves.

We'd been sitting there some time when Adrian noticed two policemen moving up the street towards us. They were identical: moustaches, reflector sunglasses, round bellies, swagger sticks, and a revolver on each right hip. They moved with a slovenly bow-legged walk, as if the street was their personal dominion. I looked away, for I'd become convinced, through my mounting paranoia, that the authorities were watching us already; but Adrian slipped off the bollard and went up to talk to them. He wanted a photo of me standing between the two policemen. I watched him explaining it to them with dread: we would be locked away before we'd spent a night in Indonesia. But, as Adrian cracked some joke, the two proud faces split into pleasing grins, and the policemen walked over to me, shook hands and took off their sunglasses, each saying how pleased he was to meet us. They struck a funny pose, pretending they'd arrested me, then moved off back into the stream of people, exaggerating their swagger to make us laugh. The agents of Suharto's Indonesia were human after all, and I felt a few of my immediate demons dispersing.

Our intentions were to spend a short time in Java, looking into the claims of the government, then to fly directly to West Papua. There, posing perhaps as health workers, or missionaries or development consultants, we could first attempt to get to the big transmigration sites. Before we started anything, however, I wanted to try to understand the Javanese a bit better. Our friendship with Walisi and the other Wekri islanders had been pleasant but superficial. In Jakarta we wanted to get to know how the Javanese were beneath the transcontinental politeness we shared, and how they might differ from ourselves.

14

Through the people who ran the grotty hotel we stayed in, and the families living close by, we began, over the course of a couple of weeks, to work out something of the way the people round us were. Though some we met were among the very poorest of all, earning perhaps two days' English wages in a year, they treated us with the greatest generosity. People who struggled to feed themselves kept offering to give us food: it ran against their codes of hospitality to let strangers pass without a meal, whatever their relative wealth. Women, in the little houses beside the hotel, kept us amused by gentle teasing, remarkably familiar after just a couple of days, and we developed the feeling, strange for an Englishman, that we were friends until proven otherwise. We felt too that the Javanese were subtle, veiled and communal people. They didn't much value individualism, and the people in those tight communities we came across reached their decisions by consensus, working around a point until a compromise was found, that everyone agreed on. I found it hard to judge the real feelings of the people I met, as they took pains to keep them shrouded, and tragedy and rage, though deeply felt, were both concealed with a smile. That subtlety was well suited to those crowded places, for there was simply no room for raw emotions. It still took me time to learn, however, how to react to a woman who smiled when her baby died.

When we felt we knew the town a bit better, and our language had improved, we set out to fulfil the first task. I wanted to know whether the government's claims about the situation in Java were really true. If the hardships and the lack of land there that it said made transmigration essential didn't actually exist, then there were good reasons for concluding that the transmigrants were being sent for unpleasant purposes. If, as I strongly suspected, things were indeed as bad on Java as the government said they were, then the issue remained open, and we wouldn't get a chance to resolve the truth of it till we'd got deeply into West Papua.

In Jakarta we found a depressingly immediate confirmation of the Indonesian view. We were, in Java, quite safe playing tourists and we moved as such into the north of the city, where long broken-down shanties were strung along the roads and railway sidings, and we stayed with a family of sixteen, living in a slum above an open sewer. They and the others packed in around them had migrated from the country, where pressure on the land had forced them out. Along with sixty-five per cent of the city's population they were working unofficially, and they picked around the leavings of Jakarta's proper economy. There were men who rode bicycle cabs, or pushed carts of food around the streets, people who fished whiteworms out of the sewers to sell to tropical fish shops, or ran on to buses when they stopped at the traffic lights, selling cigarettes or cough sweets individually. There were a few beggars there too, and rubbish-pickers and minor thieves. The men and women in the slum we stayed in seemed to be living on the very edge of survival, for if they missed just a single day's work the family would go hungry. There didn't seem to be room for anyone else to squeeze into those crowded markets.

Housing was just as miserable and cramped as the opportunities were. The slum we slept in was built of packing cases and corrugated iron, and balanced on stilts above the sewer because the space on the pavement behind it had already been taken up. Three cratelike rooms took sixteen people, without the two whites. The land—or the water—belonged in theory to the government, and when it was to be reclaimed the houses would be pushed away. There was, it seemed, just no more room for anyone else to get in; yet, every year, there were three hundred thousand more inhabitants in that town, eighty thousand of whom were refugees from the miseries of the countryside.

How much worse the countryside could be we couldn't imagine, so we went there, to central Java, to take a look. We travelled about by ponycart for a day or two, and met an old man who offered to put us up in his house. We stayed there for a week, for it was the most beautiful farming area I've ever seen. The land looked enormous—a vast volcano hanging over it, a plain disappearing off in mist at the edges—but the details were pencilled in miniature. There were the smallest brick and tile villages, living in groves of little fruit trees. Padifields radiated away from them, each one a geometric box just a few metres across, each with a person inside doing something different. As the soil was tremendously fertile, bringing forth three crops of rice a year, you could see in one glance women planting, men ploughing behind their buffaloes, teams of people harvesting with sickles, boys shouting and waving their arms to scare away birds. It looked abundant, fertile and rich. It wasn't until we had stayed there for several days, and got the farmers to show us the land they each owned, that we could see the extent of their problem.

The average farm in central Java was just a quarter of a hectare. Farms had never been big there, but they had been reduced and reduced until they could no longer support the people who lived on them, let alone produce a profit. Already forty per cent of the families—all, until a few years before, subsistence farmers—had no land at all. While the bigger landowners—those with a hectare or so—had absorbed as much of the surplus labour as they could, wages had fallen until men earned thirty pence for a full day's work, and women twenty, which was not by itself enough to feed a family. What had happened was that the population had exploded: through good medicine and sanitation it was almost four times bigger than in 1900. Farmers, as they had always done, had divided their land up equally between their sons. As the families got bigger their holdings decreased, and now the land could no longer support them. It had reached crisis point in Java. All over the countryside the people had squeezed their land for everything it could produce, and it wasn't giving them enough. The farmers were holding up, just, by finding scraps of work in other places, but the situation was due to get worse. Their children, bright, noisy and charming, were the time bomb ticking in their beds.

So in that respect the government was right, and a sweeping solution to the troubles was needed pretty fast. Whether transmigration could be that solution we had to find out for ourselves. Before we set off for West Papua, and the big transmigration sites there, we wanted to see whether the government's claims that transmigration was constructive could, in principle, be correct. In south Sumatra, just a few hundred miles north-west of Jakarta, there were some enormous transmigration complexes, that were not too sensitive for pushy tourists to get into, and we decided to take a quick look. We eased our way in as official visitors—south Sumatra was as safe to snoop about in as Java—and got to stay for a few days in the middle of the transmigration area. The site we slept in was occupied by fifteen thousand people, who were just a tiny fraction of the settlers in the region. Like the transmigrants going to all parts of Indonesia, the people we stayed with had been landless labourers or tiny farmers in Java. The government had given them bits of land in places that had been forests or swamps before, two hectares for each family, and it had built the people wooden houses and paid for them to move from Java. It claimed that transmigration would give them all that they had lacked, and in south Sumatra that seemed to be true.

Though the transmigrants we stayed with had been there for only three years, they already had gardens full of fruit and vegetables. In their new fields they were getting two crops of rice a year, for they were almost as fertile as the padis in central Java. The farmers were making enough money from the surplus to feed their families properly and clothe them, and to send their children to school. They had turned from peasants into landowners, in one swift move. In the middle of the transmigration site was a big research centre, full of Javanese and European consultants, who worked with the farmers, helping them to grow more and developing new crops. There were one or two environmental problems, where tigers and elephants had been driven out and the fisheries downstream made acid by the drainage, but otherwise the transmigration there seemed an unqualified success. No one had lived on those swamps before they were drained, so no one was made miserable by having his land removed. The farmers from Java were jubilant.

Transmigration wasn't, however, a solution to all the troubles in Java. We found out that even when, in 1985 or so, it was steaming ahead at its maximum levels, it was only moving a fifth of the extra people living on Java each year, let alone making a dent in the numbers already there. What it could do was to make life a great deal better for the small proportion lucky enough to get moved. If, in West Papua, it was doing anything like the amount of good it had brought to the people who moved to south Sumatra, then that was quite a weight to balance against any troubles it caused to the locals. To West Papua we would have to go, if it was to be us who found out what was really happening there.

It was time then for our story to begin. Our few weeks in Java and Sumatra had given me plenty of time to build up my fears. Backed by a little knowledge they had reached the state of near-clinical paranoia. Because Indonesia, spread across those three thousand miles of sea, was such a strange and loosely associated place, national integrity was perhaps at the front of the President's concerns. In all the extremities of the archipelago there had been people who felt that they should not be governed from Jakarta. Only in East Timor and West Papua had rebel groups survived, and the army seemed to have concentrated its energies on those two places. In both provinces the Indonesians had shown they were prepared to enforce their borders with rigour, and had put down dissent with the utmost ferocity. I guessed that observers were no more welcome than rebels.

All the places we especially wanted to see in West Papua were strictly out of bounds to us, as we were likely to get tourist permits for only a couple of unexciting towns. It would be no good hanging around the edges and trying to see what was happening: to get the real story, that we'd travelled all the way from England for, we'd have to land ourselves right in the middle. With my fearful imagination I had made myself a points system of the penalties for getting caught. Being found in a sensitive transmigration zone, I figured, would be deportation; a place with ethnic problems, imprisonment; on a foray with the rebels, curtains. It was not, I began to see, an inaccurate assessment.

That side of the story was scary enough, but I was getting still more worried about things we *wouldn't* be able to talk our way out of. In West Papua it was the rainy season. The forests there were the least-explored in the world. West Papua was the home of the saltwater crocodile, the orange-brown death adder and the freshwater shark; malaria, cholera and a disease called yaws that ate away your face. There were headhunters and reputedly cannibals in the south and, while we most likely had little to fear from them, we didn't possess one of the two hundred languages that the tribespeople used. There were Indonesian centres, I knew, and places where life was not hard for an outsider; but many of the parts we wanted to see were connected by mountains and forests and water, and we would have to find our own way through them. West Papua, three times the size of England, with glaciated peaks as high as sixteen thousand feet in the middle and those biggest swamps on earth in the south, was a formidable place for a roving investigation. My cowardly instincts and my coloured imagination, working full time in the oppressive weather of Jakarta, for once seemed to be pushing me in the right direction: after a few weeks on Java and Sumatra I wanted badly to go back to my girlfriend, and back home.

In other respects, however, West Papua was the most intriguing place. In parts, in the central mountains and the southern swamps especially, the people were in all respects unchanged. They had developed, in isolation, a technology that had nothing to do with the rest of the world: still in the mountains the people used stones as tools, and in the swamps, where stones did not exist, just wood and shells. In the highlands the men wore nothing but penis gourds and pigs' tusks and still fought full-scale tribal wars. In other parts of Papua people used the skulls of their ancestors as pillows to keep their souls in place, and carved huge totems of entangled figures to bring them luck before a headhunt. The tribal rebels too, in such places and elsewhere, fascinated me. Also, in the unexploited areas, there was wildlife of the most bizarre and original forms. Isolated, unresearched, many of the creatures there were likely not to be known to science.

But above all else that intrigued and terrified me about West Papua were the maps. We had the best there were, compiled from all known sources, and put together with Australian military aid for the Indonesian army. What they showed us were those mountains, the highest in either South East Asia or Australasia, with snow just four degrees south of the equator. There were forests that went on and on, with only the tiniest specks of villages in their midst, and most of those unnamed. There were those swamps, of course, that horrified me, and were reckoned in places to be entirely uncrossable; there was scrubland, just like the bush in Australia (which was three hundred miles to the south of West Papua); and there were beaches that had, perhaps, never felt a white man's foot. What we didn't see on the maps was more intriguing. There were patches, up to two hundred miles across, where there was nothing. White voids, of the sort that I'd thought were found only in children's books of pirates, crossed in places the regions we wanted to visit.

We had spent our several weeks in Java and Sumatra looking at those population troubles, at the politics, improving our Indonesian, and now I found myself committed too far to rethink our foolish plans. We renewed our two-month visa by flying to Singapore and back, got tourist permits from the police to visit West Papua, or the four dull places they wrote on the form for us, and there was nothing I could find to delay us any further. At Jakarta's airport, at dawn, an old Hercules was waiting, hissing through its broken airpipes, to carry us and some Javanese settlers to the wildest island in the world.

Chapter 3

The extent of Indonesia was horrifying from the air. We crossed the cosy padifields of Java and flew, with a rattling of bolts and a pinging of metalwork, above the island swarms of the Makassar Strait. We landed on Sulawesi, yellow, mountainous and five hours by our broken-up Hercules from Jakarta. There we reloaded and set off through the Moluccas, over Taliabu, and Buru, the wires on the ceiling shuddering into a blur, to land again in Ambon: green and mountainous islands encircled by surf, with forests running straight to the sea, and atolls in turquoise and white. Though we were missing out the greater part of Indonesia—Sumatra, Kalimantan, the island chain called Nusa Tenggara—the lands we saw below us were big enough for many nations. Already we had crossed the two great biological lines, the Weber and the Wallace Lines, where the animal life changed drastically between the islands. Now, on that domestic flight, we were about to change continents, to move from Asia to Australasia. For an hour and a half there was a black sea beneath us and then, suddenly on our right, were clouds.

For twenty minutes we saw nothing but clouds, indigo and grey, crouching close to the ground. Then they parted and below them was a black forest, broken only by brown rivers, crawling through swamps to the sea. There were beaches, long strips and sudden coves, and neither they nor the forest behind had the slightest sign of man. It was raining in places, and the clouds, the swamps below, made me feel yet again that we were doing something foolish. We got to Biak, an island off the north coast of West Papua, after twelve hours in the plane, and when it bounced down onto the runway we opted to stay there for two or three days. It would give us a chance to see the Papuans, and to settle down a little.

The first people we met weren't Papuan at all. They had boarded the plane in Sulawesi and now shared the guesthouse with us: twelve young women and a man in a leather jacket.

Despite his neat moustache and high boots, and the relaxed, seductive nature of the girls, I couldn't work out what they were doing. One of the women sauntered over to me on the verandah and pulled out a flick-knife, that she held close to my chest. I stared at the long blade.

"Could you mend this for me?" she laughed, and left me struggling, potato-fingered, with the dislodged spring, while she and her friends sat back and giggled at me. I failed to do it, and two of them, very smooth, came and sat on our beds to talk. I remained unenlightened.

"Are you, er actually, are you on holiday? No? So, you're here for work then?"

"Yes, yes, work," they giggled and looked at the ceiling.

"I see. What work do you do then?"

"Er, George," said Adrian in English, "they're tarts."

The pimp came in and sent one of them away, and a prettier girl took her place. The girls left some half hour later, aware that Englishmen were a barren pursuit, and later they ignored us, as they got down to the serious business of servicing the policemen who lounged in their vests on the verandah.

That we had crossed, within one country, into a different world, we saw when we walked down to the water's edge. Above the broken coral reef were palm-thatched houses perched on stilts. It was a fishing village, and as we walked down into it we saw people entirely different to those we had left behind, the small, fine-boned Javanese and Sulawesis and other Indonesians we had passed on the way. A woman came out of her hut, black skinned, tall, with a slow sexy movement, thick curly hair rambling off into sea-tangles. She had a strong jaw and broad bones in her face. Beside her a man came out of the gloom. I saw a beard first—the Javanese have no beards—then a heavy nose, and thin black arms with blacker curly hair on them. They were Melanesians, Pacific people: a continent apart.

I had been told by a Tamil friend that he had seen a group of Papuans at an airport once and approached them, thinking they came from his country. When they didn't speak his language he took another look, and saw that they seemed slightly different. He had possibly been right at first, however, for the Pacific people came out of the west in the European mid-Stone Age, and only much later did East Asians move down from the north—China or

Mongolia perhaps—and take over the lands in between. The spread of the South East Asians had stopped in the Moluccas, west of Papua, several thousand years ago, and moved no further until 1963, and the Indonesian takeover.

Beside the woman's house was a pig in a bamboo cage, something else far removed from the Islamic country we had come from. I stared at it for a moment, a thick black bristling thing.

"You like my pig?" she asked seductively.

"Well, yes."

"You're his brother."

"What?"

"How else would you both have such big noses?"

Further along the beach, among the coconut palms, children had scratched out a square in the sand, and were putting a little stone across it with sticks. They all stopped to stare, then someone threw a stone, and they were laughing at us and jumping up and down gleefully. A man tried to drag us into a game of volleyball, but we moved on, and came to a graveyard, where we found one fresh stone inscribed with both missionary crosses and Muslim stars: someone, in the sudden flux of cultures, was hedging the ultimate bet.

We hung around in the tea rooms and marketplace for a while, taking it all in: the rather easy-going Papuans, often laughing, their undisciplined children ragging round us, the wide-eyed interest in us and our belongings, unabashed friendly stares from the roadside. We saw one man with a grey moustache that curled away beyond his cheeks; freewheeling down a hill on a huge black bicycle with his legs in the air. Among them were Sulawesis and the odd Javanese. I noticed that they were cooler, more reserved than the Pacific people, and also that they ran nearly all the small businesses and peopled the government offices.

After two days in Biak we decided to get to work, and we booked, with some foreboding, a flight in a rather smarter aeroplane to the town of Merauké, on the south coast. There our real investigation would begin, as the people around that town were mostly transmigrants, not Papuans. They had been the vanguard of the great expansion of the transmigration programme planned for West Papua, before the price of oil fell and damaged Indonesia's economy. If, as the government claimed, transmigration was slowly coming back onstream, and some of the four million people scheduled for West Papua were on their way, more of them would go to the sites in the Merauké area than to anywhere else. Forty thousand had got there before the big slump, and several thousand more were scheduled to arrive in that year and the next, to fill some of the vacant places. To check out the stories we had heard from home we clearly had to start there, and find out whether those transmigration sites were good news for the Javanese people or not. If so that was a big point in transmigration's favour, to weigh against any harm being done, or add to the good that the government said the programme was doing in the province.

Merauké itself was not closed to us, though the transmigration sites that lay to the north of it were. We flew across the jagged spine of Papua, mountains that broke roughly from the clouds; then down across the rainforests of the foothills. Swamps flattened out away from them, enormous, sliding off towards the blue like an irregular sea. For half an hour we saw not a trace of habitation, not a mark amidst the water and ruffled swamp trees; then, quite suddenly, the forest thinned into a dry and blasted scrub, and there were rows of tin-roofed houses across the whole long view to the Arafura Sea. A Sulawesi man who sat beside me grabbed my arm and pointed: "*Itu transmigrasi*", and the word, the blunt caption to our journey, frightened me. The huts below us, many thousands of white specks against the dry red earth, were arranged in precise geometric constellations, and around them the vegetation had all gone.

As we came down over Merauké and saw the dirt roads that linked that town to the transmigration sites, I realised that travel was going to be a problem for us. If buses left for the sites they wouldn't, in common with transport all over Indonesia, depart without a great deal of fuss and wide discussion, of who was going where and what they were doing. If we travelled with other people we could expect to be arrested when we got back to the town.

The car from the airport took us past a desiccated, windswept town. Cows with xylophone ribs tottered untended along the one main road, past a single strip of shops and a huge barracks for the military police, painted strangely in effeminate pinks and blues. Low concrete houses and poor shacks were built with no relation to the sea, so that the town felt encircled by a consistent dreary wilderness, the flat land merging with the flat sea. We moved quickly into the cheapest guesthouse, feeling conspicuous in a place quite obviously unattractive to tourists. There we argued about getting to the sites. I wanted to walk, but Adrian said that would make us still more obvious, or we'd get lost in the forest if we tried not to use the roads. A motorbike, he reasoned, was what he needed. We wouldn't have to meet anyone on the track, and we could wear helmets and long sleeves to cover up our foreign skin. We wandered out into the town to find one.

There was nowhere renting bikes, or even selling any that we could later sell back. We met some Indonesian settlers lounging on machines beside the road, but they weren't prepared to let us borrow one, especially as we hedged around as to why we wanted it. We were stopped by a policeman and taken to the barracks to have our tourist permits checked, where they questioned us, gently, then told us to report every day to their immigration office. We gave up the search then and retreated to our room, where we stayed with some anxiety: I wanted to get out and up to the sites as soon as possible. We were lucky however, for the kind girls who worked in the guesthouses promised to press their men—and they each seemed to have quite a few—for a bike. After just a day of waiting a yellow trailbike sped into the guesthouse courtyard, and a Javanese man dismounted swiftly and sauntered to our window. The machine was a wreck, but we paid the high fee, and the man blessed the money on his forehead, with a twinkle in his eye.

A day later, a mile down the road—loaded with spare jerrycans and cameras, in plastic helmets you could cut open with a knife—the front tyre deflated, so we had to wheel the bike back and start again. The tyres were bald, there was no front brake, no footrests, there was oil leaking from the gearbox; so once we got the puncture mended and hit the mud roads beyond the town we started sliding all ways at once. The bike spluttered a bit and soon it stopped, and we had to kick it, randomly and viciously, all over, to get it to start again. It stopped several times, and we got more and more annoyed with it. We slid off the road and became angry with each other. The rains around Merauké had begun two days before, and we were the first to pass through the mud they'd left behind. Adrian, driving, would stick carefully to a rut, but suddenly the bike would rear off the road, and dump us, in a wave of wet clay, among the bushes alongside. Once, as we skidded on a corner, I put down my feet. The bike bucked and I was left standing bow-legged on the track, while it careered off with a sudden jolt, and dropped Adrian into a trench.

The fragments of landscape I saw through the mud were unexpected, though I had read the words that described them back in England. Coming around a corner we put up a herd of kangaroos, that bounded out from the swordgrass growing where the trees were cleared, and straightened as they leapt away, into long smooth birdlike shapes. Where the forest closed back towards the road I saw that it was composed of gumtrees, with their bark burnt black. Framed by a thunderous grey sky, it looked barren and oppressive. We passed by some small transmigration sites, not the big places we were heading for, with Javanese men wandering down the road with mattocks or waterbuckets. I felt anxious again, knowing already that nothing would be as simple as it was described in England: I was worried about our chances of discovering anything substantial. Two men, walking down the road where the forest returned, stared at us with particular curiosity; and as I turned to watch them watching us one lofted a stone into the trees, and a white cockatoo winged off. It took us three hours to cover thirty miles, and by the time we saw the biggest transmigration site, at the end of the road, we were swearing at each other.

As Salor came over the horizon it looked like rows of teeth with metal caps. The houses were in straight lines and painted white, and wore tin roofs. There had been floods after the first rains, and water still hung about on the raw fields, where planting was soon to begin. People were scattered across them, beating the ground with mattocks. Though they wore the same conical hats, rolled-up trousers and loose shirts as the people of central Java, the land they moved through was by nature far from the one they had left. Instead of the close weave of the Javanese countryside, the tiny fields and water systems, the neat round settlements and the intimacy, was a raw ugly land, of red earth, churned and broken, its long lines converging at the stormy sky. Straight rows of houses narrowed to a point, and the black forest hedged in sections of the view.

The ten months of an extended dry season had wiped any green from the view. Banana trees planted between the houses had turned brown and crisp, and hung from splintered trunks. There were grey stalks among the clods. It was hard to decide how to start. We didn't expect to find out how people's lives were straightaway. In Java we had found that they were not forthright about the ways they lived: problems were smiled away or stored up, and suc-

26

cesses were modestly glossed over. We sat down and watched for a while: a few farmers walking back to their houses for lunch, women suckling their babies in doorways, thunderclouds gathering then dispersing on the skyline. Without birds, with voices taken up and lost by the wide sky, no machinery or music, I felt already that I'd become insensitive to detail.

People were unwilling to talk to us. We told them we were white development consultants supervising the project for the government, and we'd come to do a survey of their lands; but still they were suspicious and answered questions as briefly or ambiguously as possible, looking at the ground. Some people suggested we meet the head of the transmigration site, a civil servant, and we had to avoid that. We went from house to house, waving and asking ourselves in for a talk, and we were taken round the garden plots and the big ricefields. At length we found one or two men who were prepared to talk frankly. By the end of the day I had got some sort of a picture.

Salor was in trouble. When the people there had moved in four years before it was all they could have hoped for. For the landless labourers or farmers in tiny plots, two hectares of land was a dream, worth moving two and a half thousand miles for. The government paid for everything—the flight to Papua, houses and land—and they had become in their own eyes big landowners. For the first year, while the farmers opened up their plots and settled in, the government kept them alive with fish and rice. There were handouts of fertiliser, and free seeds.

The first sowings were abortive. The farmers hadn't anticipated eight months without rain, so they planted in the dry season and the seeds died. They replanted in the wet but the rice was of the wrong variety, a cheap strain, and it was overwhelmed by disease. Without food to last until the next wet season, many transmigrants went off to Merauké to look for work. They found that people from other troublesome sites in the region had already filled a lot of the empty niches, or taken established jobs from the less commercial Papuans. They got by until the next season, however, though some had eaten their seed, and had to buy more on tick from merchants. Two months after the next plantings there were floods. There had been floods the year before and the transmigrants had assumed they were freakish, but they followed the same pattern that season and the one following. For two months their houses stood in half a metre of water. They tore planks from the walls of empty homes and built platforms to sit on. People rarely left their houses, as it was hard to get dry again. The water, for all its abundance, was fouled; they didn't know, and in both the dry and the wet people died of cholera and an unknown disease, some sort of fever that affected the bones.

The people began to get crops as they learnt to use the soil better, and some farmers had surplus rice to sell in Merauké. There was another problem. The road, that had been brick hard in the dry season and difficult but occasionally passable in the first two months of the wet, was flooded or uncrossably swampy for the last weeks of the rains and a month or two beyond. People could walk to Merauké—it took two days or more—but not with a quantity of rice that they could sell. The grain, in sacks in their wet houses, rotted, and by the time a vehicle could get down the roads most of it couldn't be sold. Even so the rice that got through met a saturated market in Merauké, whose thirty thousand people mostly farmed their own food, and that had no export links. People in Salor staved off vitamin deficiencies by irrigating patches in their gardens to grow vegetables. Only one part of the site had wells, but water could be carried over in buckets during the dry. There was a plan to build a silo, so that grain could be stored until the road was navigable. In some ways life had seemed set to improve, until they discovered their real problem.

The soil the transmigrants were farming was turning sterile. It was red, which in the tropics means an oxidised earth, poor in minerals. With the forest cover gone and the soil turned over by ploughing, it was exposed to the leaching effect of the heavy rains, that flushed out the nutrients it held. Within a few years it would be as dead as sand. There was little money for fertiliser, and a limited amount it could do anyway to redress the harm, so the farmers could only watch as their resources soaked away from beneath them. Every year the harvest would get smaller, the transmigrants' ability to buy new fertiliser would decline, their debts would increase.

One man was particularly bitter. He claimed to know why Salor flooded every year, while the ground beyond the houses was relatively dry. He said that the contractors who cleared the site and built the houses for the government had been instructed to put them on a ridge of higher land. When they turned up on the spot with chainsaws and earthmovers, they saw that a long strip just below was entirely unforested. They could halve their costs by putting the houses there rather than up on the ridge, which would take weeks to clear. So the houses went down below and the ridge was marked out for farmland. No one went in to check, and the transmigrants were moved into houses built in the wrong place. The reason why there had been no trees there was that the land lay in the bend of a river, that flooded it every year. The houses had been built on a wet season riverbed. Neither the man who told me nor the rest had any money to move to the dry ground, so they were stuck. The floods brought more than discomfort: with the first rains and the rise in the river level that followed them, two days before we arrived, a toddler had wandered out into the garden and drowned.

The houses were undecorated and had water lines two planks up from the floor. Some of them had begun to sag a little and a few had been abandoned as unsound. Insects had rotted away their supports: one woman showed me how you could rock the house by pushing one of the walls. Others had been closed up, for the owners had gone away for good to Merauké, and were working as fruit sellers or minibus conductors, like the people in the shanty in Jakarta. I asked the obvious question, to all the farmers, which received a mixed response. Some of them would stay and see what happened, some felt tied to the ground until their children were older, others would clear out after the next harvest. Not all of them, but most, would have preferred to stay in Java.

Salor stood at the end of one road, but there was a second, that ran off to the east and into sites where the conditions could be different. After a night in Merauké we set off again, already sore and tired of sliding around, and wary of the curiosity we had attracted in the town. The roads were worse as it had rained again, and twice we nearly met our deaths on unexpected corners. Erom, where we stopped, had been opened five months before, and as we approached we saw long strips of forest land cut out by the contractors but not yet farmed. I got off the back of the bike, stiff, as if I'd been riding a horse. There were the same long rows of wooden houses and beside one stood a group of men. It was odd, they didn't look at all Javanese, but they didn't look Papuan either. I went over, going up to my shins in mud.

"Hello, I'm a development consultant."

The men stared a minute, then one of them came forward. "Thank God you've come." He took my hand and held it.

We entered a house, tea was made, and an extraordinary story unfolded.

The Erom people had come not from Java but from Flores, an island eight hundred miles from Jakarta. They had sharper features and bushy hair, with precise cheekbones and fine long fingers. Some of the men wore thick woven sarongs made in Flores, with shots of silver among different greens and reds. Flores wasn't at all overcrowded by comparison to Java: indeed it was a transmigration site itself, and it took some time to work out why they had come. The governor of Flores, a man called Ben Mboi, was one of the army officers who had invaded West Papua in the failed confrontation with the province's old rulers—the Dutch—in 1962. Soon afterwards the Dutch had ceded West Papua to the United Nations, and it had later been handed over to Indonesia. As a gesture of nostalgic goodwill to the transmigration programme and the government's plans for Papua, Brigadier-General Mboi arranged for fifteen hundred people to be sent in 1987 from his island as transmigrants.

The people who went to Erom had not been poor in Flores. They were carefully selected to be model transmigrants, who would set an example to all the others moving into the area. So lots of different people were invited to join the project: teachers, civil servants, some farmers, students, who would help make the place a centre of opportunity. They would be pioneers of the self-improvement scheme that was springing up there; when they had settled into their two hectares they could branch out and help set up the development zone. Their site, they were told, was close to the markets, there were schools, a hospital, water and electricity laid on for them; and within a year they would be sending home more money than had ever passed through their hands. Some weren't told that. They were told they were going to Kalimantan, to an area they knew had excellent soils, and they'd be getting two hectares of the farmland there. So for their different reasons they signed on, sold all they had, as they were told to bring nothing, and distributed the cash among their families and friends in Flores. At the harbour, when they had all come together, there was a great big send-off with music, and those who had thought they were going to Kalimantan cried when they heard they were going to Papua, but cheered up again when the others told them how marvellous the new life would be.

They were a little disappointed when they saw the site, five months before we met them: clearly the rest of the enterprise was still catching up. There wasn't any electricity, the water was foul, some of the houses were still being built, there was no school or hospital. They began to clear the land, and they waited. The seed hadn't arrived, there was no fertiliser and no pesticide. The seed got there after two months, but as there wasn't any water it all died, and mice ate the shoots they had irrigated by hand. The dry season had been going on for five months when they arrived, and they didn't know that that year it was due to last for another five.

For some reason the deliveries of food, the rice and salted fish that was supposed to come every month during their first year, kept being delayed, and after a while they began to starve. The Flores people, more outspoken than the Javanese, got angry with the head of their project area, a civil servant from Sulawesi, and sent him packing to Merauké to find out what was happening. The food arrived on time for a while, though when we met them it had again been delayed. While they waited still for the wet season they found that the water in the holding pond behind the camp had run out. They dug three times for groundwater, and each time found it at twelve metres. But it was salty and it couldn't be used. Getting desperate, they had to use water from the ditches beside the road. The water in the pond had been dirtied as a sewerage system had not been built at Erom, but the water in the ditches carried cholera, and several people nearly died.

A few weeks before the rains were due to start they had been given some more rice seeds, so they planted those in small patches that they could keep watered with buckets. They kept at it vigorously, but the seed had all died before it was sent, so nothing came up. So they wrote home and asked their relatives to send them some of the crops they were more used to growing in Flores. When we met them they had just got seedlings of cocoa, coffee and sweet potatoes, and maize and groundnut seeds, which they had planted out under strips of palm leaf to protect them.

Most of the transmigrants had never been to Merauké. It was very hard to get there. They had been told in Flores that the town was an hour away by foot, or a short ride and a hundred rupiahs (three pence) in the minibus. Minibuses, they found, came every two weeks and cost five thousand rupiahs. It took two days to walk.

"Why didn't you come before?" asked the man who had greeted us. "We were told you would come all the time to check the site." Someone shushed him.

"Busy," I said, uncomfortably, "lots of work in the town."

"Don't you realise"—he wouldn't be hushed—"we have no money? We gave it all away in Flores. We have food only when they decide to send us some, and half of it's been eaten by the mice. Have you seen the ground?"

He took us outside. The earth in his garden looked good and black. He rolled it back. There was ten centimetres of peaty soil on top, held together like a rug by the old forest rootmat, that was quickly decaying. Underneath the earth was pale orange.

"That," he said, "is poison. Weeds won't grow on that."

"I'm sorry," I mumbled foolishly.

"So what are we going to do?"

"Well, what do you want to do?"

"Go home to Flores, of course. Do you know what I had in Flores? I had a brick house, a plantation of cocoa trees, a cow and two goats, chickens, electricity and television." He looked around him, at the house with gaps in the plank walls, a bed, a raw bench and a table he'd made from local wood, a blanket, two cooking pots. Outside was the deep mud on the path, the poison soil in the gardens, little patches of seedlings shaded over by leaves, and otherwise a muddy blankness fenced in by trees. "I sold it for this." They weren't allowed to go back to Flores: they were the model pioneers and failure would have made a laughing stock of the governor. Anyway they had no money. Erom was their home for all their lives. I began to feel that I was indeed at fault: it wasn't often I'd accepted the blame for something I hadn't done.

We were taken round the site by a growing parade of men and women, all beautiful and high-boned; the Floretian dreamy look, and I knew what they were dreaming about. Scores of children ran up and down around us, screaming and chirruping happily. I had to distract them while Adrian got some shots. Nothing we saw made it seem any better. There were a few crops that had come through and withered, green weeds, a boarded house where somebody had died. When the men tried to take us to meet the head of the site we got back on the bike promptly and left, leaving them a bit perplexed.

They were more perplexed when we came back half an hour later. A storm had upended itself on us a mile down the road and there was nothing we could do to get through it. It was torrential, and the bald tyres slithered and spun on the road while Adrian ducked down to the bars trying not to be blinded. There was nowhere in the sparse eucalypt wood to shelter, so we turned the bike around and drove back to Erom with foreboding. The Flores people took us in without a query, however, despite the resentment we could detect, resentment about the well-paid consultants who had helped get them into that mess and could ride off home on the sort of motorbike many of them once possessed. Someone took us into his house and helped us dry off, then said we could use his bed for that night. There was no need, I argued, we would sleep on the floor. "You won't," he said, "for if the rain lasts any longer it'll come up through the ground." So we agreed that we would sleep on the table, and he would borrow a blanket for us.

A candle had been lit, and a crowd of men stood round, like Red Indians with their sharp faces, and their long sarongs draped over their shoulders, as they wore them in the evenings. I began to relax a bit and they started telling us stories from home: about the three-coloured lakes in a volcanic crater, the church services (Floretians are Christians), what they had hoped to become had they stayed in Flores. One man had trained as an electrical engineer; his brother had gone to America on a scholarship to study English. Had he stayed he would have been a rich man in Flores then, and have married a girl from his village. He would not see her again as there would never now be the money to go back. The harsh rain began to soften on the tin roof, and someone who had been singing in a high reedy way which couldn't be heard above it was surprised by the quiet when it died into a patter. I was settled and just ready for sleep when a man came running in from the mud. We were wanted by the head of the unit. Please go to his house straightaway.

We went out wearily. It was dark outside, and the mud was deep, and in the headman's house it was dark also, as he hadn't lit the big paraffin lamps he'd been supplied with. I could see the lower part of his body as he sat against the wall, but not his face. He invited us to sit down and started asking questions, polite and casual at first, but getting harder as he picked up uncertainties. Which consultancy were we working for? How long had we been there? Why hadn't he seen our faces in town then? What exactly were we studying on the site?

I said I was exhausted. There were two beds in the headman's house; one had been his wife's but she had fallen ill with malaria and gone to live in his proper house in Merauké, so we could sleep on hers. Behind the wood partition we arranged ourselves head to toe on a plinth sticking out of the wall. The air was heavy and the floor below us wet mud. The head of the unit was sitting in the next-door room with another man. They waited for long enough for us to get to sleep, then I heard the headman say, distinctly, "They aren't consultants, their Indonesian isn't good enough." I rolled over and tried to shut off from it all.

I was almost asleep when a fistful of claws landed on my face and dug in, scrabbling. "Urgh, argh!" Adrian woke up. The mouse leapt away and on to his arm. "Aarr!" Other people stirred. A paraffin lamp swung round the partition and I saw the Sulawesi man's face: lean, moustached. "Huh, mice. There're plenty of those." There were. I could hear them chewing at the wood beneath my head. Another fell off the wall and scrambled over my feet. Bigger things, probably rats, scuttled across the muddy floor. That's how the seedlings had been destroyed. I drew my toenails in under the blanket, in case they ate them while I was asleep.

I was hungry in the morning, though the sight of people eating dried fish and rice didn't much appeal. The Sulawesi head was brisk with us. We had given him false names at Adrian's suggestion, but I couldn't see what good that would do: there were only two new white faces round Merauké. We'd decided to take an hour to look around and see what we'd missed, then head back and leave the town before the trouble caught up with us. But one of the men we had met the day before wandered into the head's house and very quietly said that the road had suddenly got better for biking. I paid no attention, but when I went outside he caught my arm and said, "I mean one bike's already gone, to Merauké." We hadn't reckoned with that. There was another bike on the site and the Sulawesi man had sent it off to inform the police. I pictured a roadblock, the round helmets of the military police, a khaki jeep. The other man had left twenty minutes before. The Sulawesi head tried to hold us up with some breakfast, which he hadn't offered before, but we leapt on our bike and skated away, down the road to Merauké.

Rain in the night had made the track still worse, and we kept slipping and lurching, and stalled once, but after an hour we saw the other bike, a little Vespa, with a small man hunched over it. We caught him halfway up a slope. He was a civil servant—he had the epaulettes on his jacket—a Javanese man with spectacles. I figured he'd been visiting the head of the unit and had been despatched back in a hurry. He lifted his hand in greeting, but I saw his smile tighten as we passed. When we touched the flat again he overtook us, smiling once more. His bike, with tread on the tyres, held the mud better, and he had the advantage of being alone. We had more power and could go at the holes more readily, but it was, by any reckoning, a three-legged race. We pulled past him again and accelerated hard. We slid and just kept on the road, and I heard his steady purr coming on behind. The bike hit a dry patch and Adrian opened right out: if we could get the advantage then we'd be away, but there he was, while we were at full throttle, pulling slowly ahead. We swerved, and nearly knocked him off the road. He flicked in ahead of us and held there, moving across if we tried to overtake. Adrian tried to get past him along a muddy bank, but we lost a lot of ground and he was pulling well away. We couldn't do it. The Vespa moved off steadily along the mud and we fell further and further behind. Then the bike started running out of petrol and we gave up: we'd be thrown out of West Papua before we'd even started.

There was no roadblock, however, and as the bike hiccoughed into Merauké we passed policemen on the road who didn't give us a second glance. We pulled up cautiously outside the guesthouse—there was no one there to arrest us—and sneaked into the room. Ten minutes later there was a rap on the door. It was the bossy Javanese woman who ran the house. Did we want tea or coffee? She turned in the doorway before she went. "I hear you've just been to Erom. What was it like?" I didn't understand. Had the civil servant told her and not the police? Or had he told the police too, and set her up to find out more about us? I felt uncomfortable and went out to walk round town. I got into a minibus. The conductor said, "You're one of the new consultants, aren't you? What did you make of the sites?" I got the same question in a shop I walked into. No one had known where we were going before we went, and the civil servant was the only man who had returned to town; I was confused. Back at the guesthouse there were two policemen standing in the lobby. I committed myself to my fate and walked in bravely. They smiled politely and I walked past them into our room. Later on I saw them pulling up their trousers and tucking in their shirts.

Merauké was filled with the fugitives of transmigration. Only a third of its people were Papuans, and most of the rest had come from the failing sites to the north. Many of the women had taken to prostitution: there were now so many in the small town that prices, we heard, had fallen to around forty pence. The girls in the guesthouse did a slack trade with government employees, and filled in by helping the gossipy Javanese madame to keep the place clean. Other people had squeezed their way into the crowded market: a merchant would buy a stack of bananas, a middleman would buy a bunch and sell it to a trader, who would fry them and sell them to the roadside stalls, who would sell them to passersby, sometimes, or watch them rot in competition with a dozen stalls next door. In the market women sat for a day with two pineapples in front of them, likely to make enough to buy the nutritional equivalent. Jobs that had been held by the Papuans—administration, shop assistance, driving taxis—had mostly been taken over when the first migrants fled to town, and now the Javanese competed with each other, in a stagnant market poorer than the one they'd left in Java. There were people from all the sites there—Kumbe, Jagebob, Semangga—and I heard stories of similar troubles from the whole transmigration region: of sterile soils, pests, flooding, drought, disease and inescapable poverty. We need not have gone further than the town to see that transmigration to the north was failing.

There were several reasons for failure being mooted, that explained something of the individual miseries, but didn't answer the bigger question, of why the transmigrants had been sponsored to move to a bad place. In theory the settlements should have been perfect, as there were excellent tools for selecting them and setting them up. As in Sumatra there were supposed to be consultants on the sites, Javanese and Europeans, brought in by the Transmigration Ministry to find the right places for the farms, survey them thoroughly and check the progress of the settlers. We heard indeed that there were consultants there, not on the sites but in Merauké. What they did all day we couldn't work out, for they were certainly not among the farmers, sorting out their problems.

In the case of southern Papua it seemed that either there had been no surveys or that they had been ignored. The land was almost all unsuitable for transmigration. Short of deserts it had some of the worst tropical soils in the world, with no nutrients available for anything but the sparse, long-adapted gum woodland and scrub that grew on it. It could support little groups of hunting gathering people, no more. Conditions were too thin, too extreme and too seasonally unreliable to maintain settled farming in any but the richest pockets. Something had gone wrong with transmigration, and it had overcome the infrastructure of advice and finance that supported it.

The rush to get people out of Java and the high numbers the government wanted to move might have explained a few isolated failures, like poor groundwater or a pest problem. With so many scheduled for a new life, a few could expect to find themselves with problems, but not, with the back-up of all that government money and expertise, insuperable ones. The troubles around Merauké, however, were on quite a different scale, and it seemed that every element on every site was wrong, and so far wrong that it could never be corrected. Corruption doubtless had a role to play, as it did in every Indonesian project. Corruption there was more widespread than in any other country, and it was rooted deeply in the Javanese way, as the old pre-colonial sultans used to reward their civil servants with a slice of their profits. When the sultans declined the habit persisted, unofficially, as employees each took their little bit. In a modern economy those practices could be crippling; but they couldn't, as in the Merauké case, explain a disaster of planning, as well as implementation.

Had the price of oil not dropped and the transmigration programme not been scaled down fiercely as a result, the disaster we saw around Merauké would have become a catastrophe. The forty thousand transmigrants already moved there scraped by through wringing all that there was from an impoverished town and its hinterland. There was no more to be had. Still, however, the government was moving people in—eighteen thousand in 1988 would go to Papua—and still it promised that as the economy improved or the oil price rose the full programme would be brought back onstream, and three quarters of a million people a year would be sent to West Papua. There were good transmigration sites in the north of the island, on black soils, but people had started moving there in 1966 and they were already full up. It was the red-soil areas that were targeted for the influx. The places that had been filled already around Merauké were the *best* in the region, and the soils became progressively worse, the water regime more dangerous and the markets less accessible the further from the town the new ones were sited. As the programme slowly picked up again four and a half thousand people were scheduled to go to Muting in 1988 and '89, a village five days north of Merauké by river, where the soil was barren and swampy and, a leaked government report told me, most of the houses built had already rotted away. There was nowhere there to sell surplus crops, nowhere to buy necessary extras and no one to know if the people up there—eighty crow miles across swamps from the nearest town—were thriving or starving to death. Merauké was scheduled to take half a million people. If transmigration came back onstream the new developments would be clustered round Muting, and then there would be deaths.

Until we had seen those transmigration sites our plans had been a bit woolly: we knew there were certain aspects that we had to see, but I was unsure how best we should pursue the story in Papua. In Merauké things began to seem a little clearer. What we had seen was neither a mistake nor incompetence, but something actively promoted at the highest level of government. We had to find out why that was happening: the purpose of relieving Javanese misery that the government had claimed seemed in that case to have been ruled out, so why, when it so clearly did the migrants harm, was the project continuing? The government claimed that transmigration had also been designed to help the primitive people in Papua, and give them a chance to make money and compete on equal terms with other Indonesians; they could learn from the settlers and benefit from the roads and towns that transmigration brought. Was that why the transmigration project was being pushed so hard there? Or was it, as the human rights people had told us, for something else entirely, something less wholesome, and more dangerous? We set ourselves from then on the task of answering those questions, and we began to plan a journey that would take us to where we might find clues, to some of the most sensitive parts, the most dangerous parts, of West Papua.

Chapter 4

The police left us alone in Merauké; I don't know why: perhaps we were interesting to them, perhaps not. At any rate we were able to leave without trouble, and we moved on to Sorong, in the far west of West Papua. There were transmigration sites there too, where thirty thousand people were farming red soil. Most were better, we learnt, than Merauké's, some worse. More interesting to us were traditional Papuan villages close to the transmigration area. They were more typical than those around Merauké, as they were surrounded by rainforests, not the dry eucalyptus woods found only in the south-east. By looking at the forests and the ways both the local people and the new settlers used them we could hope to unearth a few clues about why transmigration was moving in. We found a village ten miles from Sorong, on the edge of one of the big transmigration projects, and we walked in among the houses.

A man in a black Muslim's hat and bare feet came down from his stilted house to see where we were going. I told him I wanted to see his sago gardens, sago being the staple the Papuans grew.

"In the forest?"

"Yes."

"Overnight?"

"Yes."

"Wait a moment." He ran up into his house and came down a second later with a machete and a pair of flipflops. "OK. Let's go."

He sprang off on knotty legs, glancing back to see that we were following, shouting and yodelling across the wet fields to friends. Four young men ran over and joined the party, and we took a path leading from the fields up to higher ground. Yopi, short, black, with tight curly hair and deer-like eyes, was joking and talking at a great rate. There was also a shade of seriousness in him and he took care to see that we could keep up and get across the logs that made bridges over the streams. We struck up into the hills that

39

overlooked the transmigration sites, towards the sago gardens at Klassaman.

Below us the roofs of the transmigration huts were rusty brown against thin greens and orange earth. Stick figures in conical hats covered the paddyfields that filled a plain among the hills. We climbed into forest land that just in the last few months had all been cut down. The trees had not yet been cleared, and they had fallen across each other, making walking almost impossible. The trunks were huge and perfectly round, and we had to climb on to the top of one, jump down into the broken vegetation beside it, then climb up on to the next. It was fine for the Papuans with their quick small feet, but we laboured up then fell off, or got stuck in a maze of broken branches on top. Sometimes there were fallen trunks of perhaps two hundred feet to walk along, that had overlooked the other trees until just a few weeks before. Yopi said the logs would be hauled out and sent to Taiwan. In places the wood had been burnt, and we crunched through layers of ash and charcoal, spouts of soot rising up and sticking to our sweaty faces. For many miles either side of us the scene was the same, of trees felled but not yet cleared away. There were some piles of sawn planks, and the marks of wood having been dragged through, but for the most part nothing had been used.

We came at length to a little hut on thin legs, newly built, perched above the surrounding mess. Yopi called up gently and a slow woman came to the doorway. We climbed the notched pole that led up to her floor. The house swayed and creaked with our weight. The woman dug around and found Yopi some bananas, cassava and a scrawny little chicken. We left her to doze on in the middle of the broken land, within the only structure standing on the battlefield. No payment for the food had been made, and when I asked Yopi about it he appeared not to understand the question.

Grey clouds had stuck to the hills and it became very hot. Already, slipping around on the logs, I was sweating badly, and I could feel the pulse in my face. Six weeks in western Indonesia had left me unfit, and I felt clumsy behind the lithe little men pattering over the trunks. Before long the slope rose more steeply and we began to walk among standing trees. Only the most valuable species, the hard red furniture woods, had been cut and dragged away; the others stood around smashed, like guests left behind when the dignitaries have gone. We reached the crest of a hill and saw the start of the real forest, climbing up and over a mountain. Behind that, Yopi said, lay the sago gardens, and the proper village of Klassaman.

I really was unfit. Sweat ran down to my boots and I was sure I could feel my blood thickening, and my heart heaving at it as if it was treacle. Yopi bounced ahead impatiently. It would be dark in six hours, he said, and we might not get to Klassaman and the gardens in time. He kept running back, chivvying us, then springing back up ahead with a furrow of exasperation. There were good excuses to stop. The first was a sulphur-crested cockatoo, flapping like an awkward moth above the trees, and stopping at the top of a high bare branch. There were cries from over the forest—'ker-ack, kerack'—then there were four more cockatoos floating around the dead branch, angel-white against the dark clouds. They took turns to jump on to a perch and displace the others. From another direction came a deep honking, and two beasts as black as devils came into the same patch of sky. They were bigger than the white birds, with huge hooked noses that hung down far below their chins. "*Kakatua rajah!*" shouted Yopi and started calling back at them, "Aar! aar! aar!" They were palm cockatoos, the biggest cockatoos of all, and when I got closer I could see their red cheeks and shocking crests. They too landed on the branch, and they clucked and gabbled, like sinister Punches.

The forest was hot and slippery. The trees sat on buttress roots, and their trunks sweated through a skin of spines. The black forest litter had rubbed off the path to expose clay, which we floundered on. Sometimes a birdwing butterfly would slip past, caught russet and white in a lightspot on the path, and away into the darker shades of the forest. Only in places did the dark let up, and then there would be a steaming patch of sunlight, and wet leaves glistening on the floor. It wasn't a canopy forest of the sort you get in the Amazon or Congo basins. Climbing up the mountain, the trees couldn't reach a common level, the umbrella effect of the flatland rainforest, but they covered up the sky just as closely. In places in the gloom there were white lilies blazing, or dusty blue berries on top of thin stalks. Yopi said they would kill us, so we didn't try them, despite being stricken by thirst.

I found a marshy pool and demanded we stop to fill my water-bottle. Yopi tried to prevent me: there was something in it that could make me ill. I didn't understand the word, but it didn't matter because I had sterilising tablets. He looked at them, and couldn't see how they would do me any good, but shrugged to say "Suit yourself". I showed him how it was done. I lowered the can in the water, careful to keep it out of the sediment. It filled up. "And then you just put two of these in and—shit!" Leeches were winding up my arms, making for the inside of my teeshirt. There were hundreds of them. I started hopping around, trying to pull them off me before they dug in. Yopi caught me and calmed me down, and he scraped them all off with his machete, shaking his head wisely but trying not to laugh at the same time.

The rain came sizzling down. We stripped off our shirts and became all slimy, water bouncing off our sweaty skin. My trousers dragged and slowed me down, and I was less able still behind the black men in shorts who bounced and yodelled through the rain, jumping over roots with their bare feet. The water gleamed on fruit of all sorts fallen down around the path: wild green mangoes, dusky grey things, big lumps of orange plastic, heavy red husks with prickles. Nothing looked appetising enough to stop for. Yopi tripped on a dead trunk, fell, somersaulted in the same movement and came up whooping, shaking the mud off the black hat that had stuck to his head. He wasn't a Muslim, he said, he just liked the hat. He demonstrated the different shouts for calling people in the forest. When it was raining and the bass rumble in the trees cut out anything deep, you should shriek wildly, rolling your eyes to show how penetrating it was. If there was no rain, you should hit a buttress root with the dull side of the machete to make it thonk, and yodel like Tarzan. Then there were different yodels for high and low ground, though it seemed that only the yodeller could tell them apart.

The rain fell through the spiders' webs strung across the path. Their bodies were spiked and warty, sometimes sharply pyramidal, in red and white enamel. Adrian walked into a whole nest of them, and was cursing and batting at his head. Yopi pointed out an orchid sprouting high up the trunk of a tree. It was haloed by the white sky above, shot with streaks of light as the drops fell past it. The rain was clearing and the sun was coming out. The slope became steeper. Yopi put his flipflops on. "It must be serious," said Adrian, and we started winding over broken rocks and the roots that had curled in among them. Birdsong broke out as the weight of the rain lifted off, and a scarlet finch shot over our heads from its nesting hole beside the path. The sounds were entirely mysterious. I couldn't tell if they came from birds or mammals, or frogs or other people, hiding in the forest and making their own special calls. There was a deep, intermittent purring from ground level. Yopi scratched a picture of the animal in the mud: "*Mambruk, mambruk!*" Big crest. Colour? Blue. Ground-living. Eye? Red. Size? It was a crowned pigeon, three feet long and powder-blue, closer to a dodo than to anything living.

Beside the path was a pile of leaves and dirt that Yopi poked around in. He stuck his hand into the middle. "Cold." It was the nest mound of a maleo fowl, a bird like a turkey that, instead of sitting on its eggs, buried them in a compost heap, and regulated their temperature by adding extra vegetation or taking it away. The chicks were hatched by bacterial fermentation. Yopi was relaxing, as we were going to get to Klassaman by night, and he stopped to show us things. We walked into a thick sandalwood smell, and Yopi wound the resin leaking out of the tree it came from onto a twig. Was it a perfume? I couldn't see what he was driving at, so he made a dumb show of lighting the stick and sneaking through the forest, the sun shut out with his hand. *Damar*: the tribal people used it as a torch at night; they wrapped it up in palm leaves and it would burn for several hours.

The path had become less distinct, and we were tripping on trunks and buttress roots. It led down to a wide green river, lit by the chasm it made in the trees. Everyone plunged in, the five men leaping and splashing in the middle. It was shallow but quite slick and fast, and one of the men took hold of a bounder among some little rapids and sunk, so that only his nose and mouth stuck out of the water. I floated down feet first and the cramp and sweat uncoiled and I felt much better and more relaxed. Rocks on the riverside were steaming in the afternoon sun, and parakeets sped across the gap in the trees. Yopi was scanning the edges of the forest. There were orchid clusters, pink and purple flowers against the deep green, and high yellow leaves lit up by the glitter of the sun on the river. "Woo!" Yopi pointed. He and two others scrambled across the river and scuttled straight up the thin trunk of a tree, like treefrogs, their legs bunched up beneath them. Yopi had his machete and was hacking off branches, that crashed on to the riverside rocks below. The others tugged at bundles of twigs. One of the men shinned down and carried bits of the tree across to where Adrian and I sat on a rock. They were covered in *matoas*, hard-cased fruit about the size of grapes, with watery flesh inside. We ate loads. I stretched out on the rocks and closed my eyes. The sun was very good. There was a sudden noise of swans' wings and 'tronc, tronc, tronc'. I opened my eyes and the sky was full of hornbills, black and white birds swishing past, huge beaks held stiffly out ahead. I closed my eyes again.

West Papua was the only place in the world where unknown birds and mammals were likely to exist. So little was known, there were so many isolated valleys and inaccessible swamps, that almost anything could live there undetected by outsiders. Freshwater sharks had recently been discovered, and sawfish weighing half a ton, that lived high up the big rivers. Reptiles and amphibians from Papua were stacked up in museums waiting to be given names and, whenever biologists got permission to visit the place, untold wonders came back. Papua had more exclusive species than all the rest of Indonesia put together: there were birds of paradise, bandicoots, birdwing butterflies, orchids, all found nowhere else in the world, and some were confined to tiny pockets of isolated forest. While the rest of Indonesia had wildlife that was typically Asian, Papua shared something with Australia, but for the most part was unique.

Out in the Pacific, the animals and plants of Papua had evolved in isolation from Asian species. They had adapted to make use of a similar rainforest home, however. There weren't any monkeys but there was a good living to be had for an animal that could climb trees and eat fruit or leaves. In the absence of a serious alternative, kangaroos, had adapted to take their place. The tree kangaroo had retained its big feet and its long snout, but had a winding pink prehensile tail and clambered about in treetops. The absence of a tapir or a pig species (pigs were brought in more recently by man) had left a gap for a large animal that could roam about the forest floor and eat almost anything. The creature that filled it was not a mammal but a bird: the cassowary, five feet high, flightless and solidly built, with a kick that could kill a man (particularly a man because of where it kicks). All the little creatures, rat-, mouse-, squirrel- or rabbit-like, were actually marsupials, a line of mammals entirely independent from those in the rest of Asia, or Europe. Strangely enough there were no large predators in Papua, apart from crocodiles, and man. It could be that man, moving in fifty thousand years ago, had outcompeted a marsupial tiger or a marsupial wolf, but there was no evidence that anything like that had existed. The distance from other land masses and the odd evolutionary pathways meant that West Papua had ended up with creatures unlike anything else on earth.

The thing, however, that had best preserved the great diversity of wildlife in Papua was its lack of contact with the developed world. Animals such as the different birds of paradise, the extraordinary birdwing butterflies (some of them thirty centimetres across) the great variety of parrots, would have been exploited vigorously almost anywhere else in the world, and very quickly wiped out. Off the northern coasts there were the best coral reefs on earth, with fields of giant clams a mile across, herds of grazing seacows, beaches where several thousand leatherback turtles could nest without disturbance, islands occupied only by the giant sea crocodile and Nicobar pigeon. With so few people in Papua and so little disturbance from outsiders, all this had survived, while its equivalents in the rest of the world had died away.

Yopi was shouting at me. I stumbled up off the rock—my body had stiffened, I shouldn't have lain down—and followed the whooping crew back along the trail. Evening birds were gathering with their different songs. Yopi, going round a big tree, suddenly leapt forward with a sharp cry and was flailing out with his machete. I thought he'd been bitten by something, but he had disturbed a kangaroo—a ground kangaroo—and had tried to get it for supper. It was off so quickly that I didn't even see it, though we piled into Yopi's back in our haste to take a look. The path had freshened a little, and soon we saw light through the trees: there was a clearing ahead of us. "Klassaman," said Yopi with his sharp smile. He made to go ahead but stopped and sent us on. "They'll think you've come to eat them," he grinned. I stepped forward towards the banana trees that hedged the clearing. There was a log fence and beyond it a tiny hut raised above the ground. Figures dropped from it and started sneaking off towards the jungle. Yopi leapt into the light and shouted out to them: we were friends. They stood around, curious and shy, a man and two boys, uncertain where to put their hands. Yopi told them to come forward to look us over, and the man very bashfully put out his hand and grasped my wrist. "Klassaman," Yopi said again.

It was clear that Klassaman had been chosen very carefully. The little house—Yopi said there were two others further on—sat in a bowl behind the mountain which had collected a thick black soil washed down from the slopes. The same bowl shape kept the soil damp, and trees shaded the crop plants from the shrivelling sun. The clearing around the hut was thick with fruit. Ripe pumpkin vines sprawled across the ground, papaya trees each sprouted a score of breasts, there were rows of banana trees and cassava. The hut was built on the buttress stumps of the trees that had stood there before. The burnt stumps of others sat among the vegetables: the three hectares of cut forest supported twenty or so people. The deep black soil and the water that gathered there would keep them going for a long time: after perhaps twenty years they would move on and let the old bowl regain its trees. The village would have a number of sites to move between, and after a lifetime it could return to the old one, that would have regained its fertility. A small population could afford to leave the soil alone for long enough never to exhaust its resources.

An old woman was stepping through the gardens with a basket of papayas round her waist. She was bent and soft-eyed, and when she spoke she had a child's voice, husky and deeply shaded. Her wiry hair was bunched up in tufts. Two more old people emerged, men. One was blinded by cataract in one eye and his shins were bent outwards and sharp-edged. None of them had any Indonesian: they spoke Moi, a language they shared with a few thousand other people scattered around in the mountains behind Sorong. We fell to muttering to each other in different languages, nodding approval. The clearing seemed to be a sort of forest geriatric home: a few people looking after their crops and each other, sheltered from the rigours of the outside world. Yopi said the place was a proper home: the village we had met him in was just a stack of new huts built to keep the police happy. They didn't know about this other place, and it would go on as it had always done, in no fixed location, but a place with a name none the less.

A fire was burning in the hut and the old woman started boiling the bananas we had brought. In the hut were sharp-tailed dogs, fruit hanging up and bits of kangaroo skin, an incongruous plastic bucket and two metal pans: we would have to go much further into that forest to find people living just the way they had always done. The roof was woven tightly from palm leaves and the walls were planks from the trees cut to make the clearing. As the shadows faded away outside, the insects wound up and began to creak and cry. I could hear the last cockatoos and their roosting calls. Mist gathered round the trees and it fell dark.

The old woman ignored us and talked to herself or her dogs, a long low mutter that rose huskily if one of the hounds tried to grab some food. She pushed them out of the hut and they lay beneath howling. One of the old men had lit a damar candle. The resin was wrapped up in palm leaves, and it burnt with plenty of black smoke, filling the hut with a deep, somniferous perfume. Yopi made soup out of the chicken and went through all the birdcalls he knew: bird of paradise, cassowary, black-headed lory: they went on until I fell asleep. The old people had laid out mats woven from palm leaves to sleep on. They were no softer than the floor, but I was tired enough not to notice.

At dawn there was a huge eel hanging outside the hut: some-one had been down to the river before we were up. Parrots of all colours were circling around in the mist; a flock of dusky lories came and settled in the trees above us, chattering and trilling all at once. I saw a funnelweb spider reverse into its hole; it looked about the size of a mouse and had lined its burrow with thick silk. The old woman was muttering unhappily to herself: Yopi said that wild pigs had come in during the night and cut down a papaya tree with their tusks and eaten all the fruit. It didn't seem a huge loss in that overabundant garden. We set off through the forest towards the sago gardens. There was a deep river to cross, slower and muddier than the other, and we all swam across, splashing each other or bubbling underwater. Yopi pretended to drown. We had cut through the forest for some way on the other side when we came out suddenly into a magical place. The trees had been felled several years before and the crowns of a few bananas could be seen. But everything had been overrun by an extraordinary flow-ing creeper, that billowed above our heads in great waves coming down from the trees, smothering all but the tops of the banana plants. The leaves glinted and flashed like a changing sea, and we walked in among its folds as if we had held back the waters. It was the entrance to the sago gardens, or so I imagined, and I pictured a Papuan elysium beyond it.

We stopped at a broken-down hut emerging in parts above the creeper. Yopi cut into it with his machete. Inside there was an old string bag with a possum's nest within; and on the ground he found a yellowed pig's tusk. Only much later did I notice a tiny hole drilled through the root; it had once been a part of someone's necklace. I took it as a present for my girlfriend.

Instead of leading us into the magical world I had expected, the path went straight back into the forest and abruptly Yopi told us we were there. Had he misunderstood us? It was the sago gardens we wanted to see. "Yes," he pointed all around him, "sago." I had had no idea what a sago plant looked like, but I'd imagined something with big floppy leaves and a tuber underground. It wasn't till Yopi took hold of one of the branches that I saw what he was pointing at. It was an unpleasant-looking spiky palm tree: they were all around us, twenty or thirty feet tall, but overshadowed by the higher forest trees. They looked poisonous. "You eat this?" Patiently Yopi mimed out the sago-making process. You chop down the tree about three foot off the ground, and cut open the bark. Inside is a solid pinkish pith, the bit which gets eaten. You smash that up with a mattock, then arrange a system of drains made from the concave leaf-ribs of the sago tree. You mash up the pulp with water, it runs down a rib and is filtered through a mesh of bark fibres, and the grains are carried down in suspension to a trough. The flour is squeezed out into big cheeses, and when it is dry bits are broken off and rolled about in the fire.

That had been the staple diet of the lowland people in Papua for fifty thousand years. The trees were never planted; they just grew in the forest, though sometimes the other undergrowth would be cut back a bit to give them more space. They were plants of the forest floor, so always they needed other trees shading them to stop them drying out. The sago supplies were never exhausted, for the population was very low. In fact, like those of any other animal, the human numbers levelled out in response to their resources. When there was plenty of sago around a woman could have more children; when there was less she would have to cut back, as there wouldn't be enough in her area to feed them.

I knew from the reading I'd done that the only thing that could keep a system like that stable was a strict code of land ownership: if the forests were a free-for-all they would quickly be over-exploited, and populations would soar and crash. From the air, and on the ground as well, Papua looked like a wilderness, of endless forests, with occasional little villages in the middle of them. It was a wilderness—the forests were just about as they had always been—but every inch of it was owned by someone. Each sago tree, though it grew wild and was twenty miles from the nearest settlement, had a named owner, and other people had to respect that ownership; they'd be fought if they used their neighbour's resources. Every village needed all the land it possessed, and all the sago trees, for its population had grown to match what was available.

The system seemed to be extremely wasteful of land, and on first contact with it you could think it's no wonder the population's so small if it relies on what it can find in the forest. If there was more farming, more people could fit onto the land, and they could use it to the full. The truth, and the great paradox of the rainforest, is that they use it to the full already. The jungle looks like the most fertile imaginable place. Nowhere on earth is there such an abundance of different plants and animals, green from ground level to two hundred feet. Governments and settlers in South America, West Africa and Asia have mistaken it for an answer to all their land problems. The paradox is that the only thing that can grow on most rainforest soils is rainforest. In those hills behind Sorong the soil was two inches deep. Below that was solid red clay, with hardly any nutrients that a plant could use. Rainforest plants are so competitive that as soon as anything hits the ground it is sucked up. Any soil that was there before is extracted and used to make living plants. Leaves that would take months to break down in European woods are gone in a matter of days: they could not accumulate fast enough in Sorong to produce a litter deeper than those two inches. All the nutrients are stored in the trees, and if those are taken away the land goes with them. Crops planted on a rainforest soil will flourish for a few years on the litter left behind; then there will be nothing.

The Papuans learnt that through bitter experience. Early settlers burning off the forest indiscriminately would have found themselves deprived of land after just a few years. The only way they could stay alive indefinitely in an area was to keep it almost exactly as it had always been, and crop only the surplus that the forest would allow: sago, fruits, game. Only in a few places in Papua could the rules be broken—like valleys in the central highlands or the little bowl at Klassaman—where the soil was deep and stable. The land-ownership system bound people to the rules of that survival game. Land was deemed to be held not just by the living but by the unborn as well, so that the genes of someone's descendants were protected by his careful use of the forest as surely as his own were. Land was owned by a whole village, though its resources—sago, hunting rights—could be owned individually. By ancestral law, the village could never transfer the ground to anyone else, for then future generations would have nothing to live on. If even a small amount of land went missing people would either start to die or overuse the resources to keep going, so closely matched was the population to what the forest could supply.

Standing in the sago gardens, as Yopi told us about the ways to make sago grow better, I understood the implications of transmigration for the rural Papuans. The programme relied on taking over land that appeared to the government to be unused. I also saw the implications of the rainforest system for transmigration. Fertilisers and modern techniques could extend the life of the soil, but they could do nothing to avoid the inevitable equation: that before long the ground without trees would fail and crops would no longer grow.

There was a simple explanation for the uneven distribution of people between Java and West Papua. In Java, like much of South East Asia, the soils were deep, black and volcanic, some of the best soils in the world. In Papua they weren't. The land alone could support no more people there than there already were, except perhaps through a sensitive intensification of the sago crop. The empty lands that the government saw in Papua were actually full. Nowhere in Indonesia, apart from odd spots such as those swamps in southern Sumatra, was there room left for population growth based on farming.

Many of the transmigrants had found that out already. Leaving the sites close to Merauké they had moved to the town to supplement the falling yield of their soils. Around the transmigration sites planted further away from the towns, however, there were no jobs to be had, so money had to be found elsewhere. Around Sorong they found it in logging. The hardwood trees were very valuable, and for the price of an axe a family could support itself until the forest ran out. The logs were being sold to a company based in Sorong, that needed do nothing but receive the transmigrants' timber, cut it up a bit and sell it on. Still more lucrative for the settlers was the wildlife, the strange forms that had for so long been protected by isolation from the outside world. Javanese around the transmigration sites in the north and west hauled mistnets into the trees, or hired local people to collect fledglings for them. The parrots and cockatoos they caught, many—like those black palm cockatoos we saw—endangered and protected, could be sold for high prices in Sorong, to people shipping them off to Jakarta or Singapore. Soldiers brought in to organise the transmigration programme took their guns on hunting expeditions, and had almost wiped out the crocodiles—again protected and getting scarcer—in many places. The skins were being sold to a company run illegally by the man in charge of nature conservation in Indonesia, and made into shoes and handbags. The soldiers also got people to show them the trees that birds of paradise used to display in, and the stuffed birds were being exported wholesale to Singapore.

Using the transmigration sites as a focus for development, and setting up big passenger ferry services from the overcrowded islands, the government was encouraging spontaneous migrants to move into Papua and make use of its business opportunities. In a place with no infrastructure the only business is extraction. The huge reefs to the north of the island, the best reefs in the world, were being dynamited by fishermen, the shells of the giant clams broken up to make terrazzo floors, the seacows killed for their teeth (which were made into cigarette holders), the turtles caught when they came up the beach and sold as varnished souvenirs in Jakarta.

Most immediately, however, the effect of the movement of people into forest areas was to cut off the livelihood of the Papuans. Yopi told me there were three things he feared: oil exploitation in the forest, the possibility of fully mechanised logging, and transmigration. Of those he feared transmigration most. A surveyor had been to the Klassaman area, looking it over as a possible transmigration site. It had that time been rejected, as access was too difficult. If transmigration surged ahead with an improved economy, however, and a road could get round the mountain, the place would be on the list once more. Already a road had been cut east-west through the forest near Sorong for seventy-five kilometres. There were transmigration sites all the way along, and the forest had been cut or exploited for ten kilometres either side. I knew that land rights were invaluable and couldn't be transferred. As they had never been written down, however, and were not based on Indonesian law, in nearly all cases the government had deemed them not to exist, and it was government policy to pay no compensation for the land that was given to the transmigrants. The land rights were being twice ignored: once when the site was marked out, again when the new settlers wandered off to supplement their living, and assumed that the private resources of the local people were free for all.

We were back in Sorong. It was a horrible place. The Dutch had built the town from nothing to ship oil out of the interior; the Indonesians had kept the docks going, but when the price of oil collapsed there was no work and the place fell in on itself. Bands of Sulawesi men walked along the road above the broken coral beach, kicking cans or throwing stones at sea birds. Papuans got noisily drunk outside the empty oil terminal and threatened to murder each other across safe distances of road and wire fences. We were the butt of much of the dissipation: new faces, outsiders to exercise stale wits on. I was jeered walking through the market, there was a great uproar of hooting and catcalling, and a dead fish was thrown at my feet. It wasn't hostility, simply that there was nothing better to do. Failing merchants and unemployed labourers worked their frustrations out on each other. A Sulawesi man grabbed my arm in a tearoom.

"What do you think of the Papuans? Hey?"

"All right."

"You don't think they smell? No? A bit black? Have you ever seen one wash?" He threw down my arm and smiled unhappily, staring at the local labourers on the other side of the glass. In a shanty spreading along the river ex-transmigrants washed their clothes in the filthy water, and added homesickness to the frustrations of the place.

Meanwhile in the cheapest hotel in town we sat and waited for a ship to get us out of there. Someone had started building an extension but stopped; there were just a few men clearing away the rubble. They were bored all day and would come and rap on our shutters at siesta time to see what we were doing, or enter the room and watch us, whistling aimlessly, then wander out again. One evening we were sitting outside and we saw two Papuan men edge out of the shadows with arrows in their hands. They stopped about five yards away, staring fixedly at the ground as if to show that they had no intention of attacking us. They hung there for an hour, edging a tiny bit closer, looking up as if about to say something but dropping their faces again, twisting their legs about with embarrassment. Adrian cracked it only when they'd gone. "They wanted to sell us the arrows!" he said. It hadn't occurred to me.

Adrian and I argued, I don't know what about—trivial things: the dull itches of the place had got to us. We were questioned by a Javanese man who visited us in the hotel. He was young and charming, and kept slapping our knees and laughing brightly, but he wove a neat grid of questions into his conversation, and we soon knew he was a policeman. How strange that he saw two white men going down the road to the transmigration sites—it wouldn't have been us he supposed? We had, of course, police permission to visit Sorong? Where else had we been? I told him truthfully enough that we were interested in animals and had been for a walk in the forest. He dropped his flatteries and told us he'd be back when he'd checked us out.

I was homesick and disheartened, and it was past time to move on. We had got hardly anywhere towards answering the questions: in fact we seemed further still from any kind of resolution. Transmigration, far from bringing the Papuan people the benefits of development, seemed to be cutting off their traditional livelihood, without bringing anything better. The little we had seen round Sorong then seemed to discredit the government's second claim for transmigration—that it was an effort to help the Papuans get rich—but it wasn't nearly enough to be sure. As for confirming any of the human rights campaigners' views, about transmigration being a deliberately destructive policy, we were nowhere down that road. It was time to try another tack.

We had been in two places which had felt the impact of development, two transmigration centres close to moderate towns. There were other parts of Papua, however, that had had the minimum of contact with the outside world. Of those the most extraordinary was the Asmat, the largest alluvial swamp in the world, a stoneless region of twisting rivers and bog forests, draining into the southern Arafura Sea. We had heard from missionaries we'd met in Britain that there were still cannibals in the swamps, still headhunting, and the rituals and ornaments that had been around for thousands of years. We had also heard that it was just feeling the first twinges of change. It was being studied as a possible transmigration area, and logging and gold prospecting concessions had been sold in Jakarta. For those reasons it seemed like a good place to see what was going on, and to find out why the government wanted to send in transmigrants. There had long been a pencil circle round it on my map, because of the lack of change, but when we heard that the whole region had been closed to outsiders since September '86, a year before we got to Indonesia, I was itching to find out what was going on.

We played with a couple of ideas. If we flew in or took a ship to Agats, the coastal town at the bottom of the Asmat, we would be arrested on the spot. We could take a canoe around the coast and sneak up one of the rivers, but I read that the sea there was very rough, and abounded with saltwater crocodiles, which specialised in overturning canoes. To go overland across the swamps from Merauké was impossible: the rivers went straight down into the sea, and we were unlikely to find the cuts across the marshes. We were left with an option that became more attractive and more frightening as we thought it through: to fly into the central highlands, walk over the mountains, cut down to a river, hire a canoe and get into the swamp forests through the back door. Not only could we then see something of the Asmat, we would also pass through the lands of the Dani: the extraordinary agricultural people who lived with penis gourds, tribal wars and a stone technology in the mountains. Wamena, a little town in the highlands, was one of the four places for which we had a stamp on our tourist permits, so that seemed a logical starting place. I hadn't a clue what such a walk would involve—whether the mountains were passable at all, the people hostile, the forests treacherous—but I was sick of those miserable places in the lowlands, and wanted to get up and going. We burnt our money on a flight out of Sorong, before the policeman came back. At Jayapura we didn't leave the airport, and boarded a propeller plane for Wamena.

Chapter 5

The shock of seeing the Baliem Valley in 1938 must have been one of the most profound an explorer has ever suffered. Just as Richard Archbold did then, we were taking a small plane along the crest of the central highlands of New Guinea. As in 1938, the mountains were jagged and barren, unable to support more than a few tiny hamlets, and a bleak scraping of the ground that might have been farming. There was snow on some of the tops: they broke roughly through strings of cloud, peaking out yellow and grey at around fourteen thousand feet.

When the ground suddenly disappeared from below him, and Archbold found himself hanging over a valley two thousand feet deep, he saw he had discovered the last lost civilisation on earth. Sheltered in the ten-mile plain between the mountain walls was a flat green land, intricately cultivated, with clusters of round and rectangular houses, thatched and soft-looking. Around them wound irrigation ditches like spiral mazes, with heaped up greenery in between. When he landed, later, on the valley floor, Archbold found a people whose technology had for ten thousand years evolved independently of the rest of the world. They had had no knowledge of the outside, nor the influence of any technology more advanced than their own. He had seen over the mountain wall, and broken the seal on a stone-aged culture.

Fifty years later there were still the sheer walls, the sudden shock of the pastoral valley wrapped in the violent mountains. At the bottom of the valley those yellow thatched houses and the spiral mazes remained, with little black figures picked out against the green. As we wound down over Wamena the changes were just as visible: a cluster of tin roofs, an airstrip, a church and a mosque, tarmac roads connecting them. When we stepped out of the plane into the mountain air, however, it felt as fresh as if a hydrocarbon had never been ignited there. I walked out of the smoggy heat that had clung to me since landing in Asia almost two months before, and with that heavy jacket went the nerveless sloth of the lowlands. The thin air was vigorous and cool.

People outside the airport looked as if they'd never noticed the developments that had sprouted up around them. Men wearing sticks on their penises, and string hats, trod the roads that had been unpaved paths until the white men found them, towards the market whose location had never changed, that was now hedged in with Indonesian stalls. Some of them carried stone axes, that they could trade for food or pigs with other Baliem men. Women, with naked fronts, but careful to cover up their backs, waddled in beneath sacks of sweet potatoes, suspended from the bands across their foreheads. The Dani had remained proud of the way they'd always lived, and could see no virtue in the outlandish lifestyles of first the Dutch and then the Indonesians who had broken into their private world.

We joined the procession—of old men wrapping their arms around their bare chests to keep out the cold, young men painted up in soot and pigs' fat, little girls in grass skirts herding a pair of piglets—and strode off to find the police post. The idea was that we would sign in as normal tourists, then scarper out of Wamena and get into the mountains before anyone knew we'd gone. Once out of the town, we'd heard, there was nothing, not a police post, no civil service, no soldiers, until we got to Agats, one hundred and fifty miles over mountains and swamps. Away from the valley and the mountains immediately around it we wouldn't see another Indonesian.

The police questioned us about the tripod Adrian had, but tourists in the valley were quite regular, and they gave us permission to walk for up to half a day from the town: we would have to sleep in one of the registered guesthouses among the tin buildings. It was all we needed: it would be a day before they could knew we were gone and, a pass in the mountain wall permitting, we would be away out of range and up into the rockfields or mountain forests beyond the Baliem. We figured that when and if we got to Agats we would already have seen all we wanted, and the only thing the police could do there, short of shooting us and causing a diplomatic row, was to send us out the way we were going anyway. In that high thin air, free of the humid paranoia that had gripped me in the lowlands, I was exhilarated and careless.

We went to the market to look for guides. It was perhaps the only crowded place in the central highlands. The Dani women had taken up all the floorspace, and had laid out fruit and vegetables from their gardens, in fresh mountain colours: tomatoes, cabbages, carrots, sweet potatoes—it looked like a horticultural show at home. There was an excited chatter among them. I noticed bark-string bags decorated with red and yellow orchid roots, the stubs of fingers amputated in mourning, a little pig clutched to the chest of a girl like a baby. Some of the women wore dirty teeshirts they had bought in the town, but most had either the string skirt of a married person, or the grass skirt of a girl, with coloured string bags covering up their backs. I had read that you were as likely to see the bare back of a Dani woman as the bare front of an English one. The men squatted around the inside walls of the marketplace, with stone axes, crushed tobacco, salty potash from two special brinepools of the valley, shell necklaces, for sale at their feet. They wore hollow yellow gourds on their penises and no clothes. The gourds were in all shapes and sizes: long straight ones that ran past the man's shoulder, curly ones like pigs' tails, short delicate ones with a cuscus tail sticking out of the top, fat stubby ones stuffed with cloth, all hollowed from things like hard conical cucumbers and held upright with a string tied round the man's middle. Every man had something hanging down over his chest: a shell, a bit of animal fur, a bunch of special seeds. The Dani believed that the soul matter—the *edai egen*—lived just below the sternum. If it wasn't protected from acquisitive spirits it would be snatched away when they were not expecting it.

Above their heads, sitting in canopied market stalls and quite detached from the scene below, were Indonesian traders. They were selling ballpoints, soap, instant noodles, monosodium gluta-mate and tins, and sat quietly among their ordered shelves, with clean colours and cool looks. We hung around until the strange-ness of the Dani became familiar to us. I liked the look of them: their faces were strong and expressive, more deeply set than the faces in the lowlands, with folds of unusual muscle, broad noses, craggy lines. It was extraordinary to watch the heavy set flash sud-denly into a smile, the deep lines bunching up in expressive folds, brooding looks gone like smoke. When a friend turned up in the middle of a group the men all stood up briefly and said "*wa, wa, wa*" and touched him on the shoulder or the body and cleared a space for him to sit down among them. A man in another group, in the odd breathey, Dani language, was telling some sort of a story. As he got to an exciting bit the men around him all broke out with "*wa, wa, wa*" and flicked their penis gourds with their fingernails: it meant 'wow' in Dani.

We found our guides among a group of trousered Dani men standing on the edge of the market. They seemed to be runners for the Indonesians, or middlemen, for they hung round the stalls looking for a break. We met Suleman first, with a low, bearlike head, small ears, a round jaw and a moustache. He ran off to find two friends and soon brought back Arkilaus and Peres, physically two of the most extraordinary men I've seen. They were both five feet tall, with huge hands and feet, about size sixteen if ever they tried to get into English shoes. Arkilaus, perhaps forty years old, was made of lumps of muscle that stuck out in odd directions. He had calves like fissured boulders, that bunched and jumped about with the slightest twitch. His arms were like bundles of pythons tied up at one end, flailing around independently as the hand moved. Peres was only seventeen, but already he was building the Arkilaus extremities: the big muscular belly, the horse-like buttocks. For all his heavy looks, Peres was shy and ingenuous, moving from foot to foot when I stared at him. Those feet were like hovercrafts, bulging out at the sides, round and flat. Arkilaus and Peres were Yalis, from the mountains to the east, and they were shaped from twenty thousand years of climbing sheer razor-backs. There was going to be no trouble with porters.

Suleman, by dint of being first found, was elected leader. We had told him we wanted to get to Trikora, the fifteen-thousand-foot mountain due west, which we reckoned was about two or three days' walk. I didn't want to say we were going further, as word might get around. We could either persuade the guides to stay with us until we were far west, perhaps to Mbua, the first village on our map, or find someone else to take over. We reckoned on three weeks to Agats, and we couldn't expect the same people to come all the way. Suleman understood at once that we were keen not to broadcast news of our departure, and I got the feeling that Europeans and Papuans up there were automatically going to be friends.

I was glad straightaway that we hadn't tried to be tough, and had given our packs to Peres and Arkilaus. The thin, straining heat was building a little, and we soon began to assault a broad cleft in the valley walls. We followed a river that had breached the wall and was leaping down from the tops, all clean foam and rainbow sprays. Arkilaus was carrying my rucksack on his head as he didn't like the straps. In the sweet potato fields on the slopes, women, sometimes helped by little pigs, were pushing away at the mud with digging sticks and hauling out purple tubers. The sweet potato was the cornerstone of life in the Baliem Valley: all the cultivated fields were pimpled with little mounds with vines on top, sometimes spiralling around the irrigation channels maintained for years and years. If anyone ever solved the sweet potato mystery they would cast light on more than just the history of the Dani. The first outsiders assumed it had spread eastwards to West Papua in the seventeenth century, after the Portugese found it in Peru and brought it to Asia. When the Baliem soils were analysed, however, they showed that there had been a sudden change of land use about nine hundred years before that, when people started farming a much bigger area. Only the sweet potato could have allowed the Dani to expand beyond the valley and open up land on the high walls, as it clung well to mountainsides. If it was that plant which reached the Baliem Valley in our seventh century, it must have been brought by Polynesian seafarers, which would suggest that they travelled not just as far as Easter Island, but all the way to Peru, where they traded with the Indians.

As we got away from Wamena the tin-roofed houses fell back, and we went by little compounds of homes like old-fashioned beehives, with straw thatch coming almost down to the ground. These little houses were surrounded by long low barns, like triangular haystacks, about thirty feet long. They seemed to be on fire inside, as blue smoke wound up freely through the thatch. A woman came out of one of the houses, a little pig at her heels. They stared a second, she rubbed her cheek with a fingerless hand, then they went back into the smoke. The compounds had kitchen gardens: neat mounds of cabbages, taro and potatoes obscuring the ground, coming out of a black soil the very opposite of the earth in the forest lowlands. Penis gourds grew on trellises outside the round huts: some had stones tied to them to make them grow long and thin.

The materials were simple but beautifully used: the neat thatch of the huts, the drystone pig-runs beside the compounds, wickets and hurdles bound together with cane for climbing the walls.

There was a ghostbridge beside a woven fence, three sticks decorated with leaves and feathers, designed to mislead the spirits into
thinking their path was elsewhere, and missing the compound
they had come to haunt. Metal axes and knives were coming into
the valley, but all the old structures had been built with stone tools,
or points and scrapers made from bone or bamboo. The tools were
not the coarse stone chippings of the European ancestors, but axes
and adzes neatly rounded off and polished, and sharpened by
grinding, not chipping. Dani stone axes were bound to crooked
sticks with cane, and could chop down a medium-sized tree in
five minutes.

There was little time to stop and take pictures though, as we
wanted to get well clear that day, and there was still a chance of
meeting an Indonesian who might report us. Peres slipped when
he was climbing a stone wall and tore open his shin. His skin,
white on the inside, dangled down, and blood ran all over his leg,
but he didn't seem to notice until Adrian stopped him and fussed
over it with antibiotic powder and lint, whereupon he stood ox-
like until it was done, then patiently took up the pack again and
walked on. The path thinned and climbed up to meet the river
again, now smaller and breaking into little falls. We were leaving
the potato fields and winding up into the mottled mountains.

The houses gave out and we were climbing a flowery heath.
Yellow rhododendrons broke out brightly from the tweedy greens
and greys, and there were lichens and bulbous blue flowers crawling on the ground. Suleman stopped and picked up wild strawberries and chinese lanterns: the fruit in the lanterns tasted of
Stilton cheese. The path rose, then levelled into a gorge between
two hills, a stream curling through the middle. Orchids had shot
through the turf on its banks and above the sound of the water was
birdsong, echoing between the walls of the gorge. As we came
round a boulder on the path we disturbed a big black pig, which
bristled at us, then crashed off with a grunt into the forest.

There was a bridge strung from rattan vines across the stream,
a plank walkway and cane banisters woven in, making a sort of
tunnel above the water. At the other end we met an old man with
a headband made from parrot feathers and a crooked penis gourd.
His face creased up into a grin, and he took my wrist with both
hands, shaking it and saying "*nayak, uh, wa, uh, wa, uh, wa, uh, wa*",
in an odd breathey way that seemed immediately grand-fatherly

and reassuring. We had come into another village and it was already late afternoon, so we stopped for the night. There were two tin-roofed buildings among the thatched huts—a school-room and a teachers' house—the last outpost of Indonesia before Trikora and, we guessed, Agats.

The school was run by three Javanese men, smoothfaced and handsome, who had refined their isolated lives into an artistic melancholia. They played the guitar by turns, very beautifully but always slowly, as if spinning out the time, and had somehow filled the bare house with their few coloured fabrics from Java, bringing the silk patterns of a harem to the bare splintery boards. We sat beside a window with Suleman and Arkilaus while the teachers made a space for us in their own room. A young woman passed by outside. She was carrying sweet potatoes in the netbag hanging down her back, gripping the thongs around her temples. She glanced in as she passed, looked again, then ran off, yelping over the turf to the other houses. Soon there were several Papuan women clustered round the window, hardly daring to look. They would edge round for a quick glimpse, take a horrified, shudder-ing breath, then snap back out of sight. Smaller people stood below the window ledge and rose up on tiptoes until just the bright eyes came over the top. These would quickly fill with hor-ror, then vanish downwards again. We were obviously the subjects of the sickest fascination, the most appalling creatures they'd ever set eyes on. Some old men in bent penis gourds came in to sell us sweet potatoes and, though wary of us, were not too abashed to ask an outrageous price. Arkilaus took them outside, I don't know what he told them: perhaps one look at that lump of muscle made them change their minds and suggest something more reasonable.

I strolled out into the compound and stood on the hurdle beside one of those long haystack houses. Clouds had rolled onto the mountains and the air was fresh and autumnal. I couldn't see anyone inside but I waved and smiled at the gloomy entrance and a man came out to see me. He sat on the hurdle beside me and grinned back. "*Wa, uh, wa, uh, wa.*" He spoke no Indonesian, so we just nodded and grunted and shook hands several times. His wife came out of the door in the haystack to look at me, and beside her in the gloom were the eyes and snouts of several pigs, bashfully poking out from behind her string skirts like children. Pigs and people lived together in the same house, but I later found out that the pigs had little bamboo sleeping pens inside. The man had lost two of his fingers, which was unusual in men, for normally only the women had theirs cut. He would have lost someone very dear to him and hacked them off with a stone axe while he was mourning. Women could lose all of their fingers but the thumb and one forefinger: when a relative died girls of just a few years old had to present their hands as a sign of respect. An old man in the village would cut off the fingers with a stone adze, and they were hung on the walls of the houses for good luck. I had learnt this from the sparse anthropological work conducted in the time of the Dutch. Since then there had been less—few anthropologists were allowed in—and I had found only the thinnest material to read.

The teachers had cooked us a Javanese supper, while the guides were left to eat sweet potatoes around the fire in the cooking hut. It was dark and the little room full of coloured cloths flickered and drew close around us by candlelight. The teachers had wrapped up in extra sarongs and light blankets: we had climbed to eight thousand feet and it was cold, and a chilly light rain pattered on the tin roof. A chessboard appeared from a dark corner after supper, drawn on the back of a school textbook. One of the teachers laid out a set topped up with nuts and bolts and pentops where pieces were missing. I was glad I couldn't play, but Adrian set to confidently, and for several moves seemed to be winning. He had stepped into a subtle mesh, and stared helplessly as his pieces were picked off without a second's thought. It happened four times, and every time the teacher just gathered up the pieces, turned the board round and laid it out again, with the slightest smooth smile. It didn't help that Adrian kept forgetting who owned the different bits of metal and plastic, but he was no match for three years of refinement in a hut among the mountains. Another teacher took up the guitar again and began to play very gently, just louder than the light rain on the roof. It was the last outpost of East and West, the final breath of Indonesia before the clouded mountains that belonged to the Dani.

The clean light of the morning picked out all too clearly the contours of the mountains we were bound for. They stepped up over us in tiers and fissures, grey lumps emerging from the forest. They looked, said Arkilaus, closer than they were. We strode up a rocky valley, then into a dappled woodland full of mosses and black pigs.

Naked women came down through the glades with digging sticks and empty net bags, moving out towards the potato fields. We had to wait beside a log bridge as a trading party came over. They were men from the far west—Suleman said you could tell by the stubby penis gourds—and they had walked in their hairnets and parrot feathers for several days over the mountains, on their way to barter in Wamena. They were much taller than our guides, and one carried a fine bright cockerel, just as proud as they, though bundled under an arm. Others had stone axes, and bracelets woven from stiff grasses, crushed tobacco and red fruit. They were moving much faster than us, and strode quietly past, five days from home.

We were back in sweet potato fields, broken up by rills and rocky slopes that couldn't be farmed. We stopped beside some women, one of them viciously hacking up a log with the machete in her fingerless paw. They chatted in a Dani dialect with the guides. Suleman looked a little bored and scratched his big stomach. Arkilaus tried out his languages. He spoke six: Indonesian and five tribal tongues. With just another one hundred and ninety, he could have got round all of Papua. One of the women had a little pig with her that didn't leave her heels as she moved about planting potato seedlings. She would pick it up and put it behind her when it was in the way, but it kept coming back as if terrified of being left alone with other people. She had possibly suckled the piglet herself: orphaned pigs were quite often taken up, and Dani women had been seen with a baby on one teat and a pig on the other.

As we cut up further through the gardens a party of boys came running and shouting around us, not hindered by the thinning air, and the thick mud on the slopes. With them was a little crippled boy, with one leg suspended uselessly below him, but who kept up and ragged with the rest. When we stopped for another break (and the porters were getting impatient) he hobbled up to me and stuck out his fist. In it were some crumpled strawberries that he had picked from the stony patches. He dropped them into my hand then hopped away to join the others.

Arkilaus had sent a woman ahead to the first village and when we arrived men and women were already coming in from the fields with sweet potatoes to sell to us. It was a rough, weeded-over compound, not as neat as the yards down in the Baliem Valley. We sat on the ground with several old men and passed round cigarettes. The most venerable sat crosslegged in front of us. He wore a headband made of blue seeds woven together, with a cockerel feather stuck in it, and woven grass bracelets up his arms. Excitedly he started telling us a story, leaning over to grasp my arm to emphasise a point, full of facial contortions and grins and frowns and excited whispers, breaking down into "*wa wa wa wa*" when the suspense was too great. It was completely incomprehensible to us, and it might have been just an elaborate greeting.

A woman took all the potatoes and divided them into piles. The Dani recognised seventy different types, and they each had a different function. One variety would go to old men, one to young men, one could be eaten only by pregnant women. Very special-looking potatoes, as well as the first from every field, were handed over to the ancestor spirits; and the weedy ones went to the pigs. When a new potato patch was opened up, a little house was built for the soul of the sweet potato, made of twigs and grasses, much in the style of a baby's carrying net. The potato shoot was planted in the ground, it gestated, and the tubers were born at harvest. If the soulnest wasn't built the potatoes wouldn't want to come out of the ground when they were asked to, as there'd be no warm home for them to move into.

We bought about thirty kilos: enough, said Arkilaus, for four days. Suleman had to carry them, which he wasn't too happy about. As for us we had the great weight of our boots and stiff lumbersome frames to haul along, and it began to grow greater. As we left the village I wondered what special potatoes the women had picked out for us: tubers with big noses perhaps, or pale skins, or a feeble droopy appearance.

God had been Japanese gardening among the mountains west of the Baliem. We passed through a sandy-floored forest of dry pines. It changed suddenly to become a humid peaty jungle, with glimpsed birds glancing through shafts of light, and toadstools and flowers picked out brightly against the moss. Walking became a problem. Because the ground was soggy, Dani men had felled trees and lined up the trunks end to end to walk on. That was great for the pudding-footed Yalis, who jogged along the logs carrying our packs as lightly as umbrellas, but it was murderous for us, heavy boots scraping vainly at the wet moss on the trunks. If we walked slowly we overbalanced and crashed into the stinking pools and stingers underneath us. If we rushed at it we simply sailed off, and crashed, again, into the stinking pools and stingers. Every time Suleman turned round he saw one or other mud-splattered face appearing from the void beside the trunks, and a pair of arms hauling up its owner for yet another weary attempt at the slippery pole. It was funny to begin with but we soon ceased to see the joke.

We had been climbing all day and it was getting late: the sky had thickened and a chill fell down through the forest. So Suleman, who had asked advice in the potato village below, led us off along a logless path to a tiny hut in a glade. It was too low to move about in except by crawling, and the entrance was a tiny hole shaped like a lobster pot, which was clearly designed for trapping white men and leaving them to their deaths. Arkilaus covered the muddy floor with ferns, Suleman drove off the damp inside the house and on our clothes with a cheery fire, and Peres roasted the potatoes. My father, as a joke, had packed me a pot of Gentleman's Relish that I had carried about everywhere as a sort of lucky charm. So it proved to be, for the tubers were horrible without it, like dried-out dough. I didn't sleep, but listened to the rain on the thatch roof and the talk, in one of Arkilaus' many dictionaryless languages, of the three cold guides.

The log paths that we rejoined in the morning were a feat of construction. With stone axes and the brute strength of men alone, the Dani had laid tracks many miles long through the forest, huge trees joined end to end, often three or four deep, balanced on stumps to keep them off the forest floor. I ceased to admire the achievement, however. Like the little house the log tracks had obviously been designed as a trap for outsiders, and they were geared to murder anyone without a hovercraft foot and a gymnast's balance. The earnest missionaries and pugnacious reformers who must have lain dead among the slime beneath us would probably account for the complete lack of change in the area. Our troubles were compounded by our choice of the rotten logs to step on. These had the roughest surfaces, not the high polish of the nice new slimy ones, and we would land our soles comfortably on top of them, only to crash through layers of splintering wood, thorny vegetation and gurgling mud. Then we had to pull ourselves back up on to the logs, slithering and slipping, coated in mud: we'd regain our feet, then slide fluently off into the mud again. Adrian fell on some rocks once, but he was past caring so it didn't hurt.

We met a man coming the other way; like Arkilaus he wore shorts and a shirt, though very grubby. Suleman and he talked quietly in Dani for a little, then Suleman said he would come to Trikora with us, as he lived nearby and knew the area well. So I handed over the pouch of tobacco that worked as a contract for hiring guides and Abraham turned round and led the way. I had a feeling that Suleman knew how to get to Trikora and had other motives, as Abraham carried the potatoes from then on.

That made Suleman very happy and me less so as, relieved of his load, he cruised on ahead and kept waiting for us with a sympathetic look and helping hand that made me quite ready to shove him into the prickly plants. Had I but stopped to stare I'm sure I would have found the forest there an upliftingly beautiful place, as parrots chattered and black and yellow or fluorescent-blue butterflies fluttered round our heads; as it was I brushed them away angrily and stomped on through the rotten logs and mudbaths.

We were relieved after four hours. The track cut up sharply out of the peat sink, we left the logs behind and stepped out onto blessed rocks. The forest had gone and we were walking on a high path among red bushes, no higher than our heads. We rounded a corner of the track and suddenly we were in a different world. A glacial plain stepped away before us, bare and windswept, of rocks and low yellow grasses. A cold wind cut across us and echoed on the stone. Only around a distant mountain river was there vegetation, and it was nothing but a clump of tree ferns, black and otherworldly, plants that had been on earth for a third of a billion years. Suddenly it was the best place in the world to be. The wind was running, I felt dragged forward then lifted up by it: it was a place of some momentous event, a valley of dry bones, mountains of resolution. I stood back and let the rest walk on: Arkilaus and Peres plodding stoutly under the packs, Suleman striding ahead of them, Abraham rangy and thin, bent beneath the bag of potatoes, Adrian treading forward tiredly. They were all made tiny figures beneath the great black crags, little sticks crossing the ice-carved plain, while I, behind, away from people, felt the great relief that had been bubbling to come out of me ever since we stepped into the steaming crush of Asia.

I ran on and caught up with them, and we threaded across the plain towards the lowest of the mountainsides. Over the hill we found thorny scrubland, which grew huge distorted cancers full of

66

ants, that ran about wildly when Arkilaus cut one open with a machete. There were bog pools and brown thorn-living birds, feathers ruffling in the cold wind that came down from the tops. Adrian was having trouble on the slopes. He had a headache that ground with every step, and seemed to be getting worse. He wanted to lie down in the scrub and let it go, but Arkilaus was pushing us on: Trikora wasn't far. He was showing his extraordinary strength. Weighed down by my excessive pack, he marched on steadily up the mountainside, leaving even the packless Suleman labouring far behind, and us still struggling in the bog pools at the bottom. He and Peres were mountain people, and twenty thousand years in the impossible crags of the Yali had made them strong and hard enough to go up anything.

As, at last, I came over the crest, I was confronted by Trikora, on the other side of a glacial valley. The mountain climbed, through ledges and false summits, to a blunt conical top of the sheerest grey rock. There was no snow then, but the fifteen and a half thousand feet, in that thin, narcotic air, was shocking. I stopped at a bog pool to fill my canteen, and in the mud beside it I saw the prints of a man's bare feet. They were too small for Arkilaus's and I was ahead of the rest, but they were fresh. Abraham was the only man we had met that day, and he soon after starting, and I had guessed the high mountains to be unvisited and uninhabitable. Intrigued, I hurried on in the direction Arkilaus had taken. There were more slopes to climb, and soon I flagged. We had cleared eleven thousand feet, and the air was doing me no service. I just wanted to roll down in the heathery vegetation and come to rest somewhere soft.

I would rest at the top of the next rise. I was feeling dizzy, and I would wait for the others there. I waded up through clumps of yellow grass, with heavy legs and confused resolve. I pulled myself over the edge and nearly fell down again as I saw four heads peering over at me. I clambered up and there, on the windchilled top in the middle of nowhere, were four naked men sitting round a fire. Arkilaus was there too, but rather than stretching out on the heather as I immediately did, he was walking about the crest pulling up plants for the fire, using up some surplus energy. It wasn't until I had been on the ground for ten minutes that I could muster the grace to say "*nayak*" to the other men. Conversation stopped there for lack of words until Arkilaus stood still for long enough to interpret for us. The four men were Kinyum, from the west, and they had walked four days to Wamena to trade. In their net bags they had everything they'd bought: a tin of pilchards, two wads of processed tobacco, a bunch of vegetables, that was all. They were satisfied with their trading, and the bright tin of pilchards was brought out a couple of times to pass round and gloat over. I wasn't certain that they knew it was food. All that was well worth an eight-day round trip, and the four sacks of sweet potatoes they had carried in.

They had also been carrying heavy bows made out of ironwood and strung with a length of split cane, five or six feet long. The arrows were tipped with wood, elaborately carved with strange barbs and points. Some were triple-headed, for small birds, others had a single bamboo blade for tree marsupials and wild pigs. I asked Arkilaus what the points with the deep, hooked barbs were for. "*Manusia*": human beings. As I was admiring the arrows they were snatched from my gaze, and one of the young men loped off into the bushes on the edge of the crest. A brown bird had settled in the spiky branches and was swinging in the wind. The man drew but the bird flew off over the valley, leaving him silhouetted, black, with arched bow and drawn arrow, against the grey rocks of Trikora.

Adrian laboured up then, grey with pain and tiredness, his aching head held rigid on his neck. He took a look at us then tumbled over in the grass and lay face down. Peres and Suleman hailed us over his corpse and Abraham dropped the potato sack among the naked men. Arkilaus was crouching beside the fire scanning the huge plain below. He pointed. I followed his finger and tried to see.

"What is it?" I could see nothing.

"*Manusia*," he said again.

I still couldn't see though, and it was another two or three minutes before I made out the two black figures coming towards us up the glacial valley. They were running, not walking. We waited for ten or fifteen minutes, then they appeared over the crest, striding quite confidently, in full breath, crossing over and squatting beside the fire as if they'd just been down to the shops for a paper. There was a middle-aged man and a boy, both carrying bows and their sparse goods from the market in Wamena. They exchanged a word with Arkilaus and he told me they were coming with us that day, to Samera, where we would spend the night. It seemed incredible that there could be a village up there, between us and Trikora; but no, Arkilaus said, it was not a village, nor a house. He tried to explain it to me—it was a place, with a name—but I remained bemused. We marched on.

The track took us over more hills, then out across a flat rock plain, with the barest vegetation. It was bitterly cold. Adrian was now trailing badly, though helped on by Suleman. Arkilaus let me go ahead with the six hunters, and we crossed the rocks in the biting bare wind, the naked men oblivious and cheery. The plain narrowed towards Trikora and we came into a passage between two huge bluffs, leading to the mountain's northern flank.

"Trikora," I said, awed.

"Samera," they replied, with relief.

I was still confused. Yusup, the middle-aged man who had run across the plain, bounced on ahead with his bow and arrows. I did my best to keep up, clobbering through the rocks in my heavy boots. We were among tree ferns and bushes like juniper. There was a faint double whistle from behind the scrub. Yusup beckoned me to be quiet, then he answered the whistle with an exact copy. The whistle came back and he started stalking towards it. I was glad to see it was his bird arrow he had lifted to the string. Yusup kept calling, but the bird moved away, probably in search of a more likely mate than the big black one creeping towards it with crossed sticks.

Yusup bounced on along the passage between the high rocks, and it narrowed and the rocks hung over us more blackly. Then he sprang up one side of the gorge and disappeared among the bushes. I waited down below: he was probably having a pee. But soon there was a whistle and a call that sounded like Dani for "Come on". I struggled up the wall behind him. Breaking through the bushes I was suddenly beneath a ledge of rock. It was blacked by repeated fires, and it fell back into a long and shallow cave.

"Samera," said Yusup.

Soon a fire was crackling in the rock cleft, and the other Dani were unwrapping sweet potatoes to poke into the flames. The guides came along and Arkilaus and Peres, quite unaffected by the walk, were lumbering back and forth to the cave with huge bundles of firewood, which they piled up until the flames were licking the tar on the ceiling. Adrian sat in the back of the cave, out of the smoke, and stared at the gorge that ran up to Trikora. Streamers of rain were wavering down it, propelled by the strong mountain wind, and the rocks of the gorge took on shapes and faces as the light fell; I imagined people out there climbing among the stones and coarse grass, then there was no more light and the valley disappeared.

Within the cave was a stone-aged scene. The Kinyum sat around their fire in penis gourds, their naked skin lit with the same glow as the black rocks around them. The flames spurted up and crackled on the ceiling whenever they threw on more logs and every so often a man would roll a potato out of the fire and slap it as if killing the heat. The floor was carpeted with several inches of feathers, from little birds shot by hunters on their way over the mountains, and plucked and cooked in fires like that one, which had probably blackened the roof of the cave for tens of thousands of years. We had a separate, more modest fire, and Adrian and I had wrapped ourselves up in our sleeping bags, already very cold. We nibbled unhappily at sweet potatoes. Abraham and Suleman chatted in Dani, glancing all the time at the Kinyum around the big fire. Perhaps they would abscond and leave the hunters to carry our packs. I read for a while with a torch, then turned about to see how Adrian was, and caught a frightened little possum in the beam. It had big black eyes and thick fur bundled up against the cold, and it twitched its whiskers uncertainly at me.

"Oh look," I said in Indonesian, "what a nice possum."

Adrian picked up his camera to take a photo of it.

"*Makan*," said Abraham and whacked it with a stick from the fire. He threw it over to the Kinyum, who fell on it and rolled it in the flames before breaking the body into pieces and eating it: skin and bones and head. I felt a little jealous.

Brown fleas had invaded my sleeping bag so again I didn't sleep, but lay close to the fire. When the rest of our party had nodded off I heard a noise start up from the fire of the Kinyum. It sounded like dry grasses scraping in the wind. Then a bigger one came up beneath it, deeper and louder, like rocks rolling on the bed of the sea. It rose and fell beneath the reedy sound, that pitched up higher then suddenly died. The deep noises came in again, then the high refrain once more, soft and creaky. The Kinyum were singing.

Adrian was very ill in the morning. His throbbing headache had become a migraine and he lay on the bed of grass and feathers immobile with pain. We reckoned it was a trapped nerve in his neck, jolted into the gap between his head and his vertebrae by those endless falls from the logwalk. Arkilaus massaged him with his huge black hands, but it did no good, so he lay rigid on the floor of the cave, only turning his head away when offered a sweet potato. I suggested to Suleman that we spend the day climbing Trikora, giving Adrian a chance to recover. So Arkilaus and Peres stayed with him and Suleman and I set off up the slopes of the mountain. On the way we stopped and watched Yusup, the compulsive hunter, stalking another bird. As he followed it through the scrubby bushes I realised that it was the extremely rare golden-winged bird of paradise, that lived in a few isolated valleys in the highlands. I wasn't sure that it should be impaled on the end of a three-pronged arrow, but it would have been hard to explain that to Yusup. He trailed it for fifteen or twenty minutes, hiding behind the juniper and crawling out along the rocks when it wasn't looking. Eventually he got right underneath it, hidden in a bush just four feet below his quarry. With stealth he drew back his bow, aimed steadily and fired. He missed. The bird fluttered off noisily: the arrow had passed a clear foot above its head.

Suleman and I pushed on up. We were climbing a ring of rocks above the gorge. Two high waterfalls had broken from it, and they hurtled down on to the rocky plain below, rivers snaking away to a distant lake. We climbed a long tussocky slope, then Suleman, who couldn't see much point in going on if it wasn't taking him nearer to home, sat down in the grass and said we had probably done enough. So I told him he could stay there while I went on to see how high I could get. He bounced up and raced me over the next rise, that zoomed up to a sharp hogsback close to the summit. It was a hard climb through springy vegetation, all knees and elbows. We cleared the ridge and found ourselves on a knife-edge so narrow that we couldn't stand up for fear of falling off. So we straddled it with our legs and pulled ourselves along until we gained a barren slope leading to the sheer rock walls. We couldn't climb them there so we wound on round the mountain, failing to find a route up the remaining thousand feet.

We came at length to a bare limestone pavement, quite flat, perhaps two acres of crumbling criss-crossed stone. Looking closely I saw that it was covered in fossils: huge bivalve molluscs with ribbed shells, fourteen thousand feet above their proper habi-

71

tat, thrust there by the impact of Australia with the New Guinea plate. I explained to Suleman what they were and he was fascinated, poring over the surface with his hands behind his back like a geologist, picking out the crispest specimens. I stepped to the edge of the stone pavement and stared out across the view.

There were clouds in the east, but to the west I saw endless mountains crowded one upon the other, stepping off into the thin blue air. Among them was a purely pyramidal peak, blue, and streaked and capped with snow. It was Punchak Jaya, sixteen thousand feet, the highest mountain on the continent. One hundred miles away it still stopped the scanning eye, a focal point in the inestimable field of rocks. Across the empty mountainscape there wasn't a sign of people, not a sound, no wind, no birds, nothing. I shouted out, wondering if Adrian would hear me in the cave far below. The sound filled all the empty space, bouncing from wall to rock wall and throbbing above the glacial valley below us, towards the distant lake I saw, the mountains beyond that, the blue, uncharted, uncrossable lands of swamps and snaking rivers I pictured lying beyond them. But Adrian didn't hear, and when the shout wore out we wended back along another route, confident that Trikora was unscalable without ropes. Suleman's newfound love of geology was short-lived: he threw the fossils in his hand at a bird we disturbed in the bushes.

Back in the cave we had to make a decision. Adrian felt a little better and had been tottering about the rock ledge and the valley floor below; but he said the pain came back after just a couple of hundred yards. He was determined to go on, however. If he turned back then, he said, he would get to Wamena and fly straight home. He wasn't enjoying the trip very much, and hadn't been getting the photographs he'd wanted. Failure here was all it would take to finish his trip. Also, by our map, the next village—Mbua—was the same distance from us as Wamena. A landing strip was marked there, probably a missionary drop, and maybe an aeroplane could pick him up if he was still ill. He'd get there, even if Arkilaus had to carry him.

That took us to the question of guides. I was confident that someone could help us, for the Kinyum at least, who had remained in the cave, were to move off in our direction. When I told the four porters our intentions, Arkilaus immediately agreed to come. His only concern was Adrian's health. He seemed to have decided for Peres and Suleman as well, for they instantly fell in behind him. It had become clear that Arkilaus was really in charge, and resented the imposed lead of Suleman. The roles had shuffled themselves into a natural order, based, I suspected, on sheer physical strength. As for us, our place in the pecking order had declined rapidly from that of the great white hunters leaving Wamena: now we just paid the money and did as Arkilaus said.

The problem was Suleman's pregnant wife, who would worry about his disappearance. Arkilaus, however, said that Peres should go back and tell her, and clear up some of his own loose ends as well. He was worried about the boy's safety in the woods though, so he told Abraham to go back with him, in case he fell ill. Yusup the hunter agreed to take their place. He knew the paths and he could help us among the people to the west.

I sat again at night beside the prone figure of Adrian, watching the Kinyum. They seemed so well suited to those mountain tops: fit, both self-sufficient and sociable, resistant to the cold, having small needs. White men were nothing in that place, about as well adapted to the habitat as a fish in the Sahara. I had expected people to be captivated by us, and shy; but they were neither, and simply got on with their own lives, hardly acknowledging our presence. Yusup looked pained when I tried to talk to him, as if he felt sorry for the two corpse-coloured fools who made such a meal of the simplest trip.

I dreamt all night about food. Hot chocolate and apricot fruitcake kept reappearing, and I dreamt I was consuming them sitting by the fire in the cave. When Adrian woke up he groaned "Harrods Foodhall" and rolled over to dream about it again. Food was now a serious problem. We had brought nothing with us, and I craved something energising like sugar or chocolate: sweet potatoes weren't doing the trick, and they were also dropping like bombs through my alimentary tract. Adrian hadn't been eating at all, he was too ill. He was no better when he woke again after another orgy in the Foodhall, and we found that even the sweet potatoes had run out, and we would have to go on with nothing. His migraine returned, but he decided to go on and see what happened. I gave Abraham and Peres extra tobacco and cash, and they slipped down from the cave and ran off across the gulley. They became smaller and smaller, then vanished into the fields of rocks and yellow grass.

Chapter 6

It was slow, slow work lumbering across the next plain, with its dense tree ferns and knee-deep mud. All the joy of the mountains had dissipated and been replaced with dull discomfort. Adrian, resting on a stick, kept shouting and hanging his head, in serious pain, and Suleman announced that it would take us five days at least to reach Mbua. After two hours, in which we covered little more than a mile across the moor, Adrian stopped and got Yusup to divest his pack for a moment. He dug around in it then we carried on. After that he appeared to become much better, and we plodded more surely over the plain. He told me after a bit that he'd taken a morphine tablet.

"But those are only for emergencies, they're dangerous!"

"If you knew how I felt," said Adrian tiredly, "you'd think it was a bloody emergency."

From then on he said he was floating over the grass, and it was all happening to someone else. I rather envied him that, for dullness and the strong urge to lie on the ground had taken me over.

We came to the end of the plain after four hours and started to climb a steep slope of bogs and burnt bushes. It rose a thousand feet, and by the time I reached the top I was angry: with myself for being feeble, with Adrian for being ill, with Arkilaus, Suleman and Yusup for being so sickeningly fit and able. Adrian had battled on bravely and it wasn't long before he joined us—but he looked so ill that I felt we should make a bed or a coffin right there. The morphine pill was wearing off and, though it wasn't my illness, I argued with him about taking another one. We rested for a while then started to descend, and encountered another of those startling changes in the landscape. The eastward slope of the mountain had been in sunlight, but the west lay in cloud that Yusup said was permanent. The ground fell away almost sheer beneath us, invisible in the white fog. At first the vegetation consisted of platforms of protruding branches, which we had to jump on to, six or eight feet at a time, as there was no path and no bare ground. It was nerve-wracking, launching ourselves into the white void, being caught and bounced by the springy trees; jumping again, like a marmoset. Then, as we cut down deeper into the cloud, the forest changed suddenly once more.

It became a magical children's garden, padded like a safe cell. Everything was cushioned in two feet of moss. Only the tips of twigs emerged and sprouted sudden pale leaves, otherwise all the trees had been turned into crouching animals, their finest branches thicker than arms, hunched menacingly in the mist. It was like being in bed. You could throw yourself down the slope and land any way you pleased, as every fall was cushioned. You couldn't tell if there were rocks or logs or just a void beneath you, and it didn't matter. Fantail wrens floated out of the mist and displayed among the monstrous shapes, and I could hear golden-winged birds of paradise buzz past, unseen.

The slope evened out abruptly; but the growing sound of a waterfall was well below us. We were back on slippery log roads and they were hazardous and miserable, coated with leeches rearing up to sniff us out. Suddenly, as impatience took a violent hold on me, we came out into a clearing in the forest and there was a tiny hut, palm-thatched, wadded with moss. Arkilaus had asked the Kinyum, who had left the cave before us, to send ahead for food, and in the hut were two women, an old one in a rough jerkin and a shy girl with a grass skirt and a simple grass necklace. They had brought potatoes and sweet potato leaves, which we could eat as a salty vegetable. We posed outside for a photograph: Yusup in his penis gourd, a black plastic bag on his head; the twentieth-century highlanders hard and black against the mossy shapes of the hut and the forest behind; the women confused by the unaccompanied tripod staring at them; two feeble, wet, utterly exhausted whites, raising limp versions of a grim smile.

After a damp night interrupted by diarrhoea, we crossed the waterfall at the bottom on a pair of thin sticks, which sagged and buckled over instant death. There was another short climb, then a long and painful descent, which took us out of the moss forest and back on to rocky trails. At the bottom we came suddenly upon a party of men in red parrot feathers, sitting on a rock. They stared for a second, unsure. There were bows and arrows on the rock beside them. Then one man jumped up and the rest followed, taking our wrists and shaking vigorously, saying "*wa, wa, wa*," and some new word that wasn't "*nayak*". They joined our straggling chain and greatly improved its appearance, laughing and chattering or shouting "*Wa!*" and flicking their penis gourds when someone said something funny. The trail led into fields and soon we were shaking the hands of women as well. One I took had no fingers at all and the soft paw was rather horrifying till I remembered that finger-cutting was commonplace, and possibly no more traumatic than school injections.

We had come into the village of Iniyei, and here were the huts, messier than those of the Baliem Valley Dani, of rough boards and untidy thatch, but looking no less comforting. The whole village gathered around flat rocks, old men sitting on one, young men on another, women standing around a third. Only one man was in clothes, and he completed the grubby suit of Disney teeshirt and ragged shorts with a homemade guitar, whose two notes he strummed over and over as Arkilaus bargained for potatoes. The whole village watched us, gently, intent. One woman picked nits from the head of another, who in turn was weaving a net bag as she looked on from the rock. Arkilaus stared at the potatoes brought to him, turning them over thoughtfully. Sugar cane was brought and laid at his feet as well. I felt dizzy. The guitar strummed, the place was still, the eyes all on us. Arkilaus stood and pondered.

When Arkilaus suggested we buy a pig to cook from the villagers neither of us had any notion to resist him; and presently a half-grown pig was herded in. Arkilaus bargained it down to twenty thousand rupiah, about seven pounds. The owner came with us, to carry the pig over the steep bits, and despite its gentle smile and trusting look I couldn't help thinking of all its roasted meat. The pigman heaved it onto his shoulders when we got to the rocky bits of the mountains, and released it to trot along beside us when the slope smoothed out. From Iniyei onwards the mountains became worse, running from steep slopes to sheer razorbacks. Even Arkilaus was now flagging behind Yusup and the pigman, who knew the routes, and held the muddy ground well with their splayed toes.

Pigs were at the centre of Dani life. The furry grey animal running along beside us was the most important thing they possessed. Some men we saw had lost the top halves of their ears, most likely as a result of the loss of a favourite pig. In total misery at his desertion a man would hack off his ears with a bamboo knife. Pigs were treated very much like people: sometimes Dani men would whisper into their ears, urging them to be good and get fat. They were often fed on cooked food, and allowed to sleep close to the fire at night. Like children the pigs were considered to have souls, but to be unaware of the religious taboos they should observe; so they were forgiven for rooting in the spirit gardens, or eating food forbidden to the owner's clan. For all that, pigs were killed in huge numbers when necessary, which was only on special occasions.

Nothing important could be done without slaughtering pigs. When war was to be waged, pigs were first consulted, then killed and offered to the ancestors to bring good luck. Pigs were the essential part of the brideprice, and a man couldn't hope to take more than one wife unless he had a lot of them. The great *gains*, the most senior village elders, could marry up to ten wives each if they had enough pigs. Boys couldn't be initiated without eating lots of pork, and first having a live piglet held in front of them to charm the bad spirits out of their chests. When the pigs had been killed the boys could go through the mock battles, cold and hunger needed to make them into men. Funerals were also attended by slaughter: the spirit of the dead man was first appeased by being offered plenty of cooked meat, then driven out before he could lay hands on it by men rushing through the compound hurling rocks and shouting. The spirit then had to go and live in one of the Dani ghosthouses: mysterious square huts that only one foreigner had ever been allowed to enter, full of bundles of dried grass bound up to look like humans. If he came sneaking back to the compound to cause trouble he'd be shouted at and told "You go away!"; alternatively he could be called up to help with a war or a ceremony. Spirits were taken for granted by the Dani, and their incorporeal presence wasn't considered alarming.

Almost all the marriage, initiation and remembrance ceremonies took place at once, in a great pigfeast held by an alliance of villages every four or five years. The pigs that had been so carefully tended and fattened up were nearly all killed, and there followed three or four weeks of astonishing gluttony, during which some people might eat several whole pigs, being sick in between to fit more in. The more that was eaten the more favourably the ancestors would regard the village and the better would be the anticipated marriages or battles: which was fine for all the Dani, except for the pigs.

None of us was sorry when, soaked and exhausted, we broke out on to a hilltop and were told by Arkilaus that we would make an early stop to cook the pig. We stood on a grassy knoll below the high mountains, with two old rough huts, and little birds at eye-level in the treetops. The Dani men built up a pile of stones and covered it with firewood. Then Arkilaus took out a cleft stick that he kept in his string bag, some seedhusks and a bundle of thatch from a house. He pressed the stick into the tinder, and ran a strip of dry rattan vine rapidly through the cleft. Very soon smoke broke from the pile of thatch, which he blew into flames and added to the stock of wood. As the fire roared Arkilaus killed the pig with a rock, then burnt off the outer layer of skin. Yusup and the pigman dug a pit with sticks and sharp rocks, about two feet deep. When the fire had burnt low they took the hot rocks from beneath it with sticks and put them at the bottom of their hole. Then they covered them with long grass, threw potatoes and edible ferns on top of that, and laid on the bits of butchered pig, more potatoes, some squashes from Iniyei, more ferns; then they wrapped up the bundle with the grass that stuck up from the bottom of the hole and weighed it down with rocks. Suleman poured water from my canteen down the sides, and steam shot up and percolated through the package.

We left it for an hour and a half, then the men unwrapped the bundle and the feast began. Arkilaus chopped up the pig and being, I think, a little contemptuous of the untrousered Dani, gave them the gristly bits. We finished the pig in an hour: guts, brains, bones and all. The guts, wrapped round hot stones, were a bit like crispy bacon rind; we managed to crack and splinter up the bones till only the big joints and clavicles were left. I remembered, watching Suleman trying to stuff the best part of a leg into his mouth, fat bubbling down his chin, that he was supposed to be a converted Muslim, or so he had told us on the way to Trikora. His eyes bulged from behind the bloody bone. "I am," he dribbled, "but"—another huge bite—"I'm also a Dani." I felt like one of those deep-sea fish that swallows things bigger than itself. Again I didn't sleep, rolling about and scratching at the fleas.

Dawn was like a waking in the trenches, the wet grey light bringing on nothing but homesickness and cold and the prospect misery. Adrian was still in pain. We stuffed our kit back into the rucksacks, scoured around for scraps from the night before, of which there were none, and looked out of the tiny doorway onto grey rain running down the sides of the axehead mountains. Arkilaus wanted to leave straight away, so we stepped out into the black mud. The pigman went back to Iniyei, and the rest of us stumbled and slithered down the first long slope, into a gorge, and a rushing cold river. We had to breast up it for an hour, and Suleman and Adrian, dragged far behind by Adrian's sickness, went up the wrong feeder stream. Arkilaus had to run back to find them and I was left shivering on the bank, the cold all the way inside me. When he got to them, Adrian had just been saved by Suleman from death beneath a waterfall: they had climbed a rockface to get round it and Adrian had slipped. Suleman caught his hand just as he began to fall, and held him dangling until he could find his feet on the rock once more.

We left the river and started to climb the cliff that hung over it. We used our arms more than our legs, hauling ourselves up and kicking the empty air, elbows jammed among the roots, water streaming over our shoulders. Where there were footholds they were filled with mud, and once my boots slipped away and touched the void, leaving me dangling from a lump of rock. Through all that Arkilaus and Yusup bore up grimly under the packs, planting strong feet firmly in the cleft of a root, pushing themselves up on one leg, pulling themselves through with knotted arms. We were all painted with mud, our skin and clothes indistinguishable.

Going down was worse. It was a more or less a double-sided cliff, and we slipped and tumbled freely over the roots and into the trees. If one of the Dani men fell he would whoop and shout and all three would laugh, which saved Arkilaus's pride and Suleman's temper. But if we fell down it was just another slip into despair; one descent closer to the point at which I just sat down and refused to go any further. At the top of the second axehead Arkilaus and Yusup began to argue about the route. For all Arkilaus's assurances it was clear that we were lost. Adrian didn't even have the energy to sit down and put his head in his hands: his whole body was now infected with pain. Had I been generous enough to see it, I would have recognised the sheer grit which had dragged him that far.

When the guides set off again, on a different route, I hurried forward to catch up with Arkilaus, intent on getting out of that awful place as soon as possible. I fell and tumbled down a slope, through thorny lianas, ending up wedged in a tree a hundred feet below. Having got there I decided to beat on down and try to rejoin Arkilaus at the bottom. I pushed through but soon became ensnared in prickly palms, full of leeches and biting ants. I looked about and saw I was lost. I started shouting, and for ten minutes there were no replies. Then I heard Suleman's voice far above me, and I had to work back up for half an hour towards his patient calls, arriving shamefaced in front of him and the stricken Adrian.

As Yusup and Arkilaus tried to lead us out of our mess we tacked across the sharp tops, ending up on the wrong side of a mountain we'd already climbed. They found what looked like a path, and started leaping down the course of a freely falling stream. I didn't care about falling over any more: in the cold water I was quite insensitive. Only one thing stood out among a tumble of mud and rocks; the overpowering smell of chocolate. There was nothing to see, but I stood still for a full minute, willing it to appear.

It was mid-afternoon. We had walked for nine or ten hours and the rain was sliding down. Arkilaus had stopped making promises about getting close to Mbua, or finding another village. We were lost. I was quite happy to die, as long as it didn't involve any climbing. Suddenly we emerged onto a broad path, and soon there were the signs of feet and pigs' trotters. We stumbled down and followed it into a valley, then up onto a long grassy slope with houses at the top. No one had any idea where we were, but none of us seemed very worried by that. We sloshed through potato fields and past tethered pigs and into a compound of round and square houses streaked with mud and rain. Old men ran out shouting, and jumped up and down around us saying "*wa wa wa*". Strong hands grabbed me all over, there were arms round my shoulders, and I was bundled into the hut and sat right next to the fire, while the old men blew vigorously at it to get me warmed up, still saying "*wa wa*" between every breath. Seeing I was still cold an old man with a deep muscled face took my hands in his and started talking to me earnestly, persuading me in his language that I ought to warm up, or my spirit might get cold.

Arkilaus didn't speak the language, and I had to get a three-way interpretation through Yusup, who didn't know the first tongue but found one they shared. The local people had to translate into the language Yusup knew, he had to translate it into a language Arkilaus knew, Arkilaus had to translate it into Indonesian, and I had to translate it into English for myself. It was excellent to lie by the fire and listen to the incomprehensible talk. Like the Dani to the east, the men made little speeches, in turn breathy and excited, with lots of repeated words, like "*ngai ol, rokom rokom rokom rokom rokom rokom rokom rokom rokom rokom bubed de en*". The repeated words were probably a way of counting: the Dani weren't very interested in numerals, so to say "twenty pigs" they said "pig" twenty times. It made them sound gentle and unassertive.

The fire burnt between four pillars inside the hut. These held up a tarred bamboo ceiling just four feet from the ground, with a hatch leading into the upper chamber. The house was made for midgets, with a doorway I could only get through on my belly. Had we met no people in the Dani we would have guessed that everyone was two feet tall. Men were crawling in all the time, first surprised by us then delighted, scurrying over and hugging us and grinning. Soon there were fifteen people in the tiny round hut, all talking hurriedly in great breathy sentences. It was the men's house, where most of the men of the village would sleep, leaving groups of women and children to sleep in their own huts. It seemed that men and women very rarely slept together, and indeed hardly ever had sex. Women had no sex for up to five years after bearing a child, so even the old men with lots of wives hardly got a look in. Like most of what the Dani did, the penis gourd seemed designed simply to confound anthropologists, for all the likely explanations would have suggested that they were very sexy people.

I could see the men more clearly when the fire flared up, and in the hallucinatory glow of the flames some of them looked just like people I knew at home. The local doctor was there: the same beard and bald head, a string of shells in place of his stethoscope and a penis gourd where his neat checked trousers would have been. There was also Adrian's uncle: a resemblance Adrian hotly denied, perhaps because he'd never seen him in pigfat and soot before, with a row of seeds stuck to his forehead. There were some men in cassowary feather head-dresses, and others with huge bunches of vegetation stuck in their armbands, glistening and dripping as they came in out of the rain.

Adrian wanted to take a photo of one man, so he dug in his bag and brought out a packet of salt, which we'd heard was a luxury in the mountains. The man took it with delight, posed as

Adrian then Arkilaus then Yusup told him for his photo, then crawled out of the hut and ran off into the rain. He came back a minute later with two big handfuls of cooked pork, left over from a ceremony a few days before, and gave it to us with exhortations and many "*wa wa*"s.

I looked around in the hut for a box of ancestor stones. In some men's houses special slatey stones from rivers were kept, that contained some of the power of the village's greatest dead. They were brought out and dressed up when some special help was required. Very important dead people needed a lot of looking after: all spirits were likely to turn malevolent, and an important one could cause a lot of harm. Some men were so grand that they had to be looked after in the village, whether they were alive or not. So in some places there were smoked corpses hung from the eaves, or sitting in wooden chairs in the middle of the men's houses. The stones would come out for a battle or a famine, or at the initiation of the boys. There weren't any in our hut, however, and I don't suppose they would have let me see them if there were.

The Dani rolled cigarettes from little leaves and passed them around. They tasted like good cigars. Then an old man in the circle round the fire told a story, in a flat regular voice, as if it was his turn to read the sermon. The other men seemed to like it though and there was lots of "*wa wa*"-ing in the middle. They let the fire burn down, then everyone moved towards the front of the hut and crawled through the hole in the ceiling. There was a sleeping chamber full of smoke and dust, very warm from the fire below. We all rolled along the creaking floor until our bodies were wedged in tightly, like penguins ready to weather a blizzard. Adrian and I didn't get into our sleeping bags as it was warmer to be amongst the bodies, with arms and legs wrapped round each other. Straightaway the Dani were asleep, tangles of black legs and arms, snoring deeply, with just the yellow penis gourds sticking out at daft angles.

I lay there examining my perceptions: I had expected stone-aged people to be brutal hulks. The people around me had proved themselves the very opposite of brutal, and seemed to be a lot more skilled at fitting in with each other and their surroundings than the warring and polluting societies of the Personalheadset Age. Outsiders—ourselves too—had judged them by their technology, so pronounced them atavistic, without seeing the subtler sides of

1. A house in the Jakarta shanty

2. *Left:* Rubbish picking from an open sewer

3. *Right:* Central Java, the deceptive idyll

4. Successful transmigrants in Sumatra: the inherited teeshirt tells the story

5. The road the government promised: Adrian on the way to Salor

6. Isolation and sterility at Salor

7. Planting
deforested land

8. With Yopi on the
path to Klassaman

9. A break in the forest

10. The market in Wamena: the Dani below, the Indonesians above

11. *Left:* Sweet potato fields in the Baliem Valley

12. *Above:* Hunting mountain birds

13. Into the rock passage with the Kinyum

14. The Kinyum in the Samera cave

15. The hut in the moss forest: *left to right* Adrian, George, the potato women, Arkilaus, Suleman and Yusup

16. Arkilaus bargaining for potatoes

their lives: the ease, the calm, the hospitality that had reached or retained a higher state than ours. They were, I felt in the smoke and muggy warmth of the chamber, better developed in the ways that counted. All we had was a different way of living, not a better one. We needed advanced technology for ours, they didn't.

Adrian stood up suddenly, clutching his stomach. "Oh shit." He was on the wrong side of the smoke chamber from the hatch, and between them was a battlefield of bodies. I could hear his mind working, and the deep breath of decision when it came. He launched himself through the chamber, trying to plant his feet in spaces between the men. Among the peaceful snores and twitching of sleeping men I heard the 'crunch—ouf!, crunch—urgh!' of disintegrating penis gourds.

Joy was tempered by disbelief the next morning when Arkilaus told us we would reach Mbua that day. We had been building the place up as a luxurious pleasure palace set incongruously among the rigours of the mountains, where we could rest and get Adrian out if necessary. The possible airstrip with possible landings had shifted in our minds to a smart tarmacked runway, with a regular shuttle of DC-10s, an airport lounge and prim stewardesses. There would be shops, selling Garibaldi biscuits and tinned peaches, and a hotel with deep feather beds and waitresses carrying trays of draught bitter. As the image had become more ridiculous, the possibility of ever getting there had become more remote, until Mbua was simply an abstraction that we strove towards, the foot philosophers bound on an endless quest through metaphorical mountains.

Adrian's migraine seemed to have eased through the previous day, and in the morning he pronounced it gone. It its place he revealed a growing pain in his feet, that he said was quite set to become worse than the first disease. Suleman looked at them and said, "*Tsh, sepatu makan kaki*"—your shoes have eaten your feet— and it was true, to an extent. Instead of heels he had two gaping depressions pouring blood and slime. The plastic straps and polymer canvas of his expensive American boots grinned at the damage they'd done, and I was selfishly grateful to my heavy Bulgarian leather. He wrapped up his feet in bandages and lint, but his hobble from the hut was painful enough to watch.

We set off with a big group of women from the village, all carrying net bags of potatoes on their backs. We slowly climbed three thousand feet, then we stopped at the top of the mountain, and Yusup told Arkilaus that it was all downhill from there. We stumbled for a while, but then the path smoothed out and broadened and soon we were striding beside a happy chattering stream, with palm trees leaning over it and wild strawberries on its banks. It wound on down and down, but gently, then the path broadened again and led onto a hilltop with a cluster of huts. From there we looked down and saw, in the lap of the valley, the faery citadel of Mbua. Four or five rusty tin huts were clustered round a stream, with a few bananas and sweet potato patches beside them. There was nothing that looked like a runway.

We wandered down the slope. Children and young women in grass skirts were sitting in a field under the sun, following a Dani teacher in a simple recitation. Below them we came to a length of mud and sinter, sloping down the hill at about forty degrees and ending abruptly at a rockface. No one knew what it was. People in penis gourds and string skirts emerged from thatched huts, and out of one of the tin buildings in the middle came the strange apparition of a man in clean white clothes, striding among the bare skin and tribal decorations. He came forward to greet us, both bemused and confident, with a guarded smile. He was a mission teacher, a Papuan man taught by white Protestants, who was running the school there on their behalf.

"Welcome to Mbua," he said grandly, sweeping his hand round to show the extent of his kingdom, the five tin huts and the strip of mud.

"Where's the airfield?" I said rather abruptly, short of social graces after eight days in the mountains.

"There of course." He pointed to the sintered mountainside. "We built it all ourselves."

"Planes land on that?"

"Oh yes! Well, not as yet. But it was all our own work."

As we had really known all along, there was nothing to buy there, no sugar, no chocolate or beer, but plenty of sweet potatoes. I was a little suspicious of the teacher as I knew that the Protestants were self-protective and didn't like interference; but he seemed friendly enough, and put us up in a bare room in one of the tin buildings. The roofs and some of the wooden panels had been dropped in by a government helicopter to make the school buildings, but otherwise the head teacher and his assistant had been left to their own devices, and anything else they wanted, like beds, had to be carried in over the mountains from Wamena. The white-shirted teacher had come to teach maths, sport and Indonesian, but in that little enclave in the mountains there were no maths books and nowhere for sport to be played, though he didn't seem to mind.

Arkilaus took our clothes down to the river to wash. We hadn't removed them, except our boots, for eight days, and they were heavy with mud and sweat. Then we sat in the sun outside the teachers' house in our clean but mildewed shorts while one of the teachers played a homemade guitar and a crowd of Mbua villagers gathered round us. I was immensely tired and just sat there gazing at the ring of people as if my brain had left my head. The teachers' wives boiled up some cabbages, which were very good, but did nothing to relieve our diarrhoea. We resolved to spend two or three days in Mbua, so that Adrian could rest his feet and we could both redeem our energy debts.

I paid the three guides. Yusup strode off up the track, a purposeful black figure on his way back to the Kinyum. Arkilaus and Suleman decided to stay for two days to recover their strength: they weren't happy about recrossing those mountains so soon. The tobacco we'd brought had run out, so Arkilaus was a bit grumpy, and sat in the school's cooking hut all day, his big leathery soles beside the fire. I sat with him for a bit and asked him about the Yali, and he dropped a real shocker. He claimed to be twenty-one years old, three years younger than us. I thought he was joking, then I thought he didn't know his age, but I questioned him about the date and what he could remember and what had happened before he was born, and it seemed to be true. Arkilaus, with his great square jaw, deep-lined face, balding head, huge muscles and the authority of a determined middle-aged man, our boss and bully, was twenty-one. I asked other people their ages and it seemed to tie in. Suleman was twenty, the teachers twenty and twenty-two, the most gaga, grizzled, stooped and toothless village elders a full forty years. Fifty was an exceptional age, and it seemed that the whole scale of maturation had been graded so that people grew up in every way as a proportion of the maximum. At twenty-four we were well into middle age in Mbua.

The baltering river that ran between the huts was the one we were due to follow almost all the way to Agats, and to sit beside it rebuilt a little resolution. On my map, with its white spaces and tiny scale, the river ran down a soft winding valley all the way to the village of Keneyan. There, at just two thousand feet above sea level, we could expect to find a canoe that would take us to Agats. There was good reason to suppose we were over the worst. For all the climbing and toiling we'd done, however, we seemed further away than ever from any answers to our questions. I felt rather removed from the story, and it was hard, in those cold high mountains, to switch my mind back to the transmigration sites and that puzzle they posed: namely why, when they seemed to be doing so much harm to everyone, they were being vigorously filled with people.

Our search for anything better than cabbages, beans and potatoes had come to nought, and the Gentleman's Relish had run out, so we mooned around still dreaming of apricot fruitcake and foodhalls. Adrian suggested we try to buy a chicken, as we had seen a couple scratching about, and we went out and found a man who claimed to have one. We bargained briskly with him, struck a deal but didn't pay him, and he went off to get the bird. He never came back and it turned out he didn't have a chicken after all. The teachers took pity on us. They appeared at our window on a rainy afternoon under a pink parasol and a Dani rainhood, with bows and arrows in their hands. "We're just off to get you a chicken", said the headteacher, and they ran off into the thunder among the sweet potato fields. The rainhood the headman wore was woven from long plank-like pandanus leaves, and it came down to his waist, so that he looked like a sentry box on legs. Beside him the assistant teacher looked like a hunky transvestite, as he tilted the parasol into the rain and skipped over the furrows in the fields.

The chickenhunt began in earnest, and the men disappeared down the hillside, looking warlike, emerging from time to time from behind a stump or a ridge. Horrified chickens took to the air, squawking and furiously beating their wings, woken from their quiet scratching in the mud. Arrows were loosed off randomly, narrowly missing a few fascinated villagers. Feathers flew everywhere, but none of the chickens was hit. Eventually a cockerel was separated from the flock, and the two men charged after it up the slope towards us, firing off volleys of arrows. Just as it seemed to be getting away it was struck in the wing, and came to rest in a hissing ball of feathers, which was snatched up in triumph by the teachers and paraded back to the schoolhouse. The Dani were astonished, and just stared at the two men and their prize, with its furious red eyes. The cockerel was boiled by a teacher's wife, and it was horribly tough and stringy.

It was a Sunday and the Mbua Dani were in their best, which meant any variation on the traditional theme. One old man had a broken baseball cap and a filthy canvas waistcoat that he wore above his penis gourd. He did a little dance for us with a digging stick in his hand, looking entirely ridiculous. Others had filled up the holes through their noses, some traditionally, with pig's tusks or the long beaks of mountain birds; one man with a blue ball-point through his septum: the flotsam of the missionary school finally acquiring some value.

I was sleeping in the cooking hut as the boards of the room were too cold, and when I lay there that night two men came in who had stepped straight from the Trojan Wars. They carried an air of princely menace that none of the Dani we had met possessed, and I watched them with a half-open eye, not stirring from my sleeping bag. They were both tall with thick black beards and white teeth, and fierce smiles that died fast. One wore a mane of cassowary feathers running over his head and down his back, bunches of vegetation on his arms and a huge and polished penis gourd stuffed with red cloth. The other wore a black turban with pigs' tusks sticking from the crown. He had tusks through his nose and bound to his arms and long leaves tied in rings around his stomach. They laughed together, very fierce and sudden, and their bodies were tensed as if ready for a war. They ate quickly and said very little, and seemed quite removed from the little people joking and flicking their penis gourds around them. They had left their spears outside the hut. I closed my eyes for a while, and when I opened them later they had gone, and in the morning no one knew who they were or where they had come from.

Arkilaus and Suleman left the next day, and the day after that we departed with three new guides: Bernard, straightforward and mature, an assistant to the teachers in Mbua; and Yunus and Matthias, who both looked rather puny and spoke only a little Indonesian, but seemed strong enough beneath our packs. Adrian's feet were still bad but we were anxious to hurry through the next stage and get down to Keneyan.

Chapter 7

I suppose we should have guessed that the journey was not as simple as it looked on the map from the fact that Yunus was the only man in Mbua who had been to Keneyan. He was full of assurances, however: it was easy walking and would take us only three or four days. Adrian's feet soon caused him problems though, since the scabs split almost as he started to walk, and before long he was howling and cursing horribly. He sat on a rock and refused to go on, but we persuaded him to try walking in sandals, if he bundled up his feet in socks. He tried and lo, he walked, and for the first time since Trikora Adrian was free from pain. So we descended the path along the racing river happily enough, and found that Bernard knew everyone we met on the trail. One fantastically frail old woman, so ancient that she foamed at the mouth, turned out to be his mother, and he hugged her and the brothers he met many times before going on.

A little before midday we reached a village and Yunus announced that we would spend the night there. We argued with him but he said he knew the route and there wasn't another house for twelve hours. So I suggested we push on till dark then build ourselves a hut in the forest, and he agreed reluctantly. Four hours later we came over a hill and into another village, and the men invited us to stay. I sought out Yunus, who had hidden behind the houses. He was looking very sheepish. Why had he lied about the village? The truth came out of him so mournfully that I couldn't be angry. He had never been down the river to Keneyan, he didn't know anything about the path and he had wanted us to stop off early because he'd realised he could make more money if we spent more days on the track. He started to cry and I let him be.

It was raining and inside the hut there was a great fire crackling. Outside little girls ran around with pandanus leaf rainhoods over their heads, like a herd of garden sheds. There were no stone tools in the village, but steel knives and machetes, and several men wore shorts and shirts. It seemed odd, now that we were so far from any town. There were no sweet potatoes either, and we went hungry that night, with just some little cucumbers to chew on.

In the morning we were still hungry and we pushed on from village to village looking for what I would otherwise have taken time to avoid. In no place were there any surplus potatoes to sell, as there had been a blight. We moved on, becoming hungrier and hungrier, walking well out of our way to get to villages that might have potatoes to sell, without success. At last, after searching all morning, I saw the sight we'd been looking for: a girl labouring up a slope with a full string bag on her back. Potatoes! I ran down to meet her.

"How much is the whole bag?"

She stared at me, not understanding, so I dug out some money. "Enough? We're very hungry."

Her mouth fell open and her eyes grew wide, so I dug out some more. She backed away, with a look of ghastly horror. She was clearly mad.

"It's all right. I just want to buy some food. Eat, food." I made the motions, pointing to her sack. "We can cook it, we'll make a fire." I stuck out the money again.

She looked around for help with terrified eyes. Bernard and a few villagers came down to see what the trouble was.

"Can you explain to her that we're very hungry and we want to buy that bag? I just want to eat, very soon."

The madness was infectious. Bernard backed off in terror, putting up his hands as if to ward me off, shaking his head vigorously. Perhaps the woman was a witch. I looked again, then again, for the string bag had twitched. Inside was the girl's little brother. Just a few years before there had been cannibals not far to the south, and the people were still wary of them. I tried frantically to explain, and luckily they saw the joke. I found it a little trying later on, as Bernard sniggered for most of the afternoon.

The path was taking us further from the river: we had been winding up through the mountains as the gorge was too steep to follow. Adrian and I were becoming irritable, and I felt quite sapped with hunger. Adrian was slipping and twisting on his sandals. I thought dark thoughts about him and the guides, and the stupid mountains that kept hedging off our course. Suddenly the most curious figure appeared. He bounced out from behind us:

perhaps his track had joined ours or maybe he had just materialised. He had a little pointed beard and a rapid creaky voice, and
moved his lips as if browsing on a bush. He looked like a man in
a great hurry, and had no time to talk, only to say he was heading
towards Keneyan. I determined to keep up with him and get to
wherever we were going fast, and wait there for the others.

Half-man, half-goat he pattered off through the forest. It was
weird and exotic with carnivorous pitcher plants and stagshorn
ferns breaking rudely out of the tree trunks. The Goatman talked
as we went, croaking continuously, appearing to require no breath
for the strenuous climb. He grabbed handfuls of leaves and flowers and stuffed them in his mouth, urging me through mouthfuls
to do the same. No one we'd met before had had any idea about
what could or could not be eaten in the forest: everything was
'deadly poisonous', probably because the Dani were exclusively an
agricultural people. They'd clearly taken another opportunity to
confuse the anthropologists, for unlike almost any other tribal
people they saw plants as just plants and I hadn't heard of any
medicinal uses they put them to. The Goatman by contrast could
eat almost everything, and I gingerly followed suit. There were
green parsley-like plants, bitter blue fruits, waxy white flowers that
tasted of refresher towels. The strange little man chattered as he
trotted through the dappled forest. He suddenly turned to me and
said, "You follow me and I'll get you to Keneyan in one night."
He had a special route, a short cut over the mountains, very hard
but very fast. I could come with him if I promised to run all the
way.

I sprinted back to where Bernard and Matthias were helping
Adrian along in his sandals, and grabbed a toothbrush and a notebook from my rucksack. I would see them in Keneyan. The
Goatman, who looked rickety and grey, simply bounded off, from
rock to rock, as if he weighed no more than a bouncing pebble. I
crashed after him down a precipitous slope. I could hear my
pounding blood and the breath creaking and churning inside. The
Goatman trotted quietly ahead. We came to a sheer rock wall
where a rattan creeper had been hung. He swung up it, bouncing
through the air as if an engine up above was pulling him, while I
kicked and wheezed, desperately trying to get a purchase, slipping
and knocking against the rock wall. Then he bounced away up the
mountainside, as steep as an upended slice of cake, while I, almost

drowning in sweat, coughed and choked behind him. Madly and miraculously, the old man ran up the mountainside, pausing a second to shout down at me, "Them, three nights; us, one night", then cackling in a high voice and leaping on. Through a haze of sweat I pictured myself dying violently on the mountaintop. It started to rain, and swarms of biting flies assailed us.

At last the mountain flattened out, and suddenly we were crossing a slope obliterated by a landslide, with rocks the size of houses and raw earth smothering what just a month before was forest. We crossed on to a high top, grassy, wreathed in mist, and there was a startling view of the river gorge winding far below. Bluffs like the one we had climbed plunged fifteen hundred feet to the water for miles and miles and, beyond them in the blue, far off, were plains. The Goatman pointed: "Keneyan". I couldn't see how I could do it. He ran on, up and down the small ravines of little streams, over the green mountaintops, I playing troll to his nimble billygoat. We ran into the compound of a mountaintop village and suddenly he threw himself down on the grass. "Prim Prim," he said. "Three nights to Keneyan."

I stared at him. There wasn't a trace of humour in his face. He was a loony. I verged on panic. There I was, high in the mountains in no place on the map, with a toothbrush, a notebook and a loony, almost dead and three nights from Keneyan. I sat down hard on the grass and stared at the long blue gorge, with sudden loneliness and horror welling up inside me. I would never get out, I would never see Adrian again, I would never get home. I had been there five minutes when Adrian came over the hill. He and the others had taken the short cut across some lower hills on the other side of the river, and up a smoother valley among the bluffs. The Loony glanced at them quite unsurprised, then got up and wandered into a hut without a word. "What—?" asked Adrian, but I just shook my head and listened to my heart cooling down.

At least Prim Prim had food: bananas and thick grass stems—*lilay*—that tasted of artichoke hearts. We sat in the men's hut gratefully stuffing our faces. There were even fewer traditional materials there than in the village before, and lots of the men were in shorts. The only indigenous tools were a bow and arrows against the walls, that Bernard said were poisoned. I didn't believe him and offered to prick my finger with one, but he told me my arm would drop off. Apparently the wood of the arrowheads itself was poisonous, being either the stem of a small bamboo that had the toxin in its veins, or a piece of black nibun wood, that broke up when it entered the flesh and caused a very rapid infection, fast enough to stop a wounded wild pig that was being tracked by dogs.

Anything else at all indigenous had been ditched: there were machetes, matches and empty tin cans lying around in the hut. We had guessed at the influence of missionaries as we had moved through the villages from Mbua, and Bernard confirmed it. He claimed that no one south of Mbua believed in the old spirits any more; they were all baptised Protestants. Why, though, we asked, had the missionaries succeeded in those remotest places and not in the Baliem Valley, with its roads and airport and big shiny church? Bernard said something about the Baliem Valley people being too primitive to see the light, and I assumed that in reality the missionaries, in a rather cowardly way, had been eroding the edges of the culture, before eating into its heartland. The truth, when at length I resolved some of the conflicting accounts of what had happened, was quite different, and extraordinary.

When the Dani emerged from a hole in the Apulakna Mountain at the beginning of time, they behaved and functioned very much like snakes. Whenever they became old and decrepit they could, like snakes, shed their battered skins and emerge, gleaming white and youthful again. Like snakes too they needed do little work, and food and shelter came to them unbidden. They never grew senile or died. Such was the old Dani story that everybody knew. Their Eden, so the tale went, was ruined by a little black bird, exactly like the birds that we had seen in the high fields, that had white markings on their backs and shoulders. That bird challenged a primordial snake, a cousin of the Dani, to a race. If the snake won the Dani could live like him for evermore, and retain their everlasting paradise. If the bird won the Dani would have to be like him, and die after a brief life of work. The little bird, of course, succeeded, and ever since then the Dani had been mortal and miserable. When someone in a village died, the men splashed pale mud across their backs and shoulders in the pattern of the little bird, commemorating that fateful race. The triumphant bird was said to sing the dirge 'Smear yourself with mud' in Dani.

The first white missionaries arrived in the Baliem Valley in the 1950s and urged everyone to be like them. The Dani in the

Baliem were resolute: they were proud of the way they were, and reckoned that abandoning their traditions would anger the ancestors and bring them misfortune. In fact poor harvests in the Baliem Valley had been blamed on the colonial Dutch since 1958, when traditional warfare was banned there. In the western mountains, however, around Mbua and to the west and south, the missionaries, arriving from nowhere, struck an unexpected chord. Someone noticed that, like the ancestral snake people, the new people were white and shiny. Unlike those of the Dani, often hung from the eaves of their huts, the dead of the whites were never seen, which suggested that the new arrivals didn't die. As every race claims for its progenitors, they were tall and imposing. Word spread to the effect that the ancestors had returned, and people from all over the western Dani turned up to hear what they had to say. Nothing the missionaries uttered dispelled the impression. They started preaching about eternal life, and claimed that people could be born anew, very much in the manner of the old snake-men.

What really appealed, however, was not so much the eternal life the missionaries talked about, but the good things that went with it. Watching the invaders, the people saw that they could summon up all sorts of extraordinary goods, that had been out of reach since the time of the ancestors. Like the snakepeople they did nothing that could be described as work—like digging in fields or hunting in the forest—yet every so often an aeroplane turned up from nowhere and brought them everything they needed, as well as the most fascinating luxuries. The missionaries told the Dani that if they did as they said they could inherit the gifts of the Lord. The people leapt at the chance and followed their words to the letter. The missionaries told them to burn down their houses and live in a moral way, in families. They were to destroy their old tools and take up the godly ones the missionaries had brought. They had to cover their wicked nudity with clothes, throw aside their animism and become baptised.

Through the sixties and seventies, the creed spread rapidly through the lands of the western Dani. After several years, however, people began to see that they weren't getting the rewards they had been promised. The aeroplanes and their cargoes still came only for the missionaries, the Dani still hacked away in the fields and ate sweet potatoes. They decided it was a matter of doing not just what the returned ancestors said but also what they did. Dani men studied the missionaries closely, and learnt the rituals they'd have to perform to get the goods delivered to themselves. The newly trousered but illiterate men sat down with pieces of paper they'd stolen, making rows and rows of squiggles with a pen, brows puckered, lips bitten in concentration. Others built crude tables and put vases of flowers on them, then sat around with their legs crossed, talking in reserved tones. To get their planes to land the Dani needed airstrips and, seeing the practice but not the principles, cleared the trees from mountain slopes and built almost vertical runways. Whenever a plane came over men would run to the top of the mountain with a tin can, and hiss and crackle into it, trying to persuade the plane to land on their own strip.

By 1977, when none of the promised prizes had turned up, the people of the western Dani suddenly became angry. They had destroyed or abandoned everything they valued, and received nothing in return. They revolted, and ate a lot of their missionaries, before they were bloodily crushed by the Indonesians. Perhaps the missionaries deserved no better, for it seems they did nothing to dissuade the people from their crazy version of the faith, and used it quite coldly to get what they wanted. After the revolt both the anger and the cult—the cargo cult as it was called—cooled down a bit; but a lot of the Dani had been too long away from their old beliefs to return. In Mbua and Prim Prim they had kept hold of their Protestantism, vague and confused as it was, and probably still mixed it with hopes of a return to arcadia.

There had been cargo cults all over West Papua, emerging as perhaps the logical response to the entirely illogical phenomenon of aeroplanes, that discharged fascinating cargo from out of the blue. To the west of Prim Prim, close to the snowy peak I had seen from the top of Trikora, was a whole mountain made of copper ore. Companies from Indonesia and the West went in to prospect it in the late sixties. With high budgets, the surveyors were wasteful, and left rubbish dumps outside their sealed project area. The litter was fascinating to the indigenous people, who were never allowed in to see where it came from. They made the connection between the treasure they had heard about in the mountain and the treasures they had found on the rubbish dumps, and assumed that the peak itself was full of everything they had ever wanted.

According to one of the warleaders they had only to find the special key—he said it was the jawbone of a possum, that would fit into a particular hole—to unlock the top of the mountain and release the treasures for their own use. Several villages gave up farming for a year to look for the bone, and the movement didn't fizzle away until they were close to starvation.

A similar faith, the Mandobo corned beet cult, had taken hold of a tribe living close to the border with Papua New Guinea. Like the other cults it was a response to something incomprehensible—in this case corned beef—but it might have been invented deliberately by some lascivious tribal elders. The Mandobo people's belief was that their time of blessedness was to have coincided with the 1977 election. At that time the most important ancestors would return, and weapons would emerge from a hole in the ground, arming the Mandobo against the Indonesians. There would be a terrible battle and everyone on earth would die, and only those who had dedicated their lives to the great ancestors would be resurrected. Men who in life had only one wife would have proved themselves unworthy of the ancestors' support, and would be sent to a factory to be turned into corned beef. Virginal women would turn into sea creatures or corned beef, while men with two or more wives would achieve blessedness. Just before the 1977 election there was a spate of second marriages and free love in the Mandobo region, which came to an end when the election arrived and neither ancestors nor weapons emerged from the ground.

We had been walking for a few hours the next morning on a solid, wide track, that men in penis gourds with metal shovel were still smoothing out (it was sponsored, I was told, by the omnipresent and invisible missionaries), when Yunus and Matthias wanted to stop in a village we came to. We must have descended by then to just four or five thousand feet, and it was hot, so we sat in the shade of a house overlooking the gorge. I waited half an hour and the guides didn't appear. I wandered about looking for them, and it was another half hour until I unearthed the three. They were sitting in the dark of a hut whispering. Bernard was pushed forward by Yunus, who had been shy of approaching me since his confession on the first day.

"Er, we don't want to go any further," said Bernard.

"Why not?"

"Family."

"Malaria," hissed Yunus.

"Er, malaria. There's lot of malaria down below and we don't want to go."

It was no use finding out what was really the matter. I was annoyed, and I sent them off to find some more guides, fast. They ran round seeking to recruit people in the village, obviously without much of success. Eventually they found three men who looked about ninety years old, all utterly withered and decrepit. I looked them over with a sinking heart. "Oh no."

"You all speak Indonesian?"

They stared at me blankly. Yunus whispered harshly at the old man nearest to him. He grinned and raised his hand, nodding enthusiastically.

"So how many nights to Keneyan?" I asked. He kept up his silly grin, raising his hand a little higher. Yunus slunk off behind a hut. After another half hour we dug out someone who could speak the language and looked fit. He wasn't very happy about coming, but I raised the price a little and he accepted. He was also inauspiciously called Yunus: I tried not to let it put me off. He had a thick bush of hair with a band of parrot feathers, and a rather daft grin. We also took the least shrivelled of the three toothless old men, Gandano, who was four feet tall and looked like a little squirrel monkey. He was very excited about coming on the trip, but sunk to about three feet when we put the pack on him and tottered off bowleggedly. We resolved to find a third porter on the road.

Yunus told us that the big road would take us down to a bridge across the river. It stopped there but on the other side were paths that led through the mountains for a day or so until they drew level with Keneyan. We could then recross and get into the swamps. We reached the bridge after a couple of hours. The last boards were swinging about on the surface of the torrent, tugging at the rattan hawsers that had held them up. Yunus pointed: the rattans had been cut, with a machete he said. It seemed strange to me, and slightly sinister, but it was even odder when we got back to the last village and found out what had happened. It was, a group of men told Yunus excitedly, all the fault of the *bua merah*. *Bua merahs* are phallic red spikes that grow from the crown of the *daik* pandanus palm and taste of seal's fat soaked in turpentine. They cause immediate indigestion and severe stomach cramps, and very often freely flowing diarrhoea for about three days. They are a great delicacy among the southern Dani.

A man in the village we'd reached had spent days collecting *bua merahs* from a secret place in the forest, and had brought back a sack with enough to make himself ill for months. As he prepared for the feast, another man sneaked in and swiped the sack. He flew into a terrible rage, took up his machete and ran round the village looking for someone to hit with it. Finding nobody he ran down to the bridge instead and chopped down the rattans. While it did-n't bring back his *bua merahs,* it had the equally satisfying effect of making everyone else in the village as angry as he was.

We spent the night in the village, where we were treated to a spectacular elemental display. Great thunder clouds were battling it out from the mountaintops on either side of us, firing bolts of lightning at each other. Violent rains struck the village, and a child who had been wandering lost around the compound was carried into the men's house, wide-eyed with shock and curiosity, a finger in his mouth. Afterwards the sky turned yellow and was straddled by rainbows, one passing through a bent old woman wandering out of her hut. The clouds had fallen suddenly from above the mountains to far below us in the bottom of the gorge. White cockatoos, the first we had seen since Sorong, flapped above the surface of the clouds to roost. Yunus came out and pointed down the gorge. The white river glinted from under the clouds in places, snaking round the intersecting bluffs. Far to the south, still many miles away, the mountains fell suddenly into the level blue swamps of the Asmat. On our side there were no tracks, just cliffs which dropped six hundred feet into the torrent. We would have to wait until the bridge was mended.

Yunus had found a third man, Tekir, in the village, who looked fit and was taller than the others. There was something of the Asmat about him: he was slim and muscular and longer in the face. He carried a mirror in his net bag, and Yunus and he spent hours together that evening, preening themselves and plucking out hairs from their chins. I sat in a corner wrapped up in my thoughts, wanting badly to be out of the mountains and away down the river on a boat. The journey was taking longer than I'd expected, and our tourist visas were running out. There wouldn't be a chance to send our letters home till Agats, and perhaps by then we'd be considered lost or dead. Everything I saw seemed somehow to remind me that I missed my girlfriend. Adrian had miseries of his own. His cameras were falling apart: most of the equipment already seemed to be broken or filled with fungus. The film had got wet and expanded, and was scratching or tearing when he wound on. Cockroaches had somehow slipped into one of the bodies, and he'd probably been taking detailed anatomical shots of them for the last few rolls. On top of that was yet another, perhaps inevitable, ailment. The straps of his sandals had dug in deep between his toes and burnt two holes, and he hobbled now with wounds at the front and the back: I pictured him arriving with bloody stumps in Keneyan.

An old man shuffled up and sat beside me. He got my attention then shook his head sagaciously. "*Ooh, tsh tsh*," he sighed in Indonesian, "we'll be overrun with white men before very long. Lots of them coming through here nowadays." He fell into silence.

I suddenly woke up to his words. "Lots? Of white men?"

"Oooh, many, so many."

I was excited. "Where are they?"

"Well . . ." He stuck out his fingers to count them off. "There was . . . one in . . . 1979; and again one in . . . 1984. And now you. Where it'll end I don't know." He shuffled off and sat on the other side of the hut. I curled up and thought about England.

We spent the next day watching the master bridgebuilder at work. He was a tiny old man who scurried up and down shouting instructions in a thin crooked voice. Long rattan vines had been collected from the forest and men were binding them to the logs they'd wedged into the bank on our side. The problem was getting them over to the other side and tying them on there. I couldn't see how it might be done, as the walkway was riding on the violent foam and rapidly breaking up. The little man leapt up and grabbed the two handrails of the bridge, thin rattan strips that hadn't been cut by the *bua merah* man. He held them together, then placed one foot on each vine and started to crawl along, fingers and prehensile toes clinging grimly, the thin rails sagging above the torrent. There was thirty yards to cover and beneath him a rush of water that would have killed him on impact, but he crawled steadily on along the rails and landed safe on the other bank. From there he could haul over and secure the big vines, and pull the walkway high enough for us to cross, which we did—precariously, as it creaked on its new bindings and sloped steeply towards the water—some time that afternoon.

The forest had greatly changed since Mbua. Instead of the cool silence among the trees up north, the warm air was humming with frogs and insects. The tree trunks were cluttered with creepers and flowers, and odd ferns and bromeliads covered the bark. Birds shot squawking from trees we bumped into, and every now and then you couldn't help ducking as the rush of giant hornbills' wings passed overhead. We were high on a path above the gorge, picking across rocks and roots. Seeing Yunus with my pack on his head above me, and Tekir too, lit by the moist sun that fingered through the trees, Gandano behind with a sack of sweet potatoes on his head, I could believe we were pirates crossing some wild jungle island carrying our treasure, cursing at the flies and each other as we went. The fantasy didn't last long. A few falls or hands placed on spiny trunks soon shook me out of it, and I was back in the misery of being far from anywhere, hungry, overtired and quite certain we would never get out. At the top of a long slope Yunus laid down my pack and stretched his arms. He peered through the trees then turned about.

"One more mountain," he said decisively.

"Hooray!" I yelled. "Just one more mountain!"

I danced down the next slope, stumbling and bashing into trees as I went, tripping on roots and landing in ants' nests. It didn't matter: just over the top then down to the river once more and we'd be away into the gentle valleys of the northern Asmat, and almost at the canoes of Keneyan. I hurtled up the track the other side, keeping pace with Yunus, in sheer delight that I would never have to climb through a mountain forest again. Forty breathless minutes later I reached the top. There were no trees there and we could see clearly. Far from any river, the mountains of the plateau spiked up ahead of us, endless and blue, as inviting as nails sticking from a torn plank.

"We're lost," said Yunus.

We walked on that evening, trying to find a track back down towards the river, but there was none, only sheer gorges meeting sheer mountains on the other side, with mountains beyond them, and more beyond them. Yunus was following the sun, but I watched him sag as he lost confidence in the trail he struck, and his head hung lower and lower beneath the heavy pack. The jungle was unbroken: creepers trailed over fallen rocks, roots hung over hollows in the mountain walls, the forest pressed in on us from above, throbbing and buzzing with insects. It began to drizzle, and leeches came out of everywhere, fat ones that pressed through the material of our socks and swelled up between the toes. Gandano was horrified by them, and hopped up and down screaming when one anchored to his bare foot, incapacitated until Yunus came back to calm him and scrape it off with his machete. By then others would have smelt Gandano out, and the backs of his bare legs would be wriggling with leeches, and he would be hopping around again, silent with horror. Biting flies took wind of us as well, and bombed straight into our hair, nailing us on impact.

We came at length to a broken shelter on the top of a hill. Prickly pandanus palms were growing all around, and it seemed that someone had built the hut as a place for making sleeping mats. Now it was long disused and fallen in; but an indistinct path led down from it. The others wanted to stop at the shelter and spent the night there, but I, pricked with the small hope that the path had brought, wanted to push on. Yunus shook his head as if to say, "You'll be sorry", but he shouldered the load again and moved on down. The rainclouds had thickened and now pressed against the tops of the trees, darkening our slippery way. Adrian slid helplessly in his burning sandals, shouting with pain as the straps bit in deeper. Hornbills flapped away to roost above the trees, and I careered into a trunk, falling in a sagging heap into the plants below. We came to a clearing and Yunus looked at me to say the silly game had gone on long enough. I couldn't help but agree.

The three men ran off to find materials for a shelter. We sat on our packs. "God you look miserable," said Adrian, and he raised his camera to take a photo of me sitting there. As he pressed the light-meter it fell two stops. He raised the camera to try again, pressed and it fell two more: darkness had landed on the sky like a rug. The birdsong stopped. There was a pause of a few seconds, then the bottom of the sky fell out. There was a roar like surf. I couldn't hear what Adrian said, I sat stock still, pinned to the ground by rain. The men had run back into the clearing and were working furiously, driving poles into the earth, lashing beams to them with bits of vine. There was nothing we could do but watch and, in my case, feel humble about it being my fault. The rain roared,

Gandano leapt and howled with leeches, Tekir ran about with bunches of palm leaves, binding them to the structure even as it was being lashed together. We sat and streamed.

Within twenty minutes the guides had built a stout frame with a roof of leaves, and Gandano was smoking out the leeches with a fire. It was still raining and the other two lashed more vegetation to the front of the shelter to make an overhang. Yunus laid out some leaves to sit on, and we all crowded in and shivered around the fire. Adrian and I dropped bloated leeches into the flames and watched them pop, with great satisfaction. As the dark fell, all sorts of creatures came wriggling out of the leafwork: giant ants, more leeches, a biting spider, and a lizard that fell straight down the back of my neck and out again before I could grab it. We fell asleep sitting up and leaning on each other, five miserable bodies lost in the mountains.

The weak path that led down from the clearing spiralled off illogically across the hills, doubling on itself, crossing and recrossing gulches and little streams. Trees and curtains of creeper had fallen across it. Yunus worked away with his machete; it was slow and slippery. Many times, when Yunus went ahead out of sight, I lost the path and had to call back to Tekir to see where I was. It felt like potholing, with the claustrophobic despair of a deep exploratory crawl; I wanted so badly to get out. Adrian lost his temper with the guides. He was shouting at Yunus, "Where the hell are we? Where do you think we're going?" and poor Yunus stood there shocked, until Adrian pulled himself together and turned instead to despair. At length we came to a little stream of clear water. I waded in and sat down in the middle, ladling water into my mouth. I didn't want to move. Yunus came across and tried to cheer me up. "Just one more mountain," he said tentatively.

We laboured on, up rocky gorges, down boulder fields thick with roots, over mazes of fallen logs, into peatsinks. The path would climb, dither then disappear, and we had to cut back and try again. Streams flowed in all directions so we dared not leave the track to follow one. Gandano was well behind with Adrian, still bright though clearly suffering beneath his load. Adrian said that when a big yellow land crab ran across their path Gandano had leapt back in horror and hid behind him, wailing and shouting threats at the crab, muttering assurances to himself. When Adrian persuaded him to move on, he leapt over the spot it had crossed and ran off down the path in case it pursued him. Later on Adrian fell for the hundredth time and just sat on the ground with his head in his hands, half laughing, half crying. He heard a rapid low whisper behind him and turned round to see Gandano, eyes screwed up and facing the sky, hands clutched to his chest, praying for him.

We laboured to the top of a sharp peak, heavy with sweat and water from the trees, bitten and scratched all over. Yunus looked out from the top; I didn't follow his gaze.

"One more mountain?" I asked in my most cutting voice.

He grinned round at me desperately. "Yes, perhaps, maybe it is."

Either he or I should have sailed off the mountaintop then and gone down the easy way, but I couldn't decide whether to shove or to jump. Yunus was right, however, for an hour later, on our last quiver of strength, we looked over a brow and saw the Keneyan River, churning away below us. I was too tired even to smile.

When we got to the bottom there was a mile of slippery boulders to cross before the cliffs gave out. Adrian fell from the top of one on to the sharp rocks below and I thought he was dead, but he wasn't so we carried on. Yunus judged we were still upstream of the bridge we needed to cross to get back to the Keneyan bank. If we pushed on down we should find a settlement before long and get directions. He was right again, and after an hour we stumbled into an area of cut trees and cucumber vines, a few banana trees sticking out of the mess, possums and wolf spiders running about. Yunus helped me along. "It won't be long now," he said.

The sun was shining and I lay beneath a canopy of palm leaves. A pig came rooting about with two tiny piglets. From one of the houses I could hear women's voices. I couldn't move. I shut my eyes and I was in a big garden in England: the women were making tea, it was a lazy afternoon, there were ducks quacking gently round the garden pond. I fell asleep and dozed for an hour.

When I woke I noticed that the houses round me were different from the Dani huts. They were raised a little off the ground on stilts, with high wood walls and almost flat thatched roofs. Each plank bore a handprint in white lime. There were none of the neat pigpens and gardens that there had been in the highlands, and even from where I lay I could tell that the people were not serious farmers. We were in the Asmat.

A slim dark girl, quite naked, with red beads around her neck and Egyptian eyes, brought me some sugar cane then slipped away on silent feet. Later a woman came and gave me a palm leaf sleeping mat, that she told me I should keep. I lay in the rough shelter, too drained to get down and join the others, listening to the sounds of the forest all around: a tinkle of laughter from the huts, the grunts of a mother pig. Adrian had stumbled off to sleep in a hut but I just lay there on the broken boards, imagining I was on the sea and being rocked back and forth, fading away with the declining day and falling asleep when night came.

We left in the morning with three hunters from the village. They were short, but paler and more lightly built than the Dani. Each carried an ironwood bow and straight-headed poisoned arrows, and at their feet roamed springy hunting dogs. We were a jolly-looking crowd, the villagers wound up for a hunt of several days, ourselves a little revitalised by the knowledge that there were indeed no more mountains. We were still on the plateau, but it had graded down to two or three thousand feet. There was a good path, and after an hour or two we took a branch away from it and the man in front said we had reached to the bridge. We all strode forward and piled into the back of him when he stopped dead. The rattan rails were dangling limply in the water. It had been swept clean away by a flood.

The hunters said that an hour down the bank there was a rattan slide: a creeper stretched across the water that you could swing across, hand over hand. I viewed the swirling river with some concern, but followed them back to the path and on along the riverbank. Halfway down the hunters stopped suddenly and the dogs froze and stiffened. We were sharply signalled to shut up and keep still. The men were staring up into the canopy, whispering and pointing. I couldn't see anything and thought there was a tree with special significance, perhaps something to do with an ancestor. One of the men drew his bowstring back past his ear, a four-foot wooden arrow quivering. He let go, there was a soft thwack, and a big black bird came tumbling and fluttering down from far above us, then battered off into the bushes shrieking. Everyone leapt up and gave chase, Yunus and Tekir with our rucksacks on their backs, Gandano with the sack of food on his head, the hunters and the dogs, leaving us standing bewildered on the path. Ten minutes later they all came back, with a big black maleo fowl, rangy and turkeylike, held up dead in triumph. The hunters stuffed it into one of our bags, and we eyed it greedily, wondering if it could really be for supper.

The rattan crossing—I had guessed it already—was gone, and we just sat on the bank and stared.

"We can always walk down the bank . . ." Yunus volunteered. He bent his head to the hunters and talked awhile. "If we carry on downstream for two days we can maybe ford the river there or raft it, then we can walk up the other bank just two days more and find the path again. It's swamp to the south and there aren't any tracks, but we're sure to find a way."

He gave me a timid smile: it fell away when he saw the expression he got in return. Adrian and I watched the slick river swirling, brown and white, between the rock bluffs. About fifty yards below us it flickered out and crashed into violent rapids, but at our level it looked slower. We turned towards each other. "Let's swim it," said Adrian.

The guides tried to dissuade us. Yunus kept pointing at the water. He didn't have the words but it was quite obvious to him that we would die if we went in. They sat around and looked mournful. Our notion was to swim over with a thin creeper, and use it to haul thicker ones across, so that the men and our gear could follow us. The river was about twenty yards wide, and there were jutting rocks on the far side that ran down the bank for thirty or forty feet then stopped, giving way to a smooth bare rivercliff without handholds. If we missed the rocks we'd be gone. In the rapids I could hear boulders thumping as they rolled over.

"Go on," I shouted, "go and get the bloody rattans. Hurry!"

The porters ran off startled and Adrian and I sat on the bank and stared at the water.

"Lots?" I asked. I held out two twigs. Adrian pulled and lost. We debated it a moment, but he seemed quite sure.

He took off his shoes and trousers. We waited. An hour later the guides returned with the rattans, two-hundred-foot creepers as strong as ropes. They stripped down a thin one, and Adrian looped it over his chest and shoulder. It was tough enough to pull the thicker vines across, but not to hold him if he was swept away. Any thicker and it would have dragged him down the river.

He walked up the bank until he was twenty yards or so upstream of the rocks the other side. I stood downstream with the slight chance of catching him if he went. He climbed a little way then dived. He thrashed at the brown water, a knot of spray in the thick sucking current; then halfway across he just stopped. The splashing continued but he didn't move, he just held his position in the stream. Then slowly, very slowly he pushed through, and came almost to the rocks the other side. He flailed at them and bounced back. He tried again, clawing for a hold, but missing, held back by just two feet. He was being swept off down the river. "Go for it Adrian. Fucking do it!" I ran up and down on my little patch of bank. He was passing the last rock. He thrashed out one more time and caught its mossy tail and held there, until he found the strength to pull his other arm over and catch the rock higher up. He hauled himself out then lay on the rocks like a shipwrecked sailor. Adrian didn't move for ten minutes, then he lumbered up and tugged feebly at the rattans. He couldn't do it: the strength of the current was too great.

I had taken off my boots and I stood up on the top of the bank, twenty yards upstream. Adrian had won all the medals for swimming at school, I was a flop. I dived and felt the swift tug of the water. Momentum carried me forward, and I thrashed and kicked my legs high. Then I hit the main stream. The current picked me up and stopped me dead. Adrian was screaming above the roar of the falls: "Don't let your legs drop, don't drop your legs." The banks were slipping by, waves of current were running past my head, I nearly panicked, I was sinking. I thrashed viciously at the water and broke out of the stream, and got almost to the rocks. I leapt at them. The cushion of water shoved me back. I leapt and missed again, and already I had reached the last rocks. I lunged once more, missed, and was swept on past. I was going to die. Then my arm hit the rattan bowed out in the water. I grabbed it: it wasn't strong enough to hold, but I was able to swing round on it and spin in the water. The rattan creaked. I was just off the rocks. Adrian leant over and I caught his arm. He had no strength to pull me out, but held me till I swung round into the side and grabbed a rock. I hauled myself out and collapsed.

It was a long time before we could pull a strong rattan over. We couldn't bind it to the tree, but we wound it round and held it while one of the hunters splashed across, clutching the vine in one hand. He tautened it and tied it up with great precision, and when the guides on the other side had made a cable car from a loop of cane, they pulled themselves across, hand over hand, tugging back the empty loop with a thinner strand. They carried the packs over that way, the swirling waters chopping at their heels. Gandano looked more like a baby spider monkey than ever, clinging tightly with one hand to the loop, his eyes screwed shut as he hauled himself across.

It was an hour or so before all were over and ready to march. By the time we reached the top of the rivercliff it was lashing with rain, and Adrian and I were cold and exhausted. We came after a while to a hut built on top of a little hill. Though there was no one there we climbed the notched pole and sat in the house, listening to the rain spilling over the thatch. It was a hunter's hut. The jaws of wild pigs and marsupials hung from strings on the low beams, and a cassowary's skin, writhing with vermin, was there too, like a hideous pantomime wig. Yusup took a bone down from the rafters and measured it against my own shin. It was a little longer but finer, and light.

"What do you think it is?" he asked.

I couldn't think. I knew of no mammal that tall.

Yusup made a beak with his hand: "Cassowary, of course," It was a bird.

We waited for half an hour, then we heard a man whistling between his teeth as he came up the pole. I felt suddenly guilty and a little fearful. His head came over the top, he saw us, white ghosts in his living room, and started; but he didn't fall off the pole and came in a second later with a broad grin. He was tall and skinny, with a tiny penis gourd, a bow and arrows and his prize from the hunt; a little rat. He was soon followed by four or five others, all cramming into the hut eight feet off the ground, and chattering excitedly after their day's hunting. The rat seemed to be the only trophy, not particularly impressive between all those big men, and they were awed by us when we pulled out the maleo fowl. Someone brought out maize and sweet potato leaves and a battered metal pot, and we cooked up a stew of bird and vegetables, which was very good. The rat was roasted separately, whole, with the skin burnt off, and tasted gamey and charred, rather unpleasant. I was offered the intestines coiled round the end of a stick, but I thought I'd done enough for one day. Still the rain lashed on outside. Yunus said it was a freak storm and should be over by the morning. All night long creatures fell out of the hunting trophies in the ceiling, making sleep difficult.

The rain was still racing down in the morning. We waited late—till nine o'clock—but it continued, so we trudged out heavily for the last long lap. Three of the men from the hut came with us, slipping around on the sloshy trails, raddled with leeches. The leeches got everywhere: up our shirts, down our trousers, even on the back of my neck. The holes they left bled impressively, and we looked as if we'd stepped off the set of a gruesome movie. We came to a stream, that would have been a rivulet the day before, but had become a white force, enough to suck us all away without a gurgle. We pushed down a tree to cross it. That was frightening enough, but when we got to the third exploded stream we saw that it was quite uncrossable, forty or fifty yards wide.

Yunus paced up and down a bit, then he started cutting us all stout sticks from the flooded banks. The river was furious, and boulders were marked out by plumes of water shooting many feet into the air. Yunus and two of the hunters went over first, testing every step, jamming their poles in hard beneath the rocks, swaying a second then steadying up, reaching out for another step. Then we went in. The water bulged up to my stomach in places, and grabbed my feet, trying to pull them away. I kept myself upstream of the big rocks, wedging the stick in among them. Twice I stumbled and almost went down. Gandano, with a pack on his back, simply couldn't make it. Halfway across he stopped in frozen terror, stick dug in, eyes shut, praying in a gabble, the wild water tugging at his body. Two of the hunters plunged back in, relieved him of the pack and dragged him across. He stood clutching his heart on the bank, with the air of a man amazed to be alive.

Further on the path led down to the Keneyan River. Overnight it had risen to a deadly torrent, spitting spray and gravel, heaving up pillows of water. Boulders were thocking like billiards balls. The path was supposed to go down the river beach, but that had gone, and any sort of a bank with it. We had to cut back into the woods, and soon the machetes came out and were hard at work. There were acres of pandanus palm, with twisting spiky leaves, that flicked back and tore the skin if you weren't alert. Soon the ground turned into reedswamp and tanglewood. Poison spikes clung to our clothes, and insects buzzed and fluttered round us, often trapped in the spiders' webs festooned from our heads. Still the rain spun down and the leeches wound up our legs. We

107

had to wade for half a mile at a time through flooded declivities. We crossed two more raging streams and in one, the shallower, I slipped and tumbled over, grabbing hold of a bounder underwater and holding my breath, before I could haul my head out of the water and find my feet again. We were bitten by buzzing creatures and stung across the face, but eventually the hunters cut us round to an old path on higher ground, that we followed gladly for half an hour. Then inexplicably the men left it and took us back into the swamps, winding back and forth through the blinds of undergrowth. I was convinced we were lost, but I had ceased to care. I would just trudge round and round in pointless circles till I was so snarled up in the swamps that I never had to get out again. Adrian got frustrated and muttered angrily about the guides, the rain, the vegetation.

Creepy-crawlies, driven from the ground by the flooding, hung from the plants. Once, as I was wading out of a flooded depression, Adrian looked down at me and said, "There's a spider in your hair."

"So bloody what? There're bloody spiders everywhere."

"Suit yourself."

I ran a hand over the top of my head. A creature the size of a rat leapt off and hit the ground, raising its forelegs defensively, displaying its fangs. We were both chronic arachnophobes, but neither of us was moved.

The crazy march went on for another two hours, and all the time I was saying to myself, "It can't be right, we must be lost." Then Yunus and Tekir put down their loads and the villagers led them off into the swamp, telling us to stay a while. At length Yunus returned, loaded down with huge red fruit. "*Bua merah*," he said, matter-of-factly. "You can have one if you want." I didn't even have the energy to be cross; but I knew then what tree had led the Dani Eve out of *her* arcadia. Having got the *bua merahs* we were allowed to get back to the path, which was fine and firm as soon as we regained it. Before long we saw the marks of metal saws on felled trees of the forest. We were getting close to the head of the river, a point deep enough to float trunks down to Agats for sale. We came into Asmat houses, on stilts beside a little stream. It had stopped raining and I began to feel forgiving of the day. Men came to the doors of their houses and stared at us with great curiosity.

We came out of the last of the trees, on to a track above the rivercliff, into the evening sun. The path was dry white sand, and we followed it on to grassier and grassier patches, then out on to a rough turf airstrip, with a row of tin-roofed huts beside it. A gaggle of people ran out and thronged us, shouting and cheering and asking the guides where we'd come from. Someone thrust a papaya through the crowd into Adrian's arms. We were led past more houses, through a garden gate and up the steps of a modern mission building. We had got to Keneyan.

The guides were taken to another house to spend the night, and we sat down with great relief and attacked the papaya. The villagers had followed us in. They stood around the inside walls of the house and crowded about the doorway, staring at us expectantly, without a sound. No one came out to meet us though. In contrast to the teachers' house in Mbua, the mission house was neat and well organised, with shelves for Bibles and schoolbooks, and paraffin lamps waiting to be filled. A clear mind lay behind it, and behind the rows of houses that made up the village. I asked the villagers if there were any police or soldiers in Keneyan, but they just stared on, flickering their eyes aside if I met them. It was most disconcerting.

We sat and waited and it gradually came dark outside. I became fidgety, not knowing what to expect. Still the crowd remained and stared. Suddenly the people round the door drew back, and everyone shuffled away up the room. Through the door came a man of extraordinary appearance. He wore striking white trousers and a clean teeshirt. His black face was huge; he had a square jaw that obscured his neck, a square head, startling eyes deep beneath his brow. He was thick with muscle: not the calloused workaday muscle of the villagers, but the tuned, quick figure of a sportsman.

He strode over and confidently took our hands. "Monché." I felt grubby and unpleasant beside him. "You're welcome to stay, I shall find you rooms." He went into the adjoining hall and shouted at a couple of villagers. They came out of the cookroom and he spoke to them crisply. They scuttled into their rooms and pulled out their belongings.

"It's not necessary, we can——"

"It's all arranged."

He sat down briskly beside us and asked where we had come

109

from, though it was clear he already knew. He took it in through his shadowed eyes, storing it away in a way that unsettled me. He said he was the missionary and administrator for Keneyan, and anything we wanted he could arrange. I felt uneasy. He looked up "Go on!" The villagers scattered and moved off raggedly to their homes, penis gourds, dirty skirts and shorts. Monché showed us our rooms and said we could make a donation to the mission. We would eat together later that evening. He went into his room and I heard a two-way radio crackling, which added to my discomforts and distrust of the missionary.

I wandered outside, exhausted and oppressed. A man was lounging by the gate and I asked him about canoes. There were four or five in the village, he said: yes, we could most likely get one the next day, and it could take us to Sawa-Erma, halfway to Agats. He moved away when another man came up and nodded sharply at him. I recognised him as the one who had passed us the papaya. He was thin and weaselly, with a head the shape of a wasp's. He was much shorter than me, but laid a hand on my shoulder. I thanked him for the papaya, it was just what we had wanted.

"It costs one thousand," he replied.

"I thought it was a gift." He shook his head and grinned shyly. A thousand rupiah was well over the odds for a papaya, but I took out my money and passed over a note.

"No, no." he said very gently, "two thousand."

I stared at him and he smiled so innocently back. Then he looked up beyond my shoulder. Monché was standing at the top of the steps. He inclined his head sharply and the Weasel sneaked off, turning round to flash me his frighteningly charming leer.

When supper was laid out, Monché sat there staring at us without a word. I was just about to lunge with my spoon—it was potatoes with tomatoes and squashes—when he dropped his huge head and started champing out grace. His tones were resonant, and could surely have been heard around the village. As the long supper went on, however, I began to feel I was misjudging him. He would find us a canoe, he said, so that we could leave very soon, and reliable guides to take us. We had the right passes of course? I hedged about, and he seemed to understand our trouble, taking it all in behind his darklit eyes. By the end of supper I felt he was an ally, not a threat. That evening, by the paraffin lamp, I found a scrap of mirror in my room, and shocked myself with a glimpse of my face. There was a hideous wispy beard growing on it. I shaved it off, embarrassed that I had shown myself to Monché like that.

Soon after dawn I walked around the village looking for canoes. I met two men who had them. They both suggested slightly high prices—about seventy thousand—for getting to Sawa-Erma, which was halfway between Keneyan and our destination, Agats. They could leave the following morning. I reckoned I could play them off a bit and bargain the price down. At breakfast, half an hour later, Monché said: "I hear you've been asking around for canoes." I was a bit abashed. "I told you," he said, "I'll make the arrangements."

I was piqued for a moment, but then I thought how nice it was to have someone else to sort it out. Afterwards I took a look around the village. There were no indigenous houses. All were the same: planks and tin roofs, in rows. The odd thing was that they each housed one nuclear family, a unit not recognised by either the Asmat or the Dani, for whom the village was the currency of social living. It wasn't only the houses that were different to those upstream. A little group of people followed me at about fifty yards, staring sullenly when I turned around. If I spoke to someone sitting on the rim of his house he wouldn't answer, but shyly scratch the dust with his toes: there was something both self-conscious and sanctimonious about the villagers in Keneyan, that I hadn't seen anywhere else in West Papua. They were also a poor-looking bunch, in ragged clothes. Several I saw had skin diseases we hadn't seen further north. A couple of boys were so scrofulous that they moved about painfully, skin peeling from regular round bumps like a crocodile's hide.

In the afternoon Monché asked to see our police permits. We handed them over reluctantly, the empty spaces where our stamps should have been looked horribly prominent. He stared at them a while and started copying the details into a notebook. I was unsure about him again, and I didn't like his village. Monché brought out a calendar to show us. It had been issued by Father Bill, the white fundamentalist missionary who ran the church post two days' walk to the west at Mapinduma. The calendar was printed in the high-chrome sixties way, but was made for 1985. On one side were pictures of Father Bill and his family, the missionary tall and rangy with a strong jaw and a confident smile, daughter in bunches and a print dress, three sons with centre partings, ties and toothpaste-ad grins. On the other side were mock sepia shots of the family being welcomed at the village airport, arms round the heads of the Papuans. A banner ran across the pictures: 'Praise the Lord: we're back in Mapinduma.' Father Bill was an American and it was he who gave Monché the money and authority for his construction projects.

Monché had organised the rehousing of the village, getting everyone into what the missionaries described as 'moral houses': family units. He had built an extension to the rough airstrip and was in charge of the length of level road we had stumbled onto, which he hoped one day would lead from Mbua to Keneyan. He had been born in Keneyan, talent-spotted by Father Bill and sent for training in Jayapura, the capital of West Papua. He had had no position in the village before he went away, but came back with the blessing of God, the backing of the fantastically rich mission foundation, and the impact of an earthquake. The gentle leadership of the village had no power to resist him. In three years he had transformed Keneyan, and no one would challenge his authority.

The little man who ran a kiosk selling soap and tinned pilchards was also the health worker, and he administered the medicine supplied by the mission. We were intrigued to see more products of the missionary wealth, so we asked to be let into his surgery. "Here's where I make the operations." He led us through to a table of rough planks, with a wooden cabinet beside it. He pulled a drawer and showed us his surgical kit. "A scalpel." He held up a fixed-bladed knife, blunt and pitted, sharpened many times on stones from the river. He'd done seven operations with it, including two deep internal ones, something to do with stomachs and tubes. "Tongs," he announced, for pulling out babies: raw metal, rusted red. There was also a blood-pressure gauge, that had been half-eaten by a possum. There were two syringes, but one of them was cracked and neither had needles. Of medicines there were six kinds, one for liver worms, one for headaches and four others whose labels had rubbed off. He had to treat all the ill people in Keneyan and the dozen or so surrounding villages. There was a fraction of the money in the surgery that it took to print a calendar.

Monché had found us a canoe. He came into my room and announced it with muscular gusto. He would send the owner to see me. Later there was a timid knock on the door, and a thin hand came round the edge. It was the Weasel. Down on the river beach was a very long and brand-new dug-out, just dried after being hewn from the trunk of an ironwood tree. It looked impressive, propped up on runners over the stones. It had taken two months to carve and was big enough for five people: three standing oarsmen and ourselves, sitting in the bottom with our kit. It would do nicely. How much? "One hundred and sixty thousand," the Weasel smiled. "One hundred and sixty thousand?!" I laughed drily. "You think we're mad?" The Weasel just smiled and looked out over the river. I ran back up to the village and went straight to the house of one of the men who had offered me canoes the day before. I wanted it over and done with, so I offered him the seventy thousand straight down, to leave the next day. He looked at the ground and made shapes with his toe.

"Well?"

"We cannot go, *tuan*, it isn't possible."

"Why the hell not?"

He just kept his head down, scraping circles and squares through the sand. The second man said the same. I pushed him for an answer. He didn't know, he said, then he didn't say anything more.

I offered a boy in the village five thousand rupiah—a big sum in Papua—to find me another canoe by evening. He ran off happily enough, but never came back to claim the reward. The thought of entrusting ourselves, with our fascinating packs, four days down a swamp river to an unabashed cheat, was not a joyous one. We were also short of cash and if we paid the Weasel what he asked we could be stuck for further transport. I asked Monché about the strange business of the canoes. He said we must sort it out for ourselves: it was up to the villagers whether they took us or not. If we failed to take his advice and go with the man he'd chosen, well that was our problem. It was indeed, and I saw the plain truth of it. We were too independent for that little place, and we were going to have to sweat it out until we knew who was boss.

We very soon found out. Bored that afternoon, we went to a church practice Monché was running in a classroom next to the chapel: the guise of pious Protestantism we'd adopted in his presence could only be usefully enhanced, we figured. Villagers drifted in, leaving their belongings outside: a half-eaten potato, some sacks of vegetables. Inside the men were sitting neatly on one side of the hall, while women and children sprawled about on the other. The men were singing under Monché's direction, deep voices in conflicting harmonies, a pleasing noise, not all that far from the sounds of the Kinyum I had heard beneath Trikora. The women had nothing to do with it. They talked or poked each other, the children twisted around. One child persistently threw a stone across the hall and ran among the men cackling, to pick it up and throw it on the hollow boards again.

The practice seemed to turn into a service, at first in Indonesian, then in the local language. Neither registered and the men were passive. A couple of prayers were said and a passage from the New Testament was stumbled through by a literate villager. Monché then explained it in sweeping tones, but they failed to move the rows of glazed faces. He began to preach, excitingly and boldly, his deep voice cutting through the inertia of the dull afternoon, scattering the flies that buzzed lazily about him. He punched the air with his fist, held up the Bible with acclamation, eyes shining, teeth flashing in his deep black face. The people sat stupefied.

Monché had a prayer meeting that night. While he was away the Weasel came to the mission house, propelling another man, Daniel, in front of him. Daniel explained that the Weasel's Indonesian wasn't very good (he must have had a sudden lapse) and he had asked him to come and translate. Daniel was a forceful little man. The price the Weasel had quoted he said was wrong. It was too low, and we'd have to pay another forty thousand if we wanted to get to Sawa-Erma. I lost my temper. They could piss off and take their cheating ways elsewhere. They stayed, and the Weasel simpered politely at me. He knew I had no choice. So I agreed and resolved with Adrian to pay them what they were worth, when we arrived in Sawa-Erma. The two men slunk off into the night. I heard the Weasel cackle as he shut the garden gate.

At midnight Monché came back. He was glowing with triumph, his frame rippling with revelation. Three men had died of sickness the week before and other people in the village were also ill. Monché had proved to the congregation that the dead and the ill were not true Christians, and that God had reminded them that they'd erred. He had called on the ill to renounce their evil ways and return to Christianity. Five he said were cured instantly, and the others were well on their way to recovery. The dead had also been forgiven. "You see, George, Adrian, God is a glorious God, and His love is unlimited for those who follow him."

Monché refused to let us go for two days; the guides, he said, had to say their prayers. We became more and more tense and bored, Adrian hobbling about on his broken feet, both of us wandering down to the river to wash with some of the villagers, utterly sapped by the dead, expectant nature of the place. People stared at us as if either we or they were guilty, but they couldn't decide which. The third day came and we packed our bags and put them out prominently in the front room. Could we go now? Monché was sorry but he couldn't give us the blessing we needed to embark, we would have to wait until tomorrow. We unpacked and sat each on our beds, desultorily. Monché's line on us had tautened. The Weasel passed my window with an angelic smile on his cone-shaped face.

At last, on the fourth day, Monché announced that he had prayed for us and God had said we were safe to go. The Weasel had told us that fruit and potatoes were included in his new price, so we didn't bother buying any. Monché lead an expedition down the river cliff, then for an hour through scrubby forest, until we reached a wide stony beach beside the river. We would wait there until the canoe came down from upstream, where it was too shallow to load. The river there was still fast and rocky; I found it hard to picture an unstable dug-out negotiating it, fully loaded with whites and rucksacks. While we waited little children sped through the river clinging on to logs. They lived in a village just downstream, and had walked up to Keneyan to sell vegetables. That way back took ten minutes, riding the racing current, a net bag of possessions tied to the top of the head.

Then the canoe came down, winding through the shallow rapids, the three men steering standing up, with long-stalked leaf-bladed paddles, all in tattered shorts and orange construction helmets. They looked magnificent against the gleaming grey waters, despite the fact that one of them was the Weasel. We climbed in, cautiously, and the boat sunk almost to the gunnels. The Weasel held it steady against the snickering current. The three men stood with their oars and dropped their heads to their chests. Everyone on the beach shut their eyes and put their hands in their laps.

Monché, huge among his disciples, sitting cross-legged at the edge of the water, shut his eyes and raised his hands, an apostle in a wilderness of trees. He raised his deep voice above the rustle of water and blessed us, the boat and the guides. Then we spun round, and knifed through the water, down towards the swamps.

Chapter 8

Whatever else I thought of the Weasel, he was an excellent boat-man. He guided the wobbling dug-out from the back and jab-bered instructions at the two men ahead in his high-pitched jack-daw's voice. For the whole slow afternoon the river was a series of shallow rapids, that had split and braided round shingle islands, so that the men spent more of their time in than out of the water, hauling us through the rocks and foam. When we reached a deep stretch they shot the craft down channels of racing water, which swirled around the gunnels, sometimes sweeping over the side in shocking draughts. From time to time the boat ground over rocks, and the standing men wobbled but kept their balance as it seemed to twist and bend beneath them. The boat would slew into the rapids at an angle, twist round and shoot down between the bil-lowing rockbursts, the canoe leaping forward as the current caught its hull, trying like a wild horse to flick us off. The men simply dug in their oars, steadied and turned us, and led us out into the wider waters on the other side.

The dug-out was very much overloaded as the Weasel, or Stefanus as he was known to his friends, had filled it up with veg-etables to sell in Sawa-Erma, that he had bought cheap from the vil-lagers. Eventually he had to ground the boat and stow some of the sacks away under bushes. He was sick about having to leave them there and tried to get us to reimburse his profits. Of the two other men, one was a sidekick of the Weasel's and had had some hand in building the boat. He was openly hostile: though he spoke Indonesian he wouldn't do so for us. The third man, Abeyo, had been drafted in, and he was much jollier and warmer, explaining things to us as we went down. He was far ahead in the bows, how-ever, and we could hear nothing he said above the noisy water.

We soon left Keneyan and the single village beyond it, and were passing through forest without a sign of habitation. There were no paths, no crops, no cutting. The Asmat proper, the headhunters and woodcarvers, with their feather head-dresses and war canoes, would still be well to the south of us; we'd have to wait before we could get any inkling of what was happening there, of why the government wanted to develop that area, and what the effects might be. Hornbills wheezed across the river in ones and twos; the occasional palm cockatoo and brahminy kite went past; white herons, bitterns and cormorants rose from the banks; and there were flocks of parakeets in the trees. Crocodiles, said Abeyo, were not found so far upstream. The forest was low and tangled, stopping abruptly at the bare beaches, a complex of creepers and suckers where it met the light of the open river. It was good to be passing through without exertion.

We slipped down the river till it was almost dark, slicing through the tangle of shoals and rapids; or unloading, hacking over the sharp stones of the beaches, then regaining the canoe when the water was deep enough. We stopped at length on a sandy spit beside a tributary creek, and the three men started unloading our packs and their bundles of vegetables. There were the remains of a leaf shelter on the spit, broken down and rolled over by the creepers of the jungle, probably left by traders moving down the river a year before. Stefanus was content to use its old frame and he and the others started piling fresh vegetation on top of it to make a new roof, while we built a fire on the beach. Abeyo came down and said the hut was ready, so we carried the burning sticks up. As we arrived, the hut collapsed with Stefanus underneath. He came out cursing, and snapped at the other two to go and find some proper poles; then he grinned very sweetly at us and started hacking idly at some lianas. Across the river more than a hundred hornbills were flocking above the trees to roost, wings whistling, deep voices grunting and trumpeting. The Asmat, I remembered, believed that people's souls became hornbills for a short time after death, and roamed about the tops of the trees in purgatory, before returning to their old houses.

A new shelter was built, a poor version of the house that Yunus had made. The flimsy new poles had been dug into the ground at all angles, and the covering of straggly leaves above showed scraps of the darkening sky. Storms were wheeling over the trees towards us. Adrian and I cut more leaves and piled them on to the hut, but without a lot of confidence. The rain broke and ripped clean through the covering, putting out the fire with a contented sizzle.

Our sleeping bags and the trousers hung above the fire to dry were immediately saturated, and we sat shivering and hungry as the water bounced and bucketed over our shoulders and along our bare legs. Stefanus too looked utterly miserable, and that cheered me up a little.

When the rain had cleared we repaired the roof again and took off all our clothes to dry around the new fire. The jungle was crackling with insects, and as the light of the flames grew beneath the trees, they started to move into our house. Our bodies were snowed with odd forms: beetles with horns and tusks, crickets whose antennae were four times as long as their bodies, praying mantids with frilly arms, moths the size of bats and others as light as duckdown. I was weathering the attack well enough when something landed on my bare back with feet twelve inches apart. I couldn't say anything. I just grabbed Abeyo's arm and pointed towards it. He glanced over my shoulder and grabbed the thing, wrenching the claws off my quivering skin. Something green and diabolical was thrashing around in his hand, legs and other bits beating out of either end of his fist. He threw it in the fire and rolled it over in the flames a few times. It was a giant spiny stick insect, obscene and fat and covered in thorns. The body alone was more than ten inches long. Abeyo pulled it out and dropped it in front of me. "*Makan*," he said: "Eat it." We broke it in half and gingerly chewed on the charred carapace. Green fluids oozed out of the broken ends. Abeyo ignored us for the rest of the night because we hadn't said grace.

When Stefanus the Weasel had cooked some potatoes and vegetables and brought out another of his famous papayas, the three men set to hungrily. I asked the Weasel if we could have some too. Of course, he said with a soulful smile: it's five hundred for a sweet potato, and two thousand for a papaya. There was no use in arguing that the food was included in the price. We had a miserable night, too cold and hungry to sleep, and stormed by mosquitoes.

The day started wet and unenticing. Once resigned to the helplessness of a passenger I began to feel the little ills I'd ignored when we walking. The leechbites on my legs had gone septic and were swollen up purple and yellow with excrescences. Bruised joints had expanded and gave me grief, and I moved about like an old man. The guides assailed us with prayers. There were prayers before we got into the canoe, prayers before we pushed off, prayers before the first rapids; at every change in activity we heard "*kami berdoa*"—"Let us pray"—and there was a five minute break before we could go on to the next stage. The spirit of Monché hung above us like the hornbills over the trees.

We soon came to a dangerous rush, where the river ran over a rock ledge into a plunge pool below. It was too much for the dugout, so we had to pull her into the bank and pile out into the water. It came up to our necks, and we held our arms up and breathed in snorts above the shocking cold. We couldn't climb on to the bank there, for the vegetation came thickly down to the water, so we had to tow the boat along, branch by branch, our feet often riding clear of the bottom as we made our way downstream. Spiders and crickets rained from the trees and odd golden moths fluttered about our disembodied heads. The rapids took two hours to clear, and when we got to the end of them Abeyo loaded a pile of rocks, for cooking, into the boat. There was not a single stone, he explained, in the Asmat, nothing but mud and water between us and Australia. The break came as suddenly as all the changes in Papua: turning a bend in the river we saw there were no more rocks, and the streams resolved into a single brown channel. We had left the plateau and were now in the real swamps.

With no more jumping in and out of the boat to do, I could relax and meditate a bit. The banks slipped by without a print of man, taller trees now hunching over us, and shaking off flocks of birds from time to time, startled by the orange hats of the three figures standing on the water. I had time to worry about the date. I didn't know how many days we had before we overshot our visas and would be refused re-entry into Indonesia. I tried to write a letter home but there didn't seem much point, when a postbox was such a distant prospect. I fell asleep to the swishing of the oars.

I woke up to Adrian grabbing my arm. On the bank were houses. I was immediately excited: we would see our first real Asmat. As we passed them, however, I saw that they were tumbled down, choked by the jungle. The light thatch had slipped from the broken frames. We passed three settlements like that, silent but for the lapping of the water and the cry of jungle birds. Then for several hours there was nothing, only herons and parrots, and a harpy eagle that followed us downriver, its yellow eyes fixed on mine. Where had the people gone? Fish broke the water in places; once a very large fish rushed across the surface and a shoal of smaller ones sprayed out of the water. Sawfish and freshwater sharks came up those rivers, and maybe vast fish that scientists had never seen. I heard crowned pigeons through the trees, like old pumps starting up.

By early evening we came to a row of fresher huts, and Stefanus pulled up on the bank beneath them. He shouted out but no one was there. We unloaded and hacked through the reeds with machetes. The huts were on stilts, about six feet from the ground, very lightly built, with roofs made from woven sago fronds. Inside one we saw that the floor was covered with dried leaves, through which wolf spiders scuttled away to hide. Cassowary feathers and a knife made from a bone were scattered about. Stefanus said we would spend the night there as we would find no more shelters before the darkness fell. He started cooking.

Abeyo, the only one who would talk to us, cast some light on the empty lands. There were people around us he said, but they lived inland from the river, hidden far back in the forest. While the Asmat in that area launched attacks on settlements further north—Abeyo remembered cannibal raids on Keneyan twenty years ago—they in turn traditionally warred with their southern neighbours, and remained hidden in the forests in case of hunting parties. Now there were other pressures as well, but Abeyo was vague about them. The huts we had seen were *bivak*, temporary houses where people stopped off on fishing and hunting expeditions. The Asmat were unlike the Keneyan people, he said, though the Keneyan would call themselves Asmat. They had no gardens as it was impossible to farm there: the forest flooded when heavy rains came and the soil was poor. So they stayed only a little while in one place, moving around a wide territory, gathering sago and hunting crocodiles and cassowaries. If they remained in one place they would die, for they'd quickly exhaust the forest around them.

Stefanus opened his bag and pulled out a surprise. At one of the rapids where we had left the canoe, he had killed two rock pythons. The men wrapped them up in banana leaves and baked them over the fire. That food was free, and it tasted of shellfish. We ate the skin, heads and bones as well, as we were very hungry.

There were no signs of people for another two hours downriver. The forest that had given way to mudbanks on the riverside now closed back over, and it was still but for infrequent birds and huge swallowtail butterflies, blue or green. Yellow flowers trailed in the water. Then from around a turn in the river we heard a cry. It was a man's voice, and as the oarsmen slowed up a black canoe came round the bend towards us, a single man standing in the stern, pushing vigorously against the current. He was tall and deep brown—not black—and wore a pair of tattered shorts. He slowed up and slipped alongside, grabbing the edge of our own craft. He spoke rapidly with the oarsmen, and some of the words he used were Indonesian. In the bottom of his boat was a dead bushpig, a baby with ginger stripes down its black fur, and with it were the arrows that had killed it, the first iron-tipped ones I had seen. Clearly the Asmat weren't as isolated as I had thought. His hunting companion was still in the forest, he said; they were staying at a *bivak* down one of the creeks, having left Momoko village to roam about for several days. We would reach it in two or three hours. We pushed on down. The guides sang an odd song in their own language, containing place names; something like, "Keneyan we have passed; we have said goodbye to Keneyan. Momoko we are coming; be ready for us, Momoko." The Weasel's reedy voice rendered it well: a tree-tops sound, very high and creaking.

As we progressed we saw that there were more sago trees on the banks, and then one or two bananas. Then, as we approached a twist in the river, there was the sound of drums, deep and regular, pounding through the jungle like a knocking of tree trunks. As we pushed round into view we saw giant canoes hauled up beneath waterside longhouses. Children playing beside the water ran off into the village when they saw us coming. The drumbeats grew louder as we approached. I saw that the canoes had been painted white and orange—lime and clay—and carved on the prows with the heads of crocodiles or hornbills. We pulled along the mud shore beneath the houses. I saw legs among the poles of the houses, naked women running for cover and then, as we pushed for a gap in the canoes, I saw the glimmer of tin roofs beyond the traditional huts. The lands were less wild than I had fancied.

By the time we had clambered onto the mud we were surrounded by a big crowd of villagers. The men were all clothed, in shorts and cheap shirts, and the women were pulling faded dresses over their nakedness as they approached us. We were helped up on to a log walkway and marched along in the middle of a chattering procession. Beside one of the tin huts were thirty or forty children, standing to attention. As we approached they all said, "*Slamat paggi bapak bapak*" in unison: "Good morning, misters," well rehearsed and pleasing to the ear, except that it was afternoon. "Bloody missionaries," I muttered as we were propelled towards the huts. I was wrong however. It was the hand of government, not of God. On the walls of the schoolroom was that official portrait of President Suharto, that we hadn't seen for nearly four weeks, smiling Mona Lisa-like across his jungle domain.

We were sat down and a schoolteacher ran off to make us some tea. The whole village had crowded into the room and was sitting crosslegged on the floor around us, rows of huge black eyes following our movements like a tennis match. The people looked very different to those of the plateau. They had conker-coloured skins and narrow, athletic bodies, much leaner and tenser than the pudgy Dani in the mountains. Their heads were slim and compact, ears flat against the skull, and they all had big arrowhead noses, sometimes pulled out further by holes in the septum, and curvy Egyptian eyes. The women were just as tall as the men, fit and shaven-headed, which meant they were mourning, and sexy in a capable, violent sort of way. Sitting crosslegged on the schoolroom floor they seemed a little displaced.

More appealing just then though were big plates of sago that the teacher brought through. We were starved, and we fell on them like riverine crocodiles. The sago had been bashed into pancakes and rolled up in sago flour, and was just like chewy brown bread that hadn't been completely baked. I sneered in triumph at the Weasel: we weren't going to starve to death after all. The head of the village was led in to see us. He was all wizened up and toothless and clearly no more in control of the village then his own head was in charge of his body. He shook hands happily with us, his bleary eyes miles away, and sat down beside Adrian, nodding blissfully and drooling. Adrian passed round some Dani tobacco, that was taken up greedily, and had everybody coughing in moments.

The teachers took us on a little tour before we got back in the boat. There were three tin huts but the rest were as they'd always been, one or two a little skew in the mud, longhouses and shorthouses, the big ones for men and the small ones for women. From the biggest of all, beside the water, came the drums that had woken me upstream. We were taken to the entrance and inside we saw the players. I was a little disappointed, as they weren't all feath-

ered up and ravening for the blood of outsiders, but I was fascinated too. The men grinned when they saw us and carried on,
pounding and pounding with unrelenting vigour. Three of them
were hitting wooden drums, hollowed out of tree trunks, and
shaped like eggtimers with handles on and intricately carved. The
operative bits were the skins of monitor lizards, stretched over one
end. They sang in a high, forced croak, an intricate song, much
more colourful than the elemental rumbles of the Kinyum. The
fourth man blew a trumpet made from a length of bamboo, that
had a deep hornlike note, played over and over to give the tune an
earthy resonance. It was great music.

At the water's edge we were besieged for medicines: we gave
out a few harmless drugs. Then we were pushed off with shouts
and waving, cheerfully dismissed from that odd little cluster of
huts. Further down the river a fiercely driven canoe came up
towards us, with three warriors pushing hard against the current.
As they approach, we saw that they were women, standing proud
on the water wearing only bark loincloths: two lean girls, hard and
muscular as tigers, and a grizzled old lady, who had a look of such
fierceness above the stringy root of her body that I thought we
were going to be rammed. The guides were singing again. We soon
passed the mouth of another river, bigger than ours, that spilt
slowly into our course and doubled its width. The banks now had
slipped away beneath the water, and the trees stuck out through a
floating swamp. I dozed off.

Before there were people in the Asmat, Fumeripitch—or
Windman—strode about the swamp forests, seeing the animals that
abounded in them and the fruitful sago. He found that all was ready
for human life to begin. He built a longhouse beside the river, and
in it he put the figures of people he had carved from wood. Then
he made a drum and sang and danced for a long time, and slowly
the wooden figures came to life. When they had got used to living,
their numbers multiplied, so he built new longhouses for them. But
a giant crocodile came up the river and started destroying the longhouses with its tail, trying to get at the people inside. Fumeripitch
caught it and tore it into pieces, and hurled the foul flesh of the
beast as far as he could, over the sea and away from the Asmat.
There it grew up and became the people of foreign lands.

Since then the Asmat have lived on the riverbanks, and hunted
the fierce crocodile, and its offspring. When someone dies in the

village his soul flies off to join the hornbills, or the giant black fruitbats. After that he returns to the village, where he roams around distracted, causing trouble. What he lacks is a body, so, in the way of the Windman, he has one made for him, carved out of wood, that he can occupy. He and his fellow dead are then stored in a secret room behind the men's longhouse and looked after by the men of the village, and invited to advise the men's decisions. The village is as much a place for the dead as for the living, and if the dead are not sufficiently cared for they will cause trouble.

Every so often the burden of the dead becomes too great, and they have to be persuaded to leave. A huge feast is planned, and the master carver goes into the forest to make an ancestor pole. A big buttress-rooted tree is cut down, and whittled over several weeks into a totem twenty feet high. It is made of the interlocked figures of all who have died in the last few years, the least important at the bottom, the great warleaders at the top. Carved among their bodies are the motifs of revenge: no death is natural, and all must be avenged. The top figure sports a huge and intricately whittled phallus, and the bottom stands atop a tiny canoe. The carving of the pole placates the spirits of the dead, so that they feel suitably honoured. When it is complete, a huge feast is held: cassowaries have been hunted, and wild pigs, and sago grubs, the fat larvae of the capricorn beetle. There is a great glut of eating and dancing and then, traditionally at any rate, a headhunting raid in a neighbouring village. The raid serves to show the ancestors how valiant and self-sufficient the living are, and how little they need their help. Then the dead depicted on the pole are asked to use the little canoe at its base to float off to the land of the ancestors, the place across the sea where the sun sets. All life there is the opposite of life in the Asmat. The dead are white, they live in a cold country without forests and they can be as lazy as they like.

The carving, of shields, drums and paddles, as well as the poles and ancestor figures, is abstract and symbolic, pulling fragments out of life and giving them position and significance. Navels are the centre of everything, and around them are designs based on the intestines of beetles, vaginas of crocodiles, mantids in human form, cuscus tails and hornbills' heads. The master carver uses stone axes traded from far upriver with people who swapped them with the Dani, as well as the strange hard spikes found lodged in planks that drift mysteriously up rivers with the tide. For five hundred years the Asmat had been using nails from the distant wrecks of ships whose sailors didn't even know their land existed. The shields are considered so frightening by the Asmat that they will happily go into battle with them alone and no spears.

Perhaps because of their affinity with the trees Fumeripitch carved them from, the souls of the Asmat are never easy to control, even when they stay among the living. When an Asmat dreams, his spirit wanders off to the place in the dream and there is a great danger that it won't come back. So the men use as pillows the skulls of their ancestors, to reassure the soul and persuade it to stay. For that reason too no death is natural. If a man dies in his sleep it's because an enemy has stopped his soul from re-entering his body. If he dies when awake, his spirit has been lured away by the magic of the foe. The deaths of important people then have to be avenged, which is one reason for the ferocity of the Asmat, and their headhunting and cannibalism. There is however another purpose, that is more profound.

When a boy is born he inherits the spirit of someone who has gone before. A soothsayer in the village determines whose soul he has taken and names him in some way that reflects that. That first identity, however, won't last him a lifetime, and to become a man and to get married he needs to take on the identity of someone else, ideally a living man from a hostile village. So the village is raided and a head is taken, and the boy takes on the spirit of the murdered man. Remarkably he also inherits the corpse's family relationships. The man's mother becomes his own, likewise the father and brothers and sisters. When he visits the hostile village he is welcomed like the long-lost son, symbolically suckled by the mother and feasted and made much of. In that way the hostilities between the two villages, normally started by land disputes or stolen wives, get patched up when enough heads have been taken and there are sufficient surrogate sons. That system—of war leading to inevitable peace—is brutal, but, unlike our own excesses, self-regulated. There was still a fair bit of headhunting and subsequent cannibalism in secluded parts of the Asmat: soon before we got there we had heard some men were punished for eating three girls. They had to cut the grass on Agats airstrip.

Smoke was coming through the roof of a *bivak* beside the river, so we pushed across to buy some fish. It was a fairly tumbledown hut, with reed matting on the floor and thousands of empty clam shells scattered outside. Inside was an old man with a huge punctured nose and an old woman in a bark loincloth, asleep on the mats. He sent off one of his sons, then just sat there, watching us sagely with his old wrinkled face, not nodding or smiling or responding at all as we first tried to speak to him, then looked around his temporary hut. Against one wall was a sheath of iron-tipped arrows, five feet long, almost as big as spears. There were fishing lines, knotted and cracked old nylon, and nets made of bark fibres. We left with a big silver catfish, watching the old man still staring out at us without a sign.

Rain was falling and before long we saw another *bivak*, brown thatch against the dark wall of the forest. As we came close two naked women ran inside to put on clothes; whether it was missionaries or soldiers who had made them so coy I didn't know. There were also several men there and they helped us out and into one of the frail huts. I stepped in and fell straight through the floor, as the poles had rolled apart and there were only leaves there. No one was living in the shelter, so we took it over and started making ourselves at home. We bought some sago and worked up a fire, cooking the catfish in a metal pot I'd brought. Though Adrian had paid for the fish we had to argue quite heatedly with Stefanus to get any: he'd cooked it, so he was having it. After that he sulked and thought curses at us from out of a corner. He brightened a little later and suggested that as the Asmat were all thieves he should look after our bags for the night. So I lay on them, all, and watched him like an owl until he fell asleep.

We weren't there for long, however, as the guides were in a hurry. At two o'clock I was being shaken violently by Stefanus, who was hissing, "We're late, we've got to go," in my ear. I though he was after the bags for a moment so I curled round defensively, but then I saw that the others were up, so I stuffed what I could find into my rucksack and staggered out. A few stars glittered from behind the river mist. I had no idea what was happening. I fell off the landing-pole into the boat and before I knew it the prayers had been said and we were edging down through the soft, invisible water, hearing the splashes of fish. The banks were surprisingly quiet as we passed by, the odd frog and softly spoken insect singing out, once an owl with a deep, sore-throated boom; but otherwise all was still. Occasionally we would pass a tree lit up with fairy lights, thousands of luminous specks hanging in its branches. They were fireflies, fishing for their mates. Dawn came up in yellows and watery blues and very soon there were black canoes cutting through the river mist between us and the hazy banks.

At a village we stopped in, some men brought out two dance masks to show us. They had been woven from bark cloth and were long enough to cover the whole head and torso. One had huge eyeholes and frills and tassles, and was painted bright red and white. The other was much more horrible. It was a plain cone that fitted over the body, with holes for the arms. There was only a tiny knotted beak; no eyes, no mouth. It was quite the darkest, most terrifying thing I had ever seen made by a man. People wearing dance masks took on the character of the ancestors they represented and became those people for a whole night, reliving the lives of the dead.

We stopped for only a short time in the village. It was in poor repair, old dug-outs rotting in the mud behind the houses, a torn fishnet hanging from poles, two men missing their left eyes. Before we went, Stefanus took a bottle of aspirins out of his bag and started touting them as cures for malaria, swapping each one for a cylinder of sago. He told me later that he would sell it in a village downriver. We moved on and became more and more isolated in a widening tract of water. From time to time I saw rafts of logs tethered to the banks. It was ironwood, waiting to be moved to the merchants downriver.

Abeyo stopped paddling suddenly and pointed. "*Buaya!*" Halfway across the wide channel, more a dark slick on the water than a living thing, a crocodile pushed across the surface towards us. With a flick of its tail it disappeared, leaving just a coil of water where it had been. Abeyo kept watching the spot, and was a little tense until we were well away. The crocodiles on those big rivers are salties, and they grow to be thirty feet long, the biggest reptiles in the world. In 1970 a salty with a taste for humans was caught. It had learnt the trick of flicking over canoes and eating the people inside. It had eaten fifty-five before it was killed, and had stopped all the trade between two villages. At the time of our trip, twenty miles south of where Abeyo glanced behind him nervously, another crocodile, just as big as the first one, was said to be roaming the banks of a tidal river. It had killed twelve people already and, being so big, no one knew how to catch it.

The tide had now turned about on the river and was carrying us down at twice the speed. We had been on tidal waters the whole morning, though we were sixty miles or so from the coast. Many canoes were out, as people had emerged to take advantage of the free trip to the sago gardens. There were dug-outs forty feet long, some carved and painted in tiger stripes. One overtook us crewed by six people: three men and three women, equally tall and lithe, who slicked past in perfect synchrony. All three women were shaven-headed, and one carried a child slung over her back. There were little canoes holding one or two people, and tiny ones with children in, paddling cheerily along on their way to go fishing. Some canoes carried burning fires on their sterns as their owners didn't possess matches and had to take the flames with them. They gave the boats smoking tails, like stripy dragons whizzing past in reverse. Some were on their way to market, piled high with sago flour and mats; one had a little pig under a palm-leaf tent that was stroked by a girl when he stuck his snout out. We were hailed from right across the water and stopped to allow a canoe to race up and pull alongside. They were heading back to their village just beyond us, why didn't we drop in? They handed over some sago pith, raw pink foamy stuff that people chewed like sugar cane in the lowlands.

The village was a more traditional settlement than the others we had stopped in, with just two houses, a long one and a short one. The longhouse was a room for heroes, a two-hundred-foot feasting hall, built from the thick trunks of forest trees and thatched with sago leaves. Huge beams were slung across the length of the house, making a loft, where cylinders of sago were stored. Drums and bows hung from the rafters. Every ten yards there was a square of pillars and a fireplace within it; around a couple of these women were cooking. Men and women sat in groups at the doorways smoking cigarettes. The thin smoke was caught and magnified by the watery light from the river. There were perhaps thirty people in the longhouse but it could easily have taken a hundred, and still be cool and shady and relaxing.

Some of the women were barechested, and not ashamed. They had painted their foreheads white, with lime made from burnt shells, which gave them a cool and stately look. They ignored us. A man shouted across and asked them to make us some sago dough. The village must have been pretty lax, for women are in principle only allowed in longhouses on special occasions. Like the Dani women they are said to be subject to the men but not subservient. If a man hits his wife he is either soundly hit back, or, if the woman is smaller than he, beaten up by the other women. The husband-beating can be very severe, and sometimes men die from their wounds. Women, by bringing the men a special gift of sago, are the ones who decide when to have sex, and they throw the men out of their houses when they don't want them around.

On the whole a man and wife are faithful, but two couples might agree upon a *papitch* arrangement. This is a permanent wife-swap, or husband-swap, which means that the two pairs can interchange whenever they feel like it. The arrangement might be one started between two boys, long before marriage, who could themselves have had a homosexual relationship. Swapping their wives strengthens the bonds further, and the two men will always support each other, perhaps to the death in battle. There is also communal *papitch*, when everyone sleeps with everyone else by turns. It brings the village closer together when it feels frightened by a disturbance, like the arrival of a missionary. The first missionaries to arrive were of course white and came from a land that was cold and had no forests and little call for manual work. To overcome their fear of the returned ancestors, the people would promptly swap partners and throw themselves into an orgy of *papitch*. The missionary, horrified, would react furiously, and so it would go on.

The history of the first attempts to convert the Asmat is an extraordinary one, and riddled with misunderstanding and prejudice. Up until a very few years ago people were still attempting to contact new tribes. I was told by a Dutchman of the steady nerves required to go in and make contact. The whites would take a boat upriver, looking for signs of a settlement. When they found one they would disembark and sit on the ground between the houses, waiting. The villagers would have heard the boat from far off and fled into the forest. As the missionaries sat there they knew they were being watched by hundreds of eyes they couldn't see. At length the bravest warrior would show himself and approach circumspectly, spear poised. If a missionary made a rapid movement or did anything to show his fear he was likely to be speared by the warrior, out of sheer terror. Slowly other men would emerge, and circle the extraordinary corpse-coloured beings with the utmost apprehension, ready to defend themselves. The missionaries would push out gifts and wait until they had been stared at for long enough to become familiar, then carefully get up and edge towards the boat. They would return at shorter intervals, each time leaving gifts to be picked up when they had gone, until they were no longer frightening. Then they could start pushing the people towards the changes they wanted.

Why they wanted to change the Asmat had a lot to do with what they saw as Satan's work, subverting a people who could otherwise enjoy the pleasure of being like them. Later on, some of them rediscovered the truth that assails anyone who travels for a long time: that the similarities between ourselves and other people are superficial. Beneath the shared politenesses, a common joke, the same irritations, lie moral views, tastes and understandings of the world so far apart that there is not an inch of common ground.

If an Asmat man has something stolen from him, he regards the loss as a great embarrassment and an affront to his valour. If the thief is identified he has to compensate the loser in kind, giving him something of an equal value. To make the thief more embarrassed than he is himself, the loser then gives the thief something of a greater value in return.

Only one thing is more humiliating than theft, and that is the murder of a relative. The principle is the same. Rather than killing a relative of the murderer's in return, the bereaved kills a closer relative of his own. The closer the relative is, and so the bolder the deed, the better he can transfer and overcome his shame.

Another code inconceivable in the West is that of honour in the Mappi tribes, who live in the south-east of the Asmat. To be a legend-maker in the Mappi you must exercise the greatest possible deceit. An enemy is identified, someone from another village, who has perhaps killed a *papitch* brother or stolen your wife. Rather than dispatching him immediately, to gain honour and heroism you must draw him into a confounded treachery. Over the course of many years you make friends with him, cultivating his goodwill with presents and feasts until he becomes, maybe after a decade, your very best friend. Then you kill him in the most horrible way. The more surprised he is at being killed the more honourable is the killing, so that the myth-makers in the Mappi are those who have become the most inseparable friends with their eventual victims.

All these things were used as justification by the first missionaries to wade in and change the people's lives. The Protestant Don Richardson made the good work of the missionaries famous by dramatising the awful way in which people must have lived before they were saved by God. Had he tried to see it from the Papuan point of view, he might have noticed that a lot of our habits were equally repulsive to them. To pack old people off to homes when they're no longer wanted by their families is judged to be utter barbarism by the Papuans, who value their old people highly, even when they're gaga. By contrast to those in almost every other part of the world, disabled people and the mentally ill are maintained by the other villagers and live as normally as possible. One of the Dani's greatest war leaders was crippled from birth. Perambulators, which keep a mother and baby three feet apart, garden walls and locked front doors, all would make fine material for a party of evangelical Asmat to smash in a holy fury, if they enjoyed proselytising and had the chance to travel. Headhunting and tribal battles are brutal, but contained and confined to a small scale. Until the Europeans, and then the Indonesians, arrived to do them good, wars, massacres and widespread famines were unknown to the Papuans.

In 1987 the main Catholic missions in West Papua claimed that all the villages had been contacted. I spoke to one old man, however, who said that that wasn't quite true. There was still one place, Wagin Island, where tribes remained unvisited. It was an extension of the river slobs spreading into the Arafura sea, an impassable network of swamp creeks and floating vegetation. In the middle of it all missionaries in aeroplanes had seen smoke rising from forest clearings. They had tried many times to get in and make contact, but either they'd become lost among the creeks or the villagers had vanished before the missionaries reached them.

It was time, in the longhouse, to start asking the important questions, and we began chatting to a group of men. They said that for the most part they still lived off the forest, on sago and hunted animals, but that they were having to spend an increasing amount of time out logging. They hardly got any money for it, and didn't want to do it, but when I asked them why they did it they became shy and wouldn't say. The money they got would buy the odd piece of clothing, sometimes medicine. That too was a problem, as they said there wasn't a doctor for hundreds of miles. Several people suffered from curable diseases in the village, but couldn't get treated. One man said a doctor came past the village two years before, but he hadn't known, so couldn't get his bad back fixed, and had been regretting it ever since. Transmigration, they said, was in the air, but no one knew anything for certain. They all thought that the Javanese would come in soon and told me they dreaded the prospect, as they thought the immigrants would swallow up their lands and drive the game away. They didn't like the people they had met—policemen and businessmen—but wouldn't be specific. The men became a little bashful and the conversation dried up.

The women brought us sago. This was the raw flour patted into balls and rolled roughly on the fire. It was quite revolting: a gummy black parcel with white dough inside. As a moving-on present someone brought us a big cucumber: we would be thirsty on the next stage, he said, and we couldn't drink the water in the river. As we stood outside watching some of the men hacking a dug-out canoe from a trunk of ironwood, another group offered to give our guides a hand and speed us on down to Sawa-Erma. So we left our dug-out at the longhouse and loaded into a larger one, very wide and flat-keeled. Four more oarsmen joined us, so we had seven hands. Our guides, swift on the mountain river close to Keneyan, were quite outpaced by the extraordinary oarsmanship of the swampland Asmat. The new men dug in with slim carved leaves, in exhilarating synchrony, with a tight, splashless arc.

This was the realm of the oarsman. Little walking would be done: the lands were permanently flooded, with trees sticking starkly from the water. It was hot, with light reflected and magnified by the brassy river, the swamp bushes on the banks giving no shade. The tide had slowed, and men and women were sitting out the slack on little log rafts, shaded by tents of sago leaves, with their canoes tethered alongside. For a while we saw pairs of long- and shorthouses beside the big river, some still smoking blue through the thatch. Then, as the water opened out still further, so that there was only water, we took a long view of tinroofed huts: Sawa-Erma, and the first sight of home.

Sawa-Erma was where Saati, the great war-leader, had lived until a few years before. He had taken twenty-four heads, a proud boast of his right up to his death, despite his Christian conversion and a close friendship with the Bishop of Agats. For us the village had a more immediate chill. We had heard upstream that there was a police post in the settlement; we were coming back into Indonesia. We had no permits and we were entering a troublespot that had been sealed from outsiders. I thought about it for a moment, then, tired, sunstruck, I couldn't care. Little boys were climbing a bent coconut palm and dropping into the water: with its tinroofed houses on stilts it looked like that speck of coastal Melanesia we had seen in Biak, seven weeks before. We pulled up at a landing stage. The whole village was raised above the mud, alongside wooden walkways five feet high. We marched off wearily to face the fiend, to the little police station with a red and white flag hanging limply outside.

At first it seemed there was no one in: curtains were pulled across the glass windows, a wire led from a solar panel through the crack in a shut front door. Then I heard someone grunt and get out of bed: we would have a grumpy policeman to add to our troubles. An Ambonese man in jeans, the head of police, opened the door and gazed at us sleepily, scratching his stomach. We followed him into his office and he sat us down.

"Where have you come from?"

"Wamena."

"So, if you'd like to . . . What?!"

I told him the sorry route we'd taken. He sat there shaking his head, and I reckoned we were really in for it. I couldn't be bothered to lie, and when he asked why he hadn't got any permits I told him the truth: we'd just sneaked out of Wamena and slunk into the mountains.

The policeman stared a second, then whooped, jumped up and slapped us on the shoulders. "Ha, you're mad, wonderful!" He took out his rubber stamps and decorated our permits handsomely in purple ink, chuckling all the while about us getting one over on the Wamena police. "They'll still be looking for you," he gloated. I looked at the permits. Not only was there a stamp for Sawa-Erma but also a permit entitling us to visit Agats: it was a miracle. Frankie the police chief picked up our packs and led us along to his house, where we could stay the night. His wife and the other policemen were there, and they feted us with coffee and beer, wanting to know all about the trip and what the people in the mountains were like. I had the feeling they were bored in their outpost, and that nothing could be more entertaining than the arrival of two lunatic whites. Frankie made up a good bed for us and all our troubles were over.

Except one. We had yet to pay the Weasel and his oarsmen. I'd give him the preposterous fee he had asked for first, but not the surcharge. I had been dreading the confrontation, picturing for days a furious Asmat rabble backing up one of their own. When Stefanus judged the time was right for payment he edged up to my elbow—I was sitting on Frankie's verandah—and touched it with a spiky finger. "Er, *tuan* . . ." his face was the picture of innocent expectation.

"Yes. The pay." I had already counted out what I intended to give him, so I put it down on the table. He grabbed it and counted it through. He counted it again, with dramatic consternation. I told him he must divide it into three, for they should all be paid equally. He broke it into two piles and stared from the money to me to the money again. Where, he was saying, was the money for the third man? He smiled that most hateful smile and my dreads all came to the surface. The other crewmen had come on to the verandah.

Frankie bounced out of his door: "What's the problem?"

I explained: the first price and the second price.

When I mentioned the first one he said "What?!" and when I told him the second he said "What?!!"; then he turned to Weasel and said, "What's the matter, can't you divide by three?" and deftly shuffled the notes into three heaps.

Stefanus started muttering to the other two in Keneyan.

"You can't speak Indonesian either?" asked Frankie a little cruelly. It was the only time I saw Stefanus lose his cool. He spluttered and blushed blacker, then snatched up the money and shouted at the other two to follow him, marching away down the boardwalks, colliding with a Javanese trader coming up the other way, who shoved him back. Pure, remorseless revenge very seldom comes to you, but when it does it's as sweet as it's supposed to be. I felt a little sorry for Abeyo, who would doubtless get bullied and robbed on the way back. The Weasel, I later found, had pinched my watch, my knife and my cooking pot, but it was a small price for such a gloatingly bloody victory.

News had spread through the village already that the loonies had come to town, and when we staggered like the man in the desert out to one of the little shops along the boardwalks we found to our great delight that everyone wanted to make a fuss of us. When we tried to buy a beer and cakes at the first shop, we weren't allowed to pay; in return we had only to tell the shopkeeper about our adventures and—a much greater task—put up with a tiny Papuan teacher who kept trying, and failing, to translate our Indonesian conversation into English for our benefit. We ate fried bananas, pilchards from the tin, hot condensed milk, dry biscuits and chocolate, and it seemed like a banquet at a great restaurant.

The following morning was a Sunday, and the policemen combined forces to find us a speedy boat to Agats. While everyone was at church we played with the cuscus that one of them owned, an extraordinary, very stupid giant marsupial that lived in trees. It was nocturnal, with a pointed head, no braincase and shocked, forward-facing eyes, and it had a long pink prehensile tail, that could wind round a branch and take its whole weight. People made traps for cuscuses on horizontal branches, from a loop of rope and a weight that pinned them against the bough until someone came along. This one wandered casually across the ceiling of its cage, then ungratefully ate a banana in a corner. When church was over (all the policemen were Christians) Frankie fixed us a boat for no more than the price of the fuel, that could get us to Agats by the afternoon. It was a dug-out with a flat stern and big outboard hanging off the end. A friend of the policemen's was driving. As we waved to the friendly lions whose den we had stayed in, it took off with a force that tumbled me off the pack I was sitting on. We were truly back in the land of material goods.

Chapter 9

Agats was to be the end of our troubles. We had plenty to exorcise. We had lost about three stone between us and weren't well. We still suffered from infected leechbites, and my legs were in pain: all down the shins and over the ankles the skin was swollen up, and the slightest jarr would trigger off an agonising reflex. Adrian's feet were still cracked and leaking, both the heels and toes deeply gouged, and he looked like the mermaid who had to walk on knives all her life. On top of that our visas gave us a week's life before we were thrown out of the country. We were running out of cash: now we could change some cheques in a bank. Our parents hadn't heard from us for six weeks, so we could phone and reassure them. Almost above all else we wanted to get to Singapore in time for Christmas. In Agats, one of the nine towns of West Papua, we would find medicine, a telephone, a bank, good food and an aeroplane. The expectations fell away one by one.

The very sight of Agats was inauspicious. Far from the bustling coastal town I'd expected, it seemed to consist of a couple of dozen huts on sticks beside a sludgy river. While Sawa-Erma was five feet above the mud, Agats was ten, and unrepaired boardwalks showed a mass of scrap iron and sharpened stakes below the six-foot holes that had opened up. No one seemed to care very much. A couple of soldiers wandered about with M-16s under their arms, the six or seven shops were all shut and the whole place seemed sunk in the inertia that the swamp air brought it: a little cluster of iron and wood far from anywhere and going nowhere. There was a guesthouse that charged an extortionate rate and alarming numbers of police, otherwise almost nothing: no bank, no telephone exchange, a shut hospital. Two things, however, brought limited joy to our hearts: an airstrip and an eating-house. We bought a huge meal of rice, fish, beans, cucumbers, bananas and sago cakes. The kindly Javanese woman who cooked it said we could have it on tick and pay in the evening. We were just digging in when an Papuan man, quite the most arrogant I had seen, slouched in, with sunglasses and a cigarette dribbling from his mouth.

"Where you come from, mister?" he demanded in the rudest way. We ignored him and he came back a minute later in a policeman's tunic.

"You come me," he said in arrogant policeman's English, and strode off along the boardwalks so that we had to follow, leaving our scarcely touched first supper for the flies in the eating house.

Thanks to the permit from Frankie we got through a brisk interrogation unscathed, as the arrogant little corporal didn't have the authority to override the head of police in Sawa-Erma.

"So," he asked in English, though we'd been speaking Indonesian, "where you come?"

"What?"

"Where you come!" he demanded angrily.

"Oh, we'll go to Jayapura from here, and then to Jakarta."

He leapt up, triumphantly. "Ha ha, will not can! Ha!"

That happy view was confirmed in the guesthouse. The district officer had stolen the aircraft fuel, so the state airline refused to fly to Agats any more. It seemed we were stuck. I wandered out on to the broken boards with growing horror. The nice Javanese lady from the eating-house came over.

"You can pay me now perhaps?"

"Sure, yes." I brought out the standard two thousand rupiah.

"No, no. It's ten thousand. Each."

With no food, no phone, no bank, no plane, no medicine, no Christmas, no friends, we were stuck in the smelliest little pile ever planted on an intractable crocodile-swirling swamp on the other side of the world. I lay on my bed. It was the final blow, and I nearly cried with the thought that we might be stuck in Agats for ever. I wanted my mother, I wanted my girlfriend. I would forgo all my radical pretensions for some bourgeois comfort and I tried to dream myself into some natty little garden in Kent, with a patio and goldfish in the pond. It didn't work, though it might have been that which brought forth the wizened little genie of the guesthouse, who stuck his head round the door and suggested we try talking to the missionaries.

The Catholic mission in Agats was about the only decent-looking building there. It was made of long low wooden passageways, spacious halls and a monastery, habitable despite the other miseries of Agats. In the radio room we found two odd little American men, both round and very jolly. They were much amused by us, which did little to cheer us up, and, it appeared, even more amused by our hopes of getting out, which, needless to say, did even less. They were men used, in that Indonesian backwater, to not getting what they wanted. There was, indeed, a mission plane that used the Agats airstrip; but it was fully booked for the next four weeks, so we had no hope of taking it. It seemed to have been the last option. We stumbled out in the utter most misery and I felt sick. Keeping my eyes on the treacherous boardwalks, I didn't see Father Ton till he was nearly upon us. He was the very opposite of the two men in the mission house, an extremely tall and wiry Dutchman, with a calm laconic style. I was ready to confess to the good priest all my troubles on the spot, and he suggested we come back in the evening, for there might be a way out.

We spent the day wandering among the displaced Asmat men hanging about on the waterside, and rounding up scraps of information. None of them was very happy, and all the men prepared to talk to us were deeply resentful of the Indonesians. They spoke about beatings and killings by the police, sometimes for the most arbitrary reasons, and muttered vaguely about doing something about it. They had all heard of plans to bring transmigrants in, but while it was the subject of much dread, no one had any idea when they might come or how many would arrive. A more immediate problem was logging. The men complained that they were forced to log by the big companies round Agats, and beaten or even shot if they didn't comply. Even if they did get paid it was never enough to compensate for the disease, the hunger of their children and the decay of their houses that they suffered when the logging demanded that they had to spend up to four or five months at a time in the forest. If their stories were true it was a case of genuine slave labour, that needed investigation.

The boardwalks, treacherous by day, were lethal at night, and, on the way to see Father Ton, I fell through a hole so I was dangling by my elbows, just saved from the long fall into mud and splintered wood. After that we were helped along by a charming Ambonese man with a torch. Why, I asked him, weren't the causeways repaired? There was no wood he said. I got the feeling that planning in West Papua was not all that it should have been, when there was no wood in the middle of the biggest swamp forest in the world. Father Ton had seen into our dark hearts and recognised what our inchoate souls lacked. So there, in the fridge run off the generator, were two cold beers waiting for us. There was one missionary at least who knew about the relief of human misery. Ton also told us that we had a hope of getting out. At Senggo, one hundred and twenty miles back into the forest, east of Agats, a plane was due to land in six days' time. If we could hire a motorboat in Agats there was good chance we could get there and find seats on the aeroplane. The idea was cheering enough and I felt myself relaxing; at least there would be something to do.

It was hard to believe that Father Ton and Monché, in Keneyan, were serving the same god. All Ton's talk was of looking after the people's lives, protecting them from the most violent effects of change, trying to avert the plagues and massacres that from time to time had afflicted them since their exposure to the outside world. He acknowledged that a great deal of harm had been done, and no small amount of that by missionaries, but it was time now for enlightened people to try to repair it. He didn't say a word about God or the need to baptise everybody; he gave the impression, though he didn't state it, that he didn't mind what religion the people followed, as long as they were generally good and happy.

Ton sketched the history of the missions in West Papua. The Dutch in their time had divided West New Guinea between the Protestants and the Catholics, the Protestants getting the bigger share in the north, the Catholics the swamps and scrubland in the south. It was effectively a division between fundamentalists and liberals: the reactionary Dutch Protestants and the pragmatic Dutch Catholic church, one of the most liberal of all churches. It had always been the job of the southern Catholics to tend to the earthly welfare of their flocks first and then, if there was time, to attend to the good of their souls. They recognised that the Asmat culture was more than just a pretty set of customs to keep foreigners amused, but was essential to the cohesiveness and stability of the people; that without it they would turn into the glazed creatures we had seen in Keneyan. Doubtless the Catholics were concerned to smooth off certain edges—they didn't like wifeswapping very much—but on the whole the effort was to work on what was already there, rather than to destroy and rebuild in the image of the white God.

Ton didn't make them, but the comparisons were clear enough. The Protestant missionaries remained absolutist and violently uncompromising. The Papuans were to be models of themselves and were threatened with hellfire if they didn't renounce everything that allowed them to remain different, burning their old houses, destroying their artefacts, taking on the clothes and manners of the white men they were supposed to imitate. While that sort of egocentricity and destruction had been curbed in most other countries of the world, the Indonesians gave the Protestants free rein in West Papua, and in that country, one of their last strongholds, they could maintain the full repressive assault of the nineteenth-century evangelists. I had heard from another Catholic about a trip he made that year—1987—to a Protestant outstation in the mountains. One of the first people he met was a man whose hand was dangling from his wrist as a result of a severe machete wound. How, he asked the American missionary there, could he let that man walk around in such a state? "We are here to save souls", was the curt reply. For Father Ton medicine was one of the most important jobs of the mission, for he seemed more interested in saving lives than saving souls.

Listening to Ton I realised just what a wimp I was being. A little battering on the walk had convinced me I was on the verge of death, and the thought of a few weeks' captivity in Agats was utterly crushing. Ton, unflustered by the prospect of spending the rest of his life in that hole, was the most quietly tough man I'd ever met. He had trained at a theological college in London, on an entirely theoretical course that required perfect Latin. At the end of the training, in 1950, he was about our age and, like all the Mill Hill Brothers at that time, he was told where he was to be sent, for the rest of his life. He was despatched to northern Borneo, now Sabah, where he stayed in a tiny village in the mountains until 1972, when the Malaysians became suddenly paranoid about missionaries. Then he was captured and thrown into jail for a fortnight, before being deported. He moved not back to his home, but straight out to West Papua, to take up the same work in the Asmat where, all over again, he was a foreigner.

It seemed quite clear that in their efforts to make life as good as possible for the Papuans, the Catholic missionaries had come up against the Indonesian government. Only later did I find out just how, and it wasn't the missionaries who told me. Ton and the others had been in danger of expulsion, and taking with them the good work they'd started, or the bad work they'd modified. So Ton and some of the other Catholics renounced their citizenship and became Indonesians. With their nationality went all hopes of being bailed out if they were imprisoned or threatened with death, which, I later found, was not uncommon. Until his change of nationality Ton had been able to get back to see his relatives every five years or so. Now he might or might not be allowed a passport. If he was he'd be allowed out as an Indonesian tourist: his permit would run for three months, at least one of which would be taken up in travel and bureaucracy. Then, being an Indonesian, he would have to come back to his home country, the mudhole in the south of West Papua, where he would die. It is a liberty to write all this, as he and the other Catholics had no idea we were journalists: we were just especially irresponsible tourists, and we relied on the same kindness they would have given anyone. No one else is going to chronicle it, however, and when we reached them in 1987 they had heard that as the old missionaries died no foreigners would be allowed in to replace them.

The only people in radio contact with the state airline were the police, so we went back in some trepidation to the scene of our interrupted lunch: the little room where we were interrogated. There, in the place of the swaggering yob who had dragged us off, was the commander, a crisp and charming Javanese man, who sat us down, got us a tea and asked all about the trip, but only in a friendly way. He would organise a call to Senggo, then tell the guesthouse man if there were seats on the aeroplane. We went back down to the waterside to look for a launch. We were sent to a Javanese man called Sugiyono, who, for a large fee and a small surcharge for special persuasions, could hire a boat and an engine from the army. He was prepared to take us up to Senggo in two days' time: we could wait there for three days for the aeroplane. When we got back to the guesthouse the owner had a message for us: there were just two seats left on the aeroplane and the police had booked them in our names. We had our way out.

Only then did I think about money. We pulled out everything we had and added it up. We deducted the cost of the boat, the flight, the guesthouse for two more days and found that, even without eating, or paying for accommodation in Senggo, we were short by thirty thousand rupiah: just ten pounds, but it might have been the earth. Although the Weasel had stolen one of my watches, I had had the spare hidden away, which I sold for twenty thousand rupiahs to a shopkeeper. Other than that our only fluid assets were a dozen crumpled dollar bills. With no bank to change them in we might as well have fed them to the crocodiles; but again the men of God came to our rescue, and our money was changed in the temple at generous rates. We were clear and there was a chance to do some proper snooping around. We started by chatting casually with some more of the emptied-out Asmat in the town, then we hit a stroke of luck.

On the waterfront we met a man who worked in a government office. Though we meant only to be friendly we found before long that he was angry about some of the things he had seen in the Asmat: he had a personal, if rather obscure, connection with the troubles. I can't, for obvious reasons, be more specific. We talked him slowly into a quiet tearoom on the edge of the settlement and, reluctantly, he began to tell us what he had seen and heard of since he had been posted in the swamps. He wanted to help us find out more, so we met two friends of his that evening, who independently corroborated much of what he said. I've since then been able to put the stories into a wider historical scheme, and check them with more reliable Indonesian sources.

In 1964, a year after Indonesia had taken over West Papua—or West New Guinea as it was before then—the first president, Sukarno, left the United Nations, and threw out its representatives. Some people saw that as a means of getting what he wanted done in places such as West Papua, without interference. The Dutch, the previous rulers of West Papua, had left considerable resources in the territory, as they'd been preparing it for independence and eventual amalgamation with Papua New Guinea, the other half of the island. They had, by 1950, recognised the colonial debt, and were making what reparations they could to the people on the island, by building up hospitals, industry and schools. That seems to have been one of the reasons why the President had wanted the territory. As soon as the UN went, Indonesian troops moved in and started pulling out the resources. The hospitals were emptied, the factories stripped, and everything transportable was shipped off to Java, in an effort to stave off the growing resentment caused there by the President's imprudent economic policies.

Sukarno also intended to integrate his new land as quickly as possible. The Papuans stood between him and the extraction of the vast natural resources in West Papua: timber, oil, copper and gold. He and his administration regarded them as godless savages in dire need of reform, as well as a threat to the tenure of the island, and they felt they had both a moral and a political duty to change them very fast. In the Asmat the destruction of all longhouses was ordered. Soldiers went through the villages burning the houses and destroying the carvings. Anyone who resisted them was shot. The Asmat were told to rebuild their houses on Javanese standards. They fled into shelters in the jungle, horrified by the burning of things that had seemed no more than wood and thatch to the Indonesians, but were the very stuff of life to the Asmat. Some attempted to fight back and were beaten, then shot. The Catholic missionaries tried to defend them, and were themselves threatened with death, and one father was shot through the head by a district officer. When the United Nations observers were allowed to return in 1966, they found a minor holocaust taking place, and a dispersed and terrified population that in places was starving to death.

There was little the UN or anyone else could do to stop what was happening, and the transfer of the presidency to Suharto didn't change those aspects of the Indonesian policy in West Papua. Remaining longhouses were still being torn down, and the village leaderships replaced by young Indonesian loyalists from other parts of the island. Soldiers were extracting what they could from the Asmat, and using any means to get it. Before long that meant timber. The biggest firms operating in the area were military holding companies, whose profits were used to buy weapons. Private firms also hired soldiers to boost their turnover. Asmat men and women were rounded up and sent out to cut wood. Sometimes they were given an advance payment of an axe or some sticks of tobacco, sometimes nothing, but in every case they had to fulfil a certain monthly quota. The Asmat didn't want to log. It meant that there was no time to hunt, to gather sago, bring up their children, or maintain their houses. They also knew that it was only the trees that kept them alive. As the ironwood was pulled out, the game left, and if more trees went, the sago, kept shaded and moist beneath them, dried out and died, wiping out the single means of survival in the places they had logged.

At first the Asmat attempts not to work were broken up by

threats and beatings from the traders and hired soldiers. Then the government stepped in. In 1974 the district officer of Agats, after being bribed substantially by the timbermen, had the local soldiers line up the recalcitrant tribesmen at gunpoint while he beat them with a stick for not fulfilling their quotas. As a result several communities fled into the forest. Soldiers were sent after them and they were brought back to the district officer. He beat them first with a stingray's tail, inflicting serious wounds, then a rifle, which he eventually broke over the back of one of the old men. From then on the district officer's police force supervised the unpaid logging operations, and there were beatings every month.

Two years later there was an outbreak of cholera among the people being forced to log. They blamed it on the government—which was possibly partly right, as cholera was unknown to them until then—and fled into the forest. This time they fled properly and secreted themselves in an inaccessible hideaway. Others joined them when forced to vote for the government party in the 1977 election. The fugitives armed themselves with arrows and holed up for a siege. There were a couple of failed attempts to negotiate, the rebel ranks grew, and it looked as if there was going to be a bloody battle between the Asmat and the Indonesians, with little doubt about the outcome. The Bishop of Agats, an American Catholic, stepped in and persuaded the police to let him visit the fugitives. By then they were ready to kill any outsider who approached, so he went at great risk. He talked his way in and got them to put down their arms, promising to see that they were paid for the forced logging they had done. A civil servant from Merauké arrived in Agats and sacked the errant district officer and forced him at gunpoint to hand over some of the money the Asmat should have been paid.

The Asmat thought that would be the end of the forced logging, but it wasn't. The next district officer behaved in exactly the same way, supporting the logging companies and beating up the villagers if they refused to be their slaves. It happened again and again, as each subsequent district officer treated the Asmat as the first had done. At the end of 1987, though the situation had in some respects improved, Asmat villagers were still being beaten, very occasionally killed, for resisting labour that was forced and paid, if at all, at a risible rate. What we encountered in Agats were suspicions that something more than chance lay behind the consistent behaviour of the successive district officers. Though they could prove nothing, people had begun to believe that there were higher authorities making that slave labour happen. There were two possibilities. Since many of the logging concessions in the Asmat were owned by military holding companies, run on the whole by Javanese generals, it was quite possible that the army leaders were putting pressure on the district officers, to keep their profits up. Under military rule in Indonesia that sort of thing wouldn't have been too surprising. Alternatively, and more darkly, came suspicions of pressure from somewhere higher still. Two years before we got to the Asmat the *Sydney Morning Herald* had exposed the business interests of President Suharto's family, that ran to two or three billion dollars and were largely ill-gotten. Among them was timber.

Without written records to turn to, it was hard to confirm the many rumours of villagers murdered by soldiers or the logging companies. One that we could be sure of was the killing of a young man in Sawa-Erma. At a meeting of villagers he stood up and tried to persuade them to stop complying with the demands of the loggers. He was shot on the spot by a policeman (not Frankie). The policeman was never disciplined and stayed on in the village. That the logging situation was a little better in 1987 than it had been before—though villagers were still being beaten and, as that story suggested, shot—was mostly due to the efforts of the missionaries. In 1984 they finally lost their patience with the government's repeated promises to clear it up, and they fed the story to an Indonesian paper. It blew up into a big issue for a while, and the missionaries were nearly expelled, but it was reckoned that that would cause a greater fuss than the logging. The publicity had the eventual result of a promise to pay the Asmat for the work they did. When that promise materialised it emerged that the payment couldn't make up for the economic losses the Asmat suffered through logging, still less compensate for the social problems. Confined to a single patch of forest and away from their own sago grounds, the people had been developing vitamin deficiencies they had never had before. Kept from their healthy lives in the canoes and longhouses they had developed filariasis, cholera and yaws, the disease that eats away your face, and they couldn't afford the medicine to treat it. As the adults couldn't gather food the children had to do it instead, and could no longer go to school.

17 & 18. Mbua men

19. A house in the mountains

20. *Left:* Unmarried Dani girls

21. *Below:* The master bridge-builder at work

22. Three guides lost in the forest: Tekir, Gandano and Yunus in their shelter

23. Maleo fowl, hit by
a poisoned arrow

24. The weasel and his trump:
two rock pythons from the riverbank

25. Abeyo on the prow

26. *Above:* In Agats (*left* Adrian, *right* George), but neither safe nor sound

27. *Left:* Asmat *bivak*

28. The logging ship at Ats

29. Designer isolation in Senggo

30. One of the deserted villages, Mindip Tanah

31. *Above:* 'Ja, it will go.' With Brother Kase and the mended plane at Mindip Tanah

32. *Left:* The man who crossed the OPM: no ears, few fingers

33. High tack in Jayapura

34. After the massacre: photo taken from the hip in Jayapura hospital

35. Dani war council

36. Warming up for battle

37. The war's over

All this was going on while we were there. Above and below Sawa-Erma we had seen logs moored up and waiting to be loaded by the monthly ship. The people who had cut them, I heard, were forced to do so. Still the district officer, with the help of police and soldiers, maybe Frankie too, sent the Asmat men and women out at gunpoint and beat them if they didn't fulfil their quotas. The most lucrative wood, ironwood, was by then extinct in the southern Asmat. Though the forest still stood, it was rangy and broken up, and the sago in many parts had dried out and died. The logging had spread upstream.

In the mid-eighties the Asmat had been allowed to rebuild some of the longhouses, on the big rivers where they could be clearly seen. In other parts they were still being torn down and the tribal artefacts destroyed. Twenty-five years of government in West Papua had not changed the Indonesian attitude to the people, and still government ministers described them as unclean, unintelligent and incapable of leading decent lives without direction from outside. Some people had managed to hide, and I heard that many we saw on the big rivers in the shorts and football shirts of Indonesian citizens would take them off and revert to nakedness as soon as they were out of reach. In 1971 the district officer in Agats mistakenly authorised the resumption of tribal feasts, that had been banned along with the longhouses. He wanted the people to make some ancestor poles that he could sell to tourists, but knowing nothing about the Asmat he didn't realise that a pole cannot be completed without a feast. He tried to suppress the festivities, but he got no poles; so, in a few places, with permission, they were allowed to take place. Unauthorised feasts in 1987 were still being stamped out.

Extraordinarily, despite the great rise in disease that had followed the destruction of the longhouses, the wearing of clothes and the forced logging, there was not a single doctor in the Asmat. The area was the size of Belgium and held seventy thousand people, yet there were only four or five unqualified health workers, with dispensaries similar to the one we saw in Keneyan. The hospital in Agats was one of those Sukarno had stripped in 1964, and it had never been refurbished. The doctor who had been installed there had been recalled a few months before we arrived in Agats and had never been replaced, perhaps because the posting was considered too expensive. The nearest open hospital was in

Merauké, one hundred and fifty miles away and entirely inaccessible to sick people in the Asmat. Only the missionaries supplied medicines, and they were short of money. The government had refused their request to bring foreign doctors in. Before the Indonesian doctor was recalled there had been three major cholera epidemics in the Asmat. In each case the doctor radioed desperately to Jayapura for drugs and helpers, and received just a polite request for updated statistics.

None of that helped to explain why the Asmat, a remote, infertile, fully-populated swamp, had been scheduled for transmigration. No one I met in Agats could tell me any more about it than I already knew: that the Asmat had been put on the list but the sites had not yet been cleared of trees. The proposal, with many others, was on ice, pending a resurgence in the oil price. How much better the economy would have to get before the government started to move the Javanese settlers in there I couldn't tell. But already I had one clue about why it might have been put on the list.

It came from a leaked document I had received, a sensitive one I wasn't supposed to see. It was produced for the Transmigration Department by three consultancy firms: two Indonesian ones and one from Europe. It dealt with the government's plans for moving settlers not into the Asmat, but into the zone just next door, the Mappi. The Mappi's environment was very similar: swampy, salty, undeveloped, inhabited by independent tribal people. The government had been planning to move sixty thousand settlers in and get them farming rice and tree crops. The report expressed substantial worries about those plans, due to the great problems the transmigrants might encounter; but it advised that the project nonetheless suited the government's purposes. As a result, it suggested that the transmigration area actually be expanded, to include Wagin Island. Wagin Island was the one place, the old Dutchman had told me, that still had uncontacted tribespeople. The report cited, as a purpose of the programme, and one of its requirements, the 'acculturation' of the Mappi people. I wasn't exactly sure what that word meant, but I felt I was getting nearer to some of the answers we were seeking.

On the evening before our boat was due, Ton came round to invite us to supper at the mission house. He was our guardian angel. We had just begun to get bored again and to feel the absence of that long list of things we wanted, when he appeared to answer our unexpressed need. It was an excellent supper: homemade bread, fried fish, tinned meat, then cherry cake with coffee and biscuits. Afterwards we sat out with all the missionaries drinking beer and Australian wine. I loved their pragmatism, they seemed free of everything that defined other people: age, class, doctrine, nation. Someone told us about a Catholic bishop in West Papua meeting one of his new recruits, fresh from an American theological college. "Do you smoke?" the bishop asked in a concerned way. "No, Your Grace," the brother answered thankfully.

"Do you drink?"

"No, Your Grace."

"You'd better start then, because there's damn all else to do out here."

We talked a lot about their home countries and what they missed. Ton regretted none of the comforts that we so immediately mourned, and he was wry about the troubles that beset the mission: the jumped-up little policemen, the impossible absence of supplies. "The only thing you can rely on in Irian," he smiled, "is the sun coming up in the morning. If you've got that far you've probably used up your luck for the day." As we were about to go he slipped us a big package. "For the priest in Senggo. Some Swiss biscuits he likes and a bottle of holy water. Don't drop it, it's precious." When we had left the lights of the mission and walked some way back along the causeway, I sneaked a look into the package. It was a bottle of J&B.

Sugiyono was tapping on our windows at four o'clock in the morning. The boat was ready and the engine was warming up. He needed to get to a cut through the forest before the tide went out. We gunned off, an old Papuan man steering, Sugiyono pumping oil, his brother sitting in the prow looking out for crocodiles. Forty horsepower lifted the front of the launch clean out of the water, and we were soon roaring towards a blue and purple dawn. Beside the river little settlements were marked by ghosts of smoke. Parrots were flying to their feeding grounds. When the sun was up across the water we came to a log pool. Asmat families working for the timber companies had poled their rafts of logs down to a loading bay on the riverbank. They'd parked them in a big static shoal and the owners of each raft had camped on top of it: sometimes four or five people under a sago-leaf tent. A small ship was soon to come to pick the logs up and the traders on board would check that everyone had fulfilled his quota. Smoke came out of the sago tents as the loggers cooked up for the morning.

Later we stopped in the village of Ats. The ship was moored there, covered in Javanese soldiers, and logs were being hauled up and over into the hold. On the bank a man was cutting the trunks to the right length for stowing with a chainsaw. Beside him another worked on his dug-out canoe with a stone axe. Ats was strung out along the water in a straight row of houses. A few years before, as I'd been told in Agats, it was roundish and compact, like the other large Asmat settlements. The government in Agats had been instructed that proper Indonesian villages were to be built along roads. Soldiers were sent in. They burnt down the houses and supervised the building of a road, then got the villagers to rebuild their houses, with tin roofs, alongside it. The road was a mile long, and stopped at each end of Ats.

The people of Ats, because their village was on a little dry land, were able to grow banana trees. Bananas gave them an advantage over some of their neighbours, allowing them to stay in one place for most of the year, as they made up for a lot of the sugars and minerals that they could otherwise obtain only by roaming. But the banana trees, eight thousand of them, were growing in the wrong place. They stood between the houses and the waterfront, which meant that the village couldn't be watched from the river. Soldiers came in with chainsaws one day, and cut down all the trees.

We twisted back beyond Ats and began to head into the forest. It hung brassy above the banks, hedged by sago trees as black as yews. I had the runs: twice the men had to bring the boat into a gap in the trees while I fled into the tanglewood looking for a place to put my rear. We were at full speed when we saw a dug-out coming the other way. I don't know what the man in our prow recognised, but he made us pull across and the other boat came alongside. Sugiyono borrowed a thousand rupiahs—thirty pence—from me, and something passed over into our boat, two little fistfuls like balls of coloured wool. We started up and rose out of the water again, and the dug-out poled away. The lookout man had tucked the bundles under an old coat. I took a look and I saw they were a couple of fledgling parrots, still with a few of their fluffy grey feathers, but mostly decked out in violent green and red and lilac, that looked very silly on the vulturine scruffs. When I looked a bit harder I saw that they were black-capped lories, classified as vulnerable by conservationists. In Jakarta those birds would sell for fifty pounds apiece, and I felt sorry I'd lent the money.

By mid-afternoon the water had changed from the thick clay solution of the tidal swamps to the clear humic brown of the deep forest. The banks were floating mats of reeds and as we went on we began to see people attached to them: canoes staked to the mud, with women fishing. Soon we cut down a tributary, and there were several people on the bank, waving and shouting at us. We pulled up at a wooden jetty where a battered tin boat, patched and painted and battened down with canvas, rocked in the water. Senggo; and our chances of getting out were improving.

Father Joe was a bright-eyed Austrian man with thick shoulders and a string vest. He looked us over wryly; it seemed that all the missionaries found us a bit odd. He had heard about us on the two-way radio and he had come out of his wooden house barefooted, his trousers rolled up, one white man a hundred and twenty miles upriver in the forest. He took the Swiss biscuits and holy water without comment, and sent us over to a big church hall where we could sleep on the tables. We could come back for supper at dark.

Senggo was a strange village, hard to place. Most people lived in tin-roofed houses, high and narrow, with walls made of lath, running in two rows down a bare sand track. As we passed by we saw faces in the window holes, staring at us steadily. A toddler stood in the doorway with wrinkled legs and a distended belly, screaming. Joe had told us to go and get our permits stamped at the police station: it was at the end of a row of brick administrative buildings, all hanging their flags in front of the sunset. A tiny Sulawesi man in jeans was lounging outside. He stopped us as we tried to go into the station. "Where you come from, mister?" We tried to get past but he revealed he was the head of police, so we were marched in and sat down while he pondered our forms. He looked up and asked something in a muffled voice, something we didn't catch. He asked again but still we didn't understand. Suddenly he was speaking perfect English, and it turned out to be the only phrase he knew. "I would like you to pay the administrative costs incurred by this station in handling your permits." He must have been practising it for years.

At the other end of the village was the man who represented the airline. He lived in a hovel at the back of a kiosk he ran, and had a dog-eared file where he kept the bookings. He looked in his book and tutted at us: the police in Senggo had told him nothing about any whites wanting seats, they never passed messages on. The plane was booked up: he showed us the full list. His tone showed that we weren't in trouble, however, and he explained that if we gave him a little money to buy the pilot four *urips*, he would put a couple of canvas chairs in the back of the plane. I hadn't a clue what 'urips' were: they might have been anything from exotic fruit to Asmat slaves, but I didn't think I could be doing too much harm by handing sixty pence to the definitive bucketshop.

We worked at getting to know Father Joe. He had a cool, laconic way about him that intrigued me, but he wasn't keen to talk about himself. He sat back from the table, a cigarette between his yellow fingers, a dry smile, a neat handsome face, about sixty years old, with the shoulders of a bear. There was something cunning about him, and self-sufficient: everything he did was quick and calm, from blessing the food to lighting a cigarette. Like Ton he had moved from the college in London to the jungles of North Borneo, where it seems he learnt as much from the Dayaks as they learnt from him. He got the language drinking rice wine with the villagers every morning, and almost everything else by example. He would go off pighunting in the forest and wouldn't come back until he'd got one, often after several days. He knew all the medicinal plants, and the things you could eat and drink and the things that would poison you. When he heard, in 1972, that the Malaysians were after him, he slipped into the forest and disappeared. A whole platoon went in to hunt him. Two weeks later Joe slipped over the border into Kalimantan. The platoon never came out.

He worked in Kalimantan until 1982, when he was sent to Senggo. He had got the little place as organised as possible, and everything he had touched had the clean mark of Joe Haas on it. He had made the bread on the table, the table, the pickled cucumbers, the salted fish, the lemon squash, the room we sat in, and the rest of the wooden house, with its plumbing cobbled up from scavenged bits and connected to an intricate system of rain barrels. He had rebuilt the miniature *African Queen* on the jetty and tacked up its engine with fishhooks, nails and beaten tin cans. In that contraption he had steamed up the wild rivers to the north, mooring and walking when they became too shallow. He had lived in tree-houses up the Dairan Hitam and in villages above the Eilanden River, where they still flew the Dutch flag, for they didn't know there had been a change of government. In some of the villages upriver he was greeted at first with a trembling bow, a nibun arrow fixed on him through the whole meeting: only after several visits did he achieve any trust. Several times his engine broke down when he was far upriver, and couldn't be repaired with a fishhook or a piece of bark. So he would drift down until he came to a village, hire a canoe then paddle the many days down to Agats, get the required part, then paddle all the way back: for perhaps three weeks before he returned to his boat.

He wasn't in the least proud of his exploits; they were just the way of getting about. He knew that the people weren't going to be left alone, and figured it was best that he got to them first and prepared them for the impact of development, encouraging them to do things that could one day earn them some money, or protecting them from the shock of a new lifestyle. In Senggo he was trying to set people up with something they could sell to the Indonesians, so that it didn't all go one way: he had produced a tile-making machine, and organised a wholesale trade in bows and arrows, that could be shipped out then sold as decorations, two and a half thousand miles away in Jakarta.

In Agats I had dug out a few stories about Senggo, and during the couple of days we had there I was able to string them together a bit, by wandering about and talking to people. The odd tin houses in the straight lines had been built as part of the informal education project run by the police. Lessons began with questions and answers, then the people had to put their new-found knowledge into practice. I was told that the lessons typically started like this. Q: Who lives in jungles? A: Animals. Q: Are you Indonesian citizens or animals? A: Indonesian citizens. Q: Who lives up trees? And so on. The Asmat were never actually brainwashed by the instruction, but they found that the police were much kinder to them if they gave the right answers. They were told to pull down their houses and build new ones on the approved model. They weren't initially forced to do it, they were instructed, but people found slacking in the rebuilding were badly beaten up.

The semi-nomadic life the Senggo people had led was also pro-scribed. The chief of police, the Little Sulawesi man who had asked for a bribe, believed that if the people were allowed to wander about they would get out of control. They had to spend some time in the forest, however, to collect sago. So he let selected parties go off for a week at a time, which was not enough to keep them happy, but enough to keep them alive. However, the Asmat don't have watches—they have very little sense of our units of time—and the first party came back two or three days' late. The police chief, Jon Babts, made them crawl about with their bellies on the ground like crocodiles for an hour. Then they were told to roll along the path. They rolled for two hours and the police kept kicking them. Before long they were all vomiting, by the end several were vom-iting blood, and had severe internal injuries.

We visited some of the people in the tin houses. They were very different to the traditional longhouses we'd seen on the way down to Sawa-Erma. Each house contained one family, a man and his wife living together. The house was divided into four tiny rooms, low partitions between them, which gave enough space for one person to stretch out in each. The villagers were checked to see that people of the same sex slept separately. A man told me that he found his house cold at night, as the wooden floor was bare and there was no one to sleep with. He hated the isolation, and the discomfort. People could gather in the houses to talk only if they were prepared to stand up, so the new buildings had wiped out the intimacy and spontaneity of life in the longhouses. That physical restriction was almost certainly a design feature, as was the fact that they could easily be watched. The seeds of possible revolt had been grubbed out, and with them it seemed had gone the fun and communality of the Asmat. People hung in the doorways watch-ing their neighbours across the track. By contrast to the traditional villages we'd seen, in Senggo we weren't invited in or offered food, and there was a blasted, displaced, sulky mood, not dispelled by their poor physical states: the gawky bones and swollen bellies of the children.

Upriver there had been treehouses, the extraordinary shelters that the Asmat built in places where the mosquitoes on the ground were intolerable. They were built up to ninety feet high, perched on the tops of cut treetrunks, but as stable as houses on the ground. A notched pole led all the way up, helping to keep out enemies as well. The treehouses were burnt down. In the villages that used them people now lay round smokey fires at night, trying to drive off the mosquitoes. I was told that the insects were so thick that sleep was impossible till dawn, and the birthrate had fallen away to next to nothing. There were still a very few treehouses in regions the government had yet to penetrate.

Before the police arrived, we heard, there had been no problems that couldn't be addressed by traditional law. The police brought crime to Senggo. They were responsible for the crocodile poaching in the area, going out at night with rifles to harvest them for the Head of Nature Conservation's skin factory. Several Senggo women had been raped by them and one shot dead. Villagers had been forced to hand over possessions the police wanted to sell. While we were there the villagers were in a state of great relief, because the police had had all their guns confiscated by the commander in Agats, after they tried to kill the district officer of Senggo. Apparently there had been a dispute between him and the chief of police, so the chief decided to kill him. The DO had holed up in his house with a revolver, where he stayed until loyal policemen from Agats had reached the village and disarmed Jon Babts and his merry men.

The police were just a local horror. The government had its eyes on the minerals in the Asmat, and, as I knew from reports I'd read in Jakarta, it had granted prospecting licences to several foreign firms. In 1988 the American company Conoco would be looking for oil. There was no great harm in prospecting, but the threat of a spill, if oil was found in extractable quantities, would be devastating. With tides running sixty miles inland, leaked oil could wipe out the living things in most of the Asmat's swamps, and with them would go the whole livelihood of the people there. To judge from what we'd heard it was hard to believe that the government would do much about it if it happened. More than oil, however, the Asmat feared gold. An Australian company had won a contract to look for deposited gold in the swamps round Senggo. If it found any it would pull the whole lot up: the forests, the riverbeds and villages. To make low-grade mining of that sort worthwhile perhaps a hundred thousand hectares of the Asmat forest would be stripped off, and there would be nothing the local people could do about it. Like gold concessions in all parts of Indonesia, a strike would be followed by thousands of unofficial migrants, streaming in unregulated to try their hands at digging. Something told me that the one lot of people who wouldn't make a killing from those lands were the people who possessed them.

It was good to watch Joe Haas working in the village. He would dish out medicines from his back door in the morning, teasing the patients gently so that they lost their uneasiness and were tempted to tease him back. I watched one man come to his door with a basket of lemons, that he offered for a thousand rupiahs. Joe told him that was far too low a price and he'd never survive among the new traders if he didn't recognise his own value. He started bargaining the man upwards, much to the confusion of the trader, who tried to hold his price down. Father Joe could see the funny side of disasters, and seemed able to get the villagers to see it too, as he roared around the village on an old motorbike, trying to solve marital disputes, or treat someone's sick pig, or patch up an arrow wound. He knew how far he could stand up for the villagers. He had once had Jon Babt's cocked revolver held against his head, the little man counting down from ten. It is a measure of the humility of Joe Haas that he talked his way out of it, rather than reacting angrily.

Over the three days I found that watching him changed my view of myself. What I was doing suddenly seemed less important, and I began to wonder whether journalism might really be the essential service I'd imagined. I had never before felt that what I was doing might be superficial, and simply self-aggrandising; I had never before been less hubristic. Maybe I had changed a bit already, on the way down to the Asmat, but I hadn't known it. I'd found there that my heroic view of myself was something less than well-founded, and maybe some of that had seeped in, making itself apparent as I got to know Joe Haas. Perhaps it was because I had never before met a man who seemed freed from the need for recognition.

Joe didn't like the look of our leechbites, so he made us stand in steaming salty water for an hour, feet in two buckets, then he sprucely bandaged them until we looked like amputees. It didn't do much good as we let them get dirty again, but the principle was sound. I watched him, quick and quiet. He made no friends through doing what he did. He had dropped his Austrian citizenship in order to stay in Indonesia, and the old country was unlikely to allow him back. Because he defended the Asmat, the Indonesians suspected him of being against them. Though he was greatly liked by his villagers, he was white, and in important ways that was an unbridgeable gap. He was, by necessity, self-sufficient.

The aeroplane arrived in Senggo on schedule, buzzing down over the houses like a cockchafer. Everyone ran out to see it; the whole village crowded onto the airstrip. Once, I'd heard, the airstrip had been too wet, and the plane had dug into the turf when it landed and tilted on to one propeller. The prop had smashed and a bit the size of a boomerang flew through the glass of the cockpit and shaved a layer of skin off the pilot's chin. A fraction closer and it would have cut off his head. There was a great confusion of baggage going in and out, a couple of broken black umbrellas waving around, colourful clothes, skin of all colours, soldiers shoving through it with bolt-action rifles. As I watched, the airline's representative came up beside me with a cardboard box.

"I've got the *urips*," he whispered conspiratorially.

"Oh good," I said, still having no idea what *urips* were, "can I see?"

He opened the box. Huddled in the bottom were four little balls of coloured fluff: black-capped lories. The great white conservationists had now wiped out six of one of the rarest parrot species. For all that, I must admit, I didn't send him back.

Eventually all was stowed and the passengers fought their way through. Just as we were about to board I heard a motorbike approaching. Joe wove through the mass of people. He saluted, shouted over the noise of the plane, then grinned and roared off down the grass track to get on with his day in Senggo. Much later I read that the church in that village had, long before he had arrived, been dedicated to St Joseph the Worker.

At the airport in Merauké a policeman made me turn out my rucksack. He pushed aside a stack of notebooks smouldering with information, a bag of clothes in which a tape recorder had been bundled up and hidden, and two huge machetes, pitted and rusted red. He pulled out the palm-leaf sleeping mat I'd been given in the village that Yunus the Second had found below the mountains, before we got to the last bridge that didn't exist, and had to swim the swirling river. He sniffed at it and took a hard look at me. "I think I'll keep that if you don't mind."

Chapter 10

Singapore was a shock. It was like being let loose in the toyshop, and the city seemed to be made out of food. In four or five days we put on all the weight we'd lost, circling the arcades and stuffing our faces. We stayed in one of those emptied-out flats containing eighty people: of our age, our colour, and formerly—and suddenly I saw no longer—our interests. There was a Christmas party where we all ran around and got very drunk and took off our clothes and dressed up as pirates. Then there was a New Year's party, where we all ran around and got very drunk and dressed up as women. It was great fun and it couldn't have lasted long.

Even in Singapore we were working. Adrian, having lost everything but his little pocket camera to the rain, the fungus and the cockroaches, set about replacing his equipment. He spent three thousand pounds he didn't possess on a new kit, and became over-excited running around the town trying it out. I walked into a curio shop and a furtive assistant offered to sell me a tigerskin. I returned the next day posing as an importer of wildlife, and was taken into a warehouse behind the shop, that was crammed with dead tigers, clouded leopards, birds of paradise, those black-capped lories, harpy eagles, turtles, almost every endangered Asian animal I knew of. I'd stumbled on a smuggling network from all over South East Asian, gintrapping big cats and shipping them into Singapore. The man was so enticed by the size of the orders I mentioned that he let Adrian come along the next day to take photos for our import company back home. It was a chance to repair a little of the harm we'd done to the wildlife in West Papua, and as I write the traders are being charged.

I didn't want to go back to Papua. Ten days in Singapore was long enough to stop and think too hard about the expedition and its virtues. Leaving England nearly four months before, I had been swept up by notions that now seemed to me to be false. I had been excited by the glamour of writing a book, with the intrigues and secrecy of a dangerous place to do it in. There had seemed little to lose in charging off: I hadn't been enjoying my job, I was seeing too much of my friends and girlfriend to realise I would miss them. The glamour and insouciance had fallen away and left me uncertain. I was worried too: worried about going back and getting caught, falling ill, running out of money. My girlfriend was a maddening, uncatchable dream. She couldn't write to me as I had no address, and I found it hard to imagine she was still there. Had Adrian not been with me I might have failed in Singapore. He was in some ways more resilient than me, with fewer conceits, and as we had gone on his interest in the story had steadily grown. When we weren't both stressed by our surroundings we got on well, and kept each other propped up. He got me going again.

We had dug out, on that first trip, some fragmentary facts and a few enlightening stories. I found it hard to tell, in Singapore, whether we were moving towards some answers to the questions we'd asked—about why transmigration was happening in West Papua—though I'd begun to suspect we were on the right track. It was time to get to where the real action was. Along the border with Papua New Guinea, almost all the way from north to south, rebels were fighting the Indonesian army. If the stories we'd heard from England were true they were fighting with spears and poisoned arrows, and being fought from armoured cars and jets. There was transmigration there too, and tales of extraordinary brutality that needed checking out. Somewhere in that mess there were likely to be clues. How we would get to them wasn't so clear. The troubles we had encountered so far were petty by comparison to those we might meet on the border. That was where the army had concentrated, and those effective secret services. We were probably objects of suspicion already, and I had a strong feeling we'd be watched wherever we were. Discovered without permits—and we would necessarily be without permits—snooping around the sensitive zones on the border, we could find ourselves in short, sharp and terminal trouble.

I had very little idea of what to do. The whole zone was sealed by troops and there were no official ways of entering. If we walked into the area, even if Adrian's feet could take it, we'd meet an unpleasant reception. As we flew to Jakarta I became convinced that, in one way or another, our work in West Papua had already come to an end. We'd been in Jakarta for just a day or two, however, when, out of the blue, we struck a little luck.

We had trooped off miserably to the police headquarters to get our tourist permits for West Papua, again just for our useless quota of friendly places, and I'd been relieved to find that no one had been vigilant enough to put us on the blacklist. When we had joined the queue of Javanese migrants, and were waiting to get our permits stamped, I wandered off down the corridor to find a drink of water. I couldn't find one on that landing, so I went down some stairs and through another hall. As I walked back towards the permit room I noticed the name on an open office door. It was the head of immigration police, one of the most powerful men in the force. I glanced inside and saw no one. I put my head in a little further; the room was empty. With a glance either way down the corridor, I slipped in. I had no idea what I was looking for, but I saw it straightaway: a pad of paper on the head man's desk. It had a flamboyant crest at the top and his name printed on the bottom. I looked around again, then slid it into the magazine I was carrying. I was about to leave the room when I heard military footsteps coming down the corridor. The head of immigration was returning to his office. I was trapped. But the footsteps marched on down the corridor and around the corner, and I slipped out and tried to look casual as I sauntered back to join the queue.

It wasn't the answer to all life's troubles, but it was something. We conscripted an Indonesian friend to make us a grammatical translation, and I typed out a fine letter of introduction to ourselves. To whom it might concern was asked to be aware that we were amateur naturalists on a birdwatching tour of all West Papua and that we had permission to go anywhere and stay for as long as we liked. Anyone standing in our way would have the full weight of the head of immigration police land on them. For good measure the surrogate chief of police wrote that he played golf with my father and was personally responsible for our happiness throughout the trip. I signed it in the flamboyant style of a schizoid maniac. We now had a chance of getting out of or into a very great deal of trouble.

* * *

Arso was certainly trouble. In fact the unhappily-named place was founded on it. Once there were two villages, deep in the jungle, three days' walk from Jayapura and forty kilometres from the border with Papua New Guinea. Through the time of the Dutch and for the first ten years of the Indonesians the settlements were mostly peaceful and left alone by the outside world, just two more stick-and-thatch villages tucked away in the forest. In 1973, while forty kilometres away the Australians were preparing to hand over to an independent Papua New Guinean government, the area round the two villages was a stopping-off point for West Papuan dissidents, moving between Papua New Guinea and West Papua, looking for a focus for rebellion. Like groups all over West Papua at the time, those rebels were trying to get what the neighbouring country was soon to achieve: independence, which the Dutch had promised would coincide with the Papua New Guinean autonomy.

Arrows were fired into police posts and on to armed patrols. No one was killed and the rebels slipped back into the forests they came out of. The army, unable to find them, opted for mass punishment. Settlements to the south of the two villages were bombed, and people in the area were arrested and tortured. Many people fled to where they had friends and family, in the lands on the other side of the arbitrary border. Troops moved into the two villages. Some dissidents were caught and tortured, and there were stories of men being carried out to sea and dropped overboard in sacks. In 1977, when Indonesian elections triggered another wave of separatism, rebels attacked the army posts and killed several soldiers with new metal-tipped arrows. According to the people who got out, the soldiers responded with a mass execution. I can find no figures for the numbers of men killed, but it seems that at least twelve women and five children from the two villages were shot by firing squad in the forest. The rest of the population fled.

When, after several months, some of the refugees began to drift back, they found that their two villages had been knocked down and resolved into one, called Arso, built around an army post. They were instructed to rebuild in the approved way, in designated places. Even so the returned villagers couldn't be watched at all times, as they had to hunt and gather sago in the forest. So a new scheme was devised to allow them to stay in the village without starving, and the government to clear away the forests that had sheltered the rebels. It also tied in well with the government's development plans for West Papua.

An area close to Arso had begun to receive transmigrants from Java, who were coming in to farm rice. The Papuans there were asked to join the transmigration programme, but not as rice farmers. They could grow oil palms, whose fruit could be processed by a big on-site factory, and the oil sold on the world markets. As well as the two hectares of palms each family would be given, the men would work on a big estate of oil palms owned by the factory. The project would replace fifty thousand hectares of the forest: all the area, in other words, that was sheltering insurgents. The first oil-palm plantations were opened up in 1981. To see, in 1988, how they were getting on, we took the transmigrant bus from Abepura, on the north coast, to Arso.

I knew we had a made a mistake, as soon as we arrived. Soldiers were everywhere. A few were in full uniform, but most wore football shirts above their camouflaged trousers, or civilian trousers below their tunics. All of them, however casual, carried M-16s. I didn't want to leave the bus: we filed out unhappily with a gaggle of transmigrants. Two Javanese men in full uniform stepped forward and took our arms, and we were marched away along a row of tin huts. There was a grand display of flags there and a little concrete building underneath it. We were sat down in the waiting room by the unsmiling soldiers. I couldn't draw them into conversation, and I began to feel very scared.

Lieutenant Subandi came out, in his vest. He was very fat and important. Instead of an M-16 he had two revolvers strapped around his bulging hips, like a cowboy. He smiled—gold teeth—and nodded us curtly into his office. President Suharto smiled cryptically from the wall, his hangdog vice-president baggy-eyed in the frame below. A fat hand made us sit down. Subandi sat back and looked at us, and said nothing. I scrabbled in my bag and brought out an envelope. In Jakarta a week before it had been crisp and official-looking. It was now sweaty and glaringly amateur. I tried to seem brisk. Subandi read the letter once, then again, his brow now puckering in fatty folds. "There are no birds here," he said.

"I . . . I was told by my very good friend the Head of Nature Conservation that this is a good place for birdwatching."

Subandi grunted and read the letter again. I watched his eyes. I could see the signature, now so obviously contrived, and the print of a cheap typewriter. The Javanese soldiers were stirring about on the other side of the door. If Subandi picked up his telephone and asked the radio office to contact Jakarta, there could be only one outcome. He read it a fourth time, shaking his head a little, drawing in his breath. His fingers crawled across the desk like fat maggots, moving towards the telephone. They stopped and rapped with their nails on the wood. Subandi looked up. "It seems I shall let you stay for one night in Arso," he said and he smiled that small and dangerous opening of gold teeth.

We pushed off to a far cluster of huts, very conscious of the hard stares of soldiers on our backs, and the hard metal of guns on theirs. The houses were a bit like those at Senggo, with iron roofs, but roomier. Outside them one or two old women were sitting in the dust and talking, while a man hacked up wood with a machete. Some Arso farmers were walking towards their homes and we fell in with them. When we said we wanted to stay for the night someone ran off to find the schoolteacher, who seemed to be an authority on such things. He soon came to meet us, a local man who, like everyone else, had fled beyond the border ten years before. Felix asked no questions, but took us straight to his schoolroom and sent off the farmers to find us some bedding. Someone came back with a huge mosquito net, that had 'Departemen Transmigrasi' written on the top. I began to relax.

Oil palms strode all over the bared hills round Arso, little ones like hairy spiders coming out of their holes, and big mature ones like feather dusters. Between them, depending on their age, there was mud or a thick growth of creepers. The odd burnt stump was a reminder that forest had been there before the oilpalms. We wandered through, Adrian snapping away, trigger-happy with all his new equipment, that made him lopsided with the weight of it on his shoulder. In the middle of a mature stand we came upon some farmers, talking and squatting on the ground. There were five of them, all short but heavily built, with knots in their arms and calves. They started up when we appeared, but then seemed pleased to see us, and they led us through the maze of trees, through wet mud a foot deep. When we told them what we were after two or three of the men became very excited, and their story started coming out in a rush. The bushy palmtrees had already produced fruits, little black ones nestling around the leafribs. The trees were doing well, the farmers said, the soil, as we could see, was good and dark, and there was plenty of water. They told us how many kilos you could harvest from each tree, if you wanted to.

The farmers didn't want to. There was no factory. Though the whole project depended on a factory to process the palmfruits, it had never been built. The government had promised its construction before the oil palms were planted, then had kept promising its imminent appearance, but it had never come. With no market for the fruit and no way of processing it themselves the farmers had watched it rot on the trees. The trouble, as I later found out from reports, was that the factory would have been too expensive for the government to build. While the plantation project was being planned, the price of palm oil had dived. As the project was seen to be an important instrument of government policy, however, it still went ahead, and the sago forests were cleared and oil palms planted in their place. Had the plantation been closer to the world markets, or bigger, a factory there might have broken even; but in West Papua, with just five thousand hectares of maturing palms, palm oil processing would be far from economic. Though the forest was still being cleared for the project, planting had stopped as there was no more money.

The farmers complained that they were down to their last reserves. Not only had their resources—the sago and game—been greatly reduced by the clearance of much of their forest, but they now had to share the diminished subsistence with immigrants. To work the big acreage of oilpalms the government had planned, fifteen hundred more Papuans had been brought in from other parts, to join the five hundred already living in Arso. As none of them had an income, though a few had made vegetable patches beneath their houses, they too had to compete for the sago reserves. On top of that the Javanese transmigrants, six thousand of them, hunted informally and drove away the game. To make up for an almost total loss of protein some people went for a couple of days on the other side of the Arso River to hunt, but they couldn't get back—sometimes for a week or two—if it rained and the river flooded; and they were hunting in another tribe's land, so were in danger of being killed. There had been no compensation for the loss of land, as joining the new programme was thought to be a sufficient reward. The Arso people, whose legitimate land-holding had fallen from seventy-five thousand hectares to two hundred, felt hard done by. They had never wanted to join, but feared they would all be killed if they didn't comply.

The farmers also said that the transmigrants from Java had brought new diseases, of which some of the Papuans had died. There was cholera in the drinking water, also something that caused diarrhoea, which had emerged when the water had turned red and stayed that way when the oil palms were planted. They said that the Javanese despised them and refused to talk, even when they tried to be friendly. For their part they thought the new settlers were deceitful and avaricious. It seems there was plenty of misunderstanding between the two races there: the direct, open Papuans, and the subtle, more reserved transmigrants. The new settlers knew very little about the Melanesian inhabitants and had brought with them the Javanese common wisdom that they were unintelligent, insanitary and artless. Both groups suffered from their fears as well, fears of the jungle savage struggling with fears of the mystic Hindu. The farmers said relations were getting tenser all the time: three thousand miles had kept the explosive ingredients apart, and transmigration had mixed them up. Worse still, the farmers said, were their relations with the people from Sulawesi. They had moved into some of the empty spaces left in the rice-growing area, either buying up the land or being given the surplus by the government, which was trying to encourage as many people as possible to join the scheme. They were said to be profiteering. The Arso people claimed they'd been ripped off by the Sulawesi people, who, having acquired the tribe's land for nothing, had then monopolised supplies, and charged excessively for the food required to make up for what the locals had lost from the forests. Threats of a bloody solution were mouthed, but we took them to be hollow.

There was a chance of a small factory being built one day, that could buy the fruit harvested from five thousand hectares. I heard later that if ever it did happen, the oil it produced could only be sold internally, within West Papua, as export wouldn't be viable for such a tiny amount. If so, it was likely to undercut the market in coconut oil, which was one of the main forms of subsistence for many Papuan families, who obtained the money for the food they needed by selling a couple of bottles a week. There was an equilibrium on the island that subsidised projects were likely to upset. The Arso farmers, in the meantime, deprived of their old subsistence and a new living with which to replace it, complained that the government simply didn't care about them. All that mattered, they said, was that the government's policy happened and its security plans were fulfilled, and if people were threatened with starvation as a result, that was just bad luck.

We had come to the houses of the people moved in from other parts of West Papua, a long row as in any other transmigration site. A crowd buzzed round us and we were pulled off into one of the huts, where about twenty people stood, crowded in like a student party. The boards creaked beneath us. The man who owned the house told me he had come from Waris, sixty kilometres away. The government had promised him that all would be ready before he arrived: a factory, mature oil palms to supply it, and a living for him of the kind he'd never known. Only the last promise was kept, as he was scraping by on a few weedy vegetables and the sago he could sneak out of other peoples' lands, now further and further away. He said he was close to starvation. Another promise had been concrete foundations for the houses: he claimed the wood they were built on was rotting away and they were falling down: we saw, when we had stepped outside, that it was true. We headed back towards the schoolroom. As we passed by the last of the houses a tall Arso man with a beard started shouting at us in English. It was the first English we'd heard there, no great grammar, but quite clear enough to be threatening. He was very drunk.

He lurched out of the house and down across the marshy ground towards us, shouting and waving an empty bottle. Adrian tried to get a shot: action, drunken man coming for us. The bottle whistled over and missed his head by a fraction. We walked away. "You come here. You, my brother, I kill you." He staggered over the deep mud, in a pair of tracksuit trousers too long for him, treading down the heels. "You come here. I do kung fu." We weighed the consequences of laying him flat in front of his fellows, and decided to avoid him, so we marched off through the mud and bushes, heading for a bridge across a deep green stream. His drunken breathing and splashing was coming close. The bridge was composed of just two thin poles, that I crossed first. Adrian followed and got to the middle just as the drunkard caught up. The man leapt to get at him and landed squarely on the middle of the poles. They broke and the drunkard, Adrian and three thousand pounds-worth of camera equipment flew into the murky river. I hauled Adrian out, and we left the man standing, suddenly sober, in the cold green stream. Adrian opened his camera bag and water poured out on to the path. His trip was over.

Adrian took two antihistamine pills—which worked as knock-out drops—and went to bed. In the schoolroom the camera gear was laid out like dissected organs: delicate mirrors, beautiful lenses, sophisticated electronics, wrenched open and exposed to the moist air. Felix the teacher and two of the farmers had come in to join us. When they heard what had happened they received it like a bereavement of their own. They cooked up some condensed milk and sat brooding over the equipment as if they could will it to get better. I went to bed, unaware that the three men would sit up all night to guard the gear. I woke up suddenly believing that the house was being torn down, but it was stray cows ripping up a breadfruit tree that had fallen beside the schoolroom. Rain lashed the wooden building then edged away, and a strong moon came out and searched through the chinks. Adrian snored on through his drug-induced sleep. I twisted about all night.

I watched Adrian in the morning, moving like a wooden man, putting the pieces back in his camera bag and trudging away without speaking. He took the bus back to the capital, Jayapura, and waited in a hotel. I stayed on in Arso until noon. Lieutenant Subandi collared me. He seemed convinced that Adrian had gone off to join the rebels and I thought he was going to keep me hostage. But I couldn't care, and he let me go. I went back to Jayapura, and for a while I watched Adrian trying to make some sense of the mangled pieces with fungus in the lenses. I had my own putting together to do. Arso had set me thinking on a different line, and I began to research a little more of West Papua's recent history. In every town we had stopped in till then I had made a point of collecting older information: books, reports (official ones I wasn't supposed to see) that I borrowed from friendly expatriates, stories I was told by naïve civil servants. In Jayapura it started to fit together as a consistent story, filled out by what I heard from people I met in the town.

* * *

Holland was as cruel a colonial nation as any other. Until the Second World War it kept a brutal grip on its South East Asian colonies, that it had added up to make the Dutch East Indies. West Papua, or West New Guinea, was of all of its eastern acquisitions the hardest to exploit, so it had escaped the sharp end of colonial oppression. The Dutch never moved in there seriously until 1948, when they were losing the rest of their empire and it was set to become the independent republic of Indonesia. They decided to, and managed to, keep hold of West New Guinea. It bore no relation to the rest of the old empire: it was on a different continental shelf, inhabited by a different race, with a different culture, a different stage of development, with no connections to the other islands but its domination by the same European power. They realised they couldn't hold it indefinitely, and made plans for its independence alongside the Australian-ruled half of New Guinea on the other side of the border. The island could then become one Melanesian nation, which made a lot of sense, for none of the indigenous people of either state recognised the border that had been laid across their lands.

The Second World War forced a change in the perceptions of the colonial powers, and Holland began to recognise some of the difficulties of continued dominion. A few years after the war, the Dutch began to atone for a few of the injustices they'd caused by building up their one remaining province. At first they were trying to enhance their popularity there and strengthen their hold, but later their efforts switched towards helping New Guinea towards a viable independence. This was one of the rare cases of a colonial power putting in more than it took out, as they built roads, schools and hospitals on the coast. They felt the pressure other nations were exerting for the old colonials to lose their empires, so they accelerated the process, rapidly training the West New Guineans to become civil servants, business men and parliamentarians. By 1961 fifty-one per cent of the country's administration was indigenous, and the Dutch could begin to feel they were winning the battle. By 1962 they were forced to hand the island over to Indonesia.

The force came largely from the United States, anxious to please the Indonesian president and so keep him from straying towards communism. The first president, Sukarno, had had greedy eyes on the colony for some time. It could serve him in several ways. It would bring his ailing government popularity in Java, as it would represent a victory against the reactionary colonial forces;

it was a foot into the South Pacific; and it was a chance to lay hands on some of the world's largest reserves of minerals. He made it clear that the presence of a million black people running around in penis gourds over that rich and promising land did not trouble him. So did President Kennedy. When, at the time, he was asked why it was all right for Indonesia to take over West Papua, but not all right for East Germany to isolate West Berlin, he replied: "That's an entirely different matter, there are two and a quarter million inhabitants ... those Papuans of yours are some seven hundred thousand and living in the Stone Age."

In 1962, when the United Nations had wandered into the argument to talk about a handover, President Sukarno got impatient and sent the young Major-General Suharto to take the place by force. Suharto dropped in fifteen hundred paratroopers to relieve the colony, but the New Guineans, who didn't want to be relieved, or not by the Indonesians at any rate, captured most of them and handed them over to the Dutch. It was a flop, but it added to the determination of both the old president and the man who would usurp him a few years on. Suffering increasing unpleasantness from the United States, the Dutch gave up their efforts to protect the New Guinean people, and handed over the colony to the United Nations, who took charge of it for six months, after which, in 1963, the Indonesians could have it.

Sukarno emptied West New Guinea. Shops were looted, hospitals emptied, development projects abandoned and stripped, and the good bits carted off to Java where the impoverished electorate was. He then started pushing the extraction projects into being, like the exploitation of Mount Ertsberg, eleven thousand feet of almost solid copper ore. He, and more noticeably Major-General Suharto who succeeded him, found that the people they'd taken along with the land were not at all happy about their change of fortune. Especially hard to handle were the well-educated administrators whom the Dutch had trained to run their own country. Though none of them was very pleased about their disrupted plans, quite a few were prepared to play along with the Indonesians in the hope of keeping their government posts. The Indonesians weren't interested in doing business with the 'stupid Papuans', as the press called them, and chose to suppress their resentment with imprisonment or, insecure after the coup and dreadful turmoil that led eventually to the fall of Sukarno, the more direct expedient.

169

People had been campaigning for independence even before the Indonesians moved in. Finding that self-expression was not encouraged by the new government (in fact all Papuan political parties were banned in 1963), dissenters formed armed resistance groups. These were ragged and uncoordinated. They were spurred on by some astonishing acts of brutality, that began in the very first month of the handover, when, for instance, a group of educated Papuans in Biak was kicked to death by soldiers for showing insufficient respect. The rebels attacked police posts and army camps, pathetic efforts with machetes and bows and arrows. The response was devastating, and shocked both the Papuans and outsiders. Because few of the rebels could be identified and the soldiers were understandably frightened about following them into unknown forests, the army decided on mass punishment instead. Tribal villages were strafed from the air, napalmed in 1966, or wiped out by troops with machine guns: three thousand villagers were said to have died that way in 1967.

All the while the United Nations tried to remind the presidents that there had been three conditions to the handover: freedom of speech for the New Guineans, freedom of movement and self-determination. Self-determination would come about by means of a referendum, within five years, in which every adult in the country could decide whether West New Guinea should stay in Indonesia or leave and become independent. The UN gave up on the first two conditions, but pushed hard for the 'Act of Free Choice' to take place. Even by 1965, however, Sukarno, the first president, had said it was unnecessary, as all the Papuans clearly wanted to stay in Indonesia. President Suharto felt the pressure though, and agreed to go ahead with it in 1969. In 1968 he brought in Sarwo-Edhie. Sarwo-Edhie was the soldier who had kept the Javanese communists in check three years before. An attempted coup in Java, though suspiciously beneficial for General Suharto, had been blamed on the communists, who had been gaining increasing influence with President Sukarno. General Suharto had organised the retaliation, and sent Sarwo-Edhie in to deliver it. Around half a million people were killed in Java, some of them by the army, some by villagers whipped up by the soldiers to seek revenge or, as it turned out, to settle old scores with non-political enemies. There had been six months of state-led anarchy, from which Suharto emerged victorious, his personal enemies dead or exiled; and Sukarno broken.

Sarwo-Edhie applied his techniques to the people in the highlands of West Papua. A friend of mine had dinner with him on the day, in 1969, after the Paniai massacre, when five hundred people were finished off in the western mountains. Sarwo-Edhie, who in 1988 was head of the department that teaches the principles of government, had recounted with relish the way, the unclean way, that he had despatched the last of them with his own knife. He knew what was meant by a pacification programme.

Before the Act of Free Choice, President Suharto told the newspapers that anyone voting against the government would be guilty of treason. To protect people from being thus charged, he narrowed the electorate of six hundred thousand down to one thousand and twenty-five selected tribesmen, and they were primed with threats. The UN, which was supposed to supervise the referendum, was duped at every turn. It was forced by the Indonesians to send home most of its representatives. Those remaining were denied access to transport, so they couldn't get to where the elections were taking place. On the six occasions that they actually witnessed some voting the UN observers could do nothing to stop the blatant coercion that they saw. The selected tribal leaders were arranged in decision panels and asked to vote in block, while soldiers stood behind them. Unsurprisingly there were no refusals, and the nine hundred thousand people in West Papua were recorded as making a unanimous decision to stay in Indonesia. There had never been a doubt—and the Indonesians knew it—that the referendum would be accepted by the United Nations however it was conducted, for it was politically expedient for all the major powers to humour Indonesia, and there was no political gain in supporting tribal people. The United Nations had flouted the very principles it was created to uphold, and the Indonesian takeover had become an annexation.

Resistance now began to get serious, and people fled across the border to Papua New Guinea. The Australian colonial officers there, who didn't want to get involved, sent them back, where they were killed. Mass punishment bombings on villages began, in areas where rebels had run at police posts with bows and arrows. Outsiders also heard stories of torture, with electricity, deprivation, cigarette ends; and of village pacification procedures. In one of these, a pregnant woman was cut open by soldiers, then her baby was chopped up in front of a crowd. Zealous Muslim officers took the opportunity to purge the Papuans of their areligious ways, and went around the highland villages shooting pigs.

As resistance grew Suharto tried a different tactic. At the end of 1969 he called for all the two hundred thousand children in West Papua to be removed and sent to homes in Java. There they could be re-educated to become proper Indonesians. He was dissuaded from that at length by his cabinet, and instead launched a scheme, which began in 1973, to educate the people in West Papua round to the Indonesian point of view. He called it Operation Koteka. *Koteka* is Indonesian for tail; it's also a derogatory term for a penis gourd. The philosophy behind it had been expressed by a Foreign Minister, Dr Subandrio: to "get them down from the trees even if we have to pull them down". The programme was not designed with bad intent, however, as the government thought it was genuinely going to bring the benefits of civilisation to primitive people, but it suffered painfully from ignorance and insensitivity. Teams of students, civil servants and soldiers were sent to an area for six months, to teach the locals how to dress, to cook with pots and pans, build Indonesian houses, read and write and wash like Indonesians. As well as the miseries imposed by some entirely inappropriate changes of lifestyle, the operation caused several hundred deaths. Unaware that their new clothes should be taken off when wet, the people in the Operation Koteka regions suffered epidemics of flu.

The troubles of Operation Koteka and the expectations of wondrous cargoes that the missionaries had encouraged, as well as looting, rape and the forcible curtailment of traditional ceremonies by soldiers, led to a minor Dani revolt in 1977. In the Baliem Valley police and army posts were attacked, though mostly without result, and stakes were planted in the airstrips to stop commandos landing. In response nearby villages were strafed, and in response to that fifteen thousand people in the Baliem Valley rose up against the Indonesians. As it coincided fairly well with the Republic's elections, the revolt touched sensitive nerves, and troops were sent in to put it down fast. There was heavy bombing from the air, rocket attacks and reports of napalm use. On the ground inexperienced soldiers used persuasive tactics, well documented by outsiders. The old chief of a war alliance had his throat cut into a bucket and the villagers were forced at gunpoint to drink the blood. Pigs and humans were used for bayonet practice, women being bayoneted through the vagina and cut open. Village leaders were picked up in helicopters, flown over their lands, then pushed out from several hundred feet. Any Dani who had been around when the Japanese invaded his island in 1942 must have felt he suffered from recurring dreams.

After that there was a tighter military hold in the trouble spots and discontent could be dealt with more rapidly. The next year a hundred and twenty-two people were said to have been dumped in sacks in the Arafura Sea, and there was mass punishment bombing on villages around the border. In 1981, after a Dutch camera team—whose director had a genuine letter from a government minister—got permission to film in West Papua and found a group of rebels training, a military operation went in to sort them out. Reports, probably exaggerated, gave five thousand locals dead; it was said that families were bayoneted then left outside their homes to die. When that was over, things calmed down a fair bit. Several potential leaders of resistance were held at bay by preventative detention. West Papua caused a stir abroad in 1984 when Arnold Ap, a famous Papuan anthropologist and artist, was shot while escaping from prison. Or bayoneted. Or shot while escaping from a beach, or bayoneted, all of which were versions of his death the authorities gave. Certainly his body bore the marks of having been shot, bayoneted and variously tortured enough to have killed one person several times. In 1986 rebels killed two employees of Shell Oil, which was prospecting on the northern coast, as the company was said by the local people to have ignored their land rights. The Indonesian response provoked a minor rebellion, and whether it was that, or a genuine accident, that caused the reputed obliteration of several villages by bombs released on a military exercise, no one could tell. There were confirmed reports of torture in Jayapura, when returning refugees, accused of being rebels, had nails driven into their toes, and their feet put under table legs while soldiers jumped on the tables (a torture technique said to be common in Indonesia). For all that it seemed fair to say that the government had, on the whole, become less violent as time went by. That was partly the result of better local commanders. West Papua for its first few years under the Indonesians had been a punishment post, and soldiers despatched there were among the lowest, going out with grudges, readily exercised on tribespeople. In the 1980s men with

173

better education and more experience were arriving, and the purely military problems had declined.

In their place, or so many of the Papuans I'd met had claimed, had come transmigration. The troubles they had suffered under the ruthless army commanders in previous years were quite matched by the miseries the transmigration programme brought them in the 1980s. The project was dependent on what was most essential to the tribespeople: the land they possessed. There was nothing they could do to stop their lands being transferred, and many had been shot by soldiers when they tried. As the government claimed that the tribal lands belonged to itself, it would pay no compensation, even when it was clear that the livelihood of the people was being clean cut off. Those rebel movements that persisted in West Papua were fighting, above all things, the transmigration programme.

Land removal was just the first of the troubles the transmigration programme brought. The scheme was designed—it was stated policy—to attract spontaneous migrants from other islands, who would come in to join the Javanese settlers. Life in all the Indonesian islands was hard for at least a few, and stories of forests rooted in gold and seas of suicidal fish had always drawn some of the dispossessed towards West Papua. Transmigration had made it much easier for them to get in. By making cuts into the impenetrable land and peopling it with fellow Asians, transmigration had made West Papua accessible. It had begun to look like a pioneer country, and it was attracting fugitives. Most of them were Sulawesi people—Bugis and Makassarese—hard nosed itinerant sea-people, some of whose ancestors ran the black-sailed pirate ships so terrifying to Europeans that they forever after told tales about the Bugis—or Bogey—man. That entrepreneurial character had persisted, and West Papua had become for such outsiders the land of the quick killing. They'd found that confused villagers would unwittingly sign away their fishing or hunting rights, that they had no knowledge of the marketplace, and didn't know the value of the things they tried to sell.

The transmigration department was trying to get as many spontaneous migrants over to West Papua as possible, and it was unconcerned where they came from. Anyone making his own way across could be given land on a transmigration site. This wasn't an option taken up in the infertile areas in the south and west, but it was quite vigorously pursued by migrants from Sulawesi in the blacksoil sites around Arso. A cheap government ferry service had been set up to run between Sulawesi and West Papua, and everywhere it landed it offloaded another batch of entrepreneurs: 180,000 spontaneous migrants had arrived by 1988—on top of the 100,000 government-sponsored migrants—and still they came.

The Papuans complained that some of the official transmigrants weren't interested in farming at all, and had just come over from unemployment areas in Jaya to find a new job. Having been flown across at great government expense they would leave the site after a couple of months to find a job in the nearest town. Others had worked the system out to perfection. I heard of one family that had transmigrated six times. Each time it arrived it sold the land and house it had been given, moved back to Java and reapplied for transmigration, making a decent profit as it went. That scam was not a serious problem for the Papuans, but jobs were. Papuan townspeople, many well-trained under the Dutch, were often far better qualified than the new settlers, who, frequently the poorest and least trained, were fleeing from their lack of opportunity at home. Yet the Indonesian firms and government offices that had moved over would swap their Papuan staff for Indonesians as soon as they could get them, as they disliked working with foreigners. From other occupations the Papuans had been squeezed by sheer force of numbers: as in Merauké, where they simply couldn't compete with the thrusting, often desperate, migrants, who, coming from Java, knew all there was to know about surviving in a crowded market.

What seemed to pain the Papuans above all else was the feeling that they were being swamped by people who saw no value in them or their culture. In all the transmigration regions Papuan people had been forced, often by soldiers, to adopt the standards of the settlers. They had been rehoused in model villages alongside the transmigration sites and, through intense social and administrative pressure, they had found they had to conform to the culture of people from two and a half thousand miles away. We has stopped in a resettlement village on the way back from that transmigration site at Salor, and the people there were in the same state as the villagers of Senggo and Keneyan: displaced, resentful, unhealthy and poor. Their lands had all gone, and they were trying to live like the Indonesians next door. Papuans I spoke to felt the crude efforts to change them—like Operation Koteka or army brutality—that they had suffered in the sixties and seventies had been neatly replaced by the transmigration programme.

The indigenous transmigration sites, like Arso, were deeply resented, though some, we had heard, were likely to function better than the one we saw. The transmigration ministry had announced that plantations like that oil palm estate would be a big part of its future strategy in West Papua, and it wanted to get as many of the Papuans working on them, alongside Javanese migrants, as possible. The Papuans complained that they might be working alongside the Javanese, but in every case the outsiders got the better land, the better crops and the government assistance. From what we had seen I could be pretty sure that future participants would not be politely invited to join.

I seemed to be getting there. Transmigration in West Papua was resolving into a pattern, and slowly the material we had come across earlier on was fitting into it. I had, by that stage, little doubt that it was not all that the government had said. It was clear that something of what the human rights groups had claimed for it— the unpleasant cultural and political motives they said lay behind the programme—was undeniably true. To what extent they were right, and just how transmigration might fit in with the government's other policies in West Papua, we had yet to find out. There was still a whole chapter from the story of West Papua—and we took it, transmigration—that we hadn't even looked at.

Adrian had laid his delicate instruments out across his bed, having borrowed four or five fans to point at them. He had scrubbed away at the fungus with airbrushes and lens tissues and done his best to force the pieces together again. He seemed to be winning. One lens was ruined and one camera body; but he had saved enough to go on with. After two days of amateur sedation in Jayapura he could raise a weak smile. "Let's go to Mindip Tanah," he said.

Chapter 11

The Papuans had not been taking all their troubles lying down. Even as the United Nations took charge of West Papua ahead of its transfer to Indonesia, rebel groups were forming, the old administrators shedding their suits and ties and taking to the bush. They wanted the promised independence and would have no truck with anyone taking it away from them. As the Indonesians moved in and the Papuans began to see what they could expect from indefinite rule from Jakarta, the undecided population made up its mind fast and many men took off to join the fighters. They had bows and poisoned arrows, machetes and a few old rifles found mouldering in back rooms. It was never a promising force for the recapture of West Papua. It called itself the OPM, which is roughly translated as the Free West Papua Movement. Even from the beginning, however, it could never have been considered a single movement. Like all rebel armies it was split and factionalised, but this one had the added trouble of impossible communication over mountains and swamp forests, which cut coordination down to the odd word over a muzzy radio set, and a response to rumoured wars over hundreds of miles of jungle.

Nevertheless, had they but known it, there was a considerable unanimity of purpose. It was and remained true that nearly all young men nominally supported the OPM, even though few actually got into the bush and did any fighting. Its aims, first for independence, then for an end to brutality, transmigration and cultural colonialism, had great support, though how, when and by whom they were exercised was left to the whims of fate, rusty weapons and local leadership. It was true that very few Indonesians had been killed and all conflicts had resulted in the deaths of many more Papuans, but the numbers of fighters in the bush, though low, had hardly changed, and still engaged the attentions of four thousand Indonesian troops.

For all its puny strength and the hopelessness of its cause, I was fascinated by the rebel army. It was the old dream of noble savagery: jungle warriors who knew all the tricks and trails, fighting their well-armed oppressors with bows and arrows, communicating with the noises of birds and strange signs beside the path that only fellow fighters recognised. Moreover I could be sure by then that the transmigration and the fighting were in some ways interlinked: certainly transmigration caused some of the fights, and I had a suspicion that the fights caused some of the transmigration. If we could get to the rebels, and maybe see them in action, there was a chance of picking up some more clues.

Getting to meet rebels within a military state is not a simple task and, despite the letter from our friend the head policeman, there were good reasons for being worried about moving around in the battlezones. Of all the fraught places, the most violent and the one most likely to yield contact with the OPM was Mindip Tanah. Since the troubles had begun there five years before, no tourists had entered the area, and very little was known about what was going on. From all we could glean, however, Mindip Tanah, up against the border, wedged between the mountains and the southern swamps, was in the middle of the rebel war.

There was one plane a week that flew to Mindip Tanah, which mostly carried soldiers, with the odd trader or missionary worker. It was, however, going to be our only way in, as we couldn't get there by river and were in no state, and had no inclination, for walking. The letter would have to see us through, and I was getting the chilling feeling that its luck was running out. That came over strongly while we were waiting for our plane in the Merauké airport. There was no putting off the lean policeman from Sulawesi though, and he took it all the more suspiciously for my reluctance. We got through that and boarded the juddering Twin Otter, not at all happy with the careless look of the overweight pilot, or the broken straps on our seats. I was even less happy when I found that five of our fellow passengers were soldiers and one an armed policeman, all humping weapons—four M-16s, a Chinese rifle and a submachine carbine—over our heads as they manoeuvred into their seats. They were a jolly bunch, however, and I got chatting with the army captain who was sitting next to me. He was a civil and well-spoken man. No-one asked us any embarrassing questions and I wondered, as the plane took off, whether I hadn't been overdramatising the issue:

very likely no tourists had visited Mindip Tanah because no tourists wanted to.

We flew across one hundred and fifty miles of swamp, water glinting evilly from beneath the low trees, some places swallowed by floating mats of grass and pondmoss, treacherous for anything bigger than a fly. As we made towards Mindip Tanah, low hills wormed out of the marshes, and the water resolved itself into rivers, wide ones between the jungle trees. Coming in low towards the airstrip, I saw an empty village, burnt and roofless, and I knew that we were flying into trouble.

At the airstrip there were no soldiers, but a gaggle of colourful women, all excited to see the new arrivals, of which we were the stars. They jostled through, in teeshirts and print dresses, with bright umbrellas to keep off the sun, laughing and slapping each other, and trying to pull our clothes as we went past. Everyone was short and thick-featured, though quite attractive in a robust way. They grabbed our bags from our backs and carried them for us, while we were swept along in the tide of cheap colours, out of the glaring sun and through a shady rubber plantation, down to where a rickety bridge crossed a clear green stream. It was stifling hot. The women assumed we had something to do with the mission, and we were happy for people to believe that, so we were pushed along to the pastors' building, a roomy wood and tin house on the high banks of the River Kao. There were two Dutch pastors inside, Father Cor and Brother Kase and, while they weren't pleased to see us, they sat us down and made us coffee. Cor was big and heavy, with his white hair pushed back, while Kase was all sinews and old skin, bald and slightly jumpy-looking. They spoke only a small amount of English, so we got by in Indonesian, which made me feel uneasy. Father Cor said we would have to report ourselves to the police and he would help us to do it. It was the last thing I wanted.

My plan had been to get our bearings in Mindip Tanah, find some guides and head off towards the border that day, before anyone knew we had come. I reckoned we could find the rebels beyond the last of the villages, in the deep forest that everyone else there kept away from: that if we got to the right spot and stood around for long enough we would eventually be picked up by them. Because of a local myth about the friendly intentions of white men we knew we would be safe with the rebels. The plan had already been compromised by the soldiers on the plane: they would certainly tell their colleagues in Mindip that we'd come over with them, and I imagined that someone would be roundly beaten up until he told them where the guides were taking us. The girls at the airstrip, bound to talk, had made it even harder, and now I realised that the stop at the mission house had rendered a quick flight impossible. If we fled then we would get not only ourselves but also the missionaries into a lot of trouble, for it would be assumed, quite wrongly, that they were in cahoots with their fellow whites.

When Father Cor was ready we meekly followed him along the sandy track towards the police building. The village seemed to have been built for everything but villagers. We passed two huge schools, one for boys and one for girls, the army headquarters—which had a violent mural of an Indonesian soldier triumphing under fire—and the district officer's complex, rattling with type-writers. There were houses for government employees, a football pitch, a Sulawesi man's shop, and not a single Papuan hut that I could see. The only thing we were likely to discover in that village was the colour of the prison walls, and I approached the police house with rising dread as, headmasterly, the Father led us on, as if towards a caning in his study.

The post was run by a little Javanese man with teeth sticking out at all angles. He kept us standing for a moment, then pointed to a bench and flashed his crooked fangs a second, without mov-ing his eyes. I had told Cor we had general permission to travel through Papua, but he had misunderstood, perhaps on our behalf, and he told the commander that we had special permission to be in Mindip Tanah. I brought out the letter without conviction and stared hard at the ground while the policeman read it, again, and again, and again. Then he looked up, I looked up, and he folded the letter and put it into his drawer. "I shall have to radio Merauké to check this up," he said. "You will stay in the mission house until I have an answer." He nodded sharply at us and flashed his teeth at Father Cor, who led us back in silence to the mission. "You should cheer up," he said, unaware of our predicament. "With friends like that how can you go wrong?"

We sat in the mission house all afternoon, not eating, though excellent food had been prepared. All our luck had rubbed off at once: it had lured us in right up to our necks, and now the wave hung over us, in an army village two hundred miles from any-where: homes, friends, task forces and ambassadors. Prison would be a lucky break. I suggested to Adrian that we make a run for it, get to the border and get the OPM to help us over, into asylum in PNG; but he suggested I find a different sort of asylum. We'd be picked up straightaway, or, without guides, get lost in the forest and die anyway.

In the evening we saw a spectacular sunset, with thunderous brown clouds growling over crystal blues, and orange parrot feath-ers touching the first faint stars. Fruit bats, thousands of them, flocked across it, the last of the sun painting them under the wings. I slept in an extinguished pastor's bed, or tried to, for thoughts whined and snapped around my head like the insects that had entered the room. Night deepened the dread and made me feel alone.

Adrian and I walked to the police house like condemned men in the morning, one in front of the other as if in chains. The police chief had us sit, and two more policemen moved about in shad-ows behind him. "We are just making the radio call now," he said, and paced a little on the floor. I heard Merauké crackle up. There was an indecipherable exchange. There was interference and the operator was whispering: he had to repeat everything he said, but wouldn't raise his voice. Then he put down the handset and called the chief over. They whispered a moment, then the chief came back to his desk. "Well we have checked up with Merauké, and they confirm your permission is valid." He pulled out the letter and handed it to us. "You may stay in Mindip Tanah until the plane arrives, but you mustn't leave the village." I praised God for the indolence of the Merauké police, who hadn't been bothered to check, and we sped off down the path towards the mission.

For all the relief of our release we were no nearer our objective than before, in fact further, as we were confined to Mindip Tanah. I chose to believe, however, that the confinement applied only to where we slept, and that we should go out as far as we dared and cut up rough about influential friends if we were blocked. We knew that the guerrillas had occupied a strip of jungle ten kilometres wide on the Indonesian side of the border, about thirty kilometres from Mindip Tanah, and that was the zone we hoped, at length to reach. The occupation in itself was not a great achievement, as no one else wanted the land. In fact there was no one there to want it.

All but three thousand of the eleven thousand people round Mindip Tanah had fled to Papua New Guinea three years before, leaving behind a wasteland. The reason, as we understood it then, arose at the beginning of the world.

The Muyu tribe, whose people lived in Mindip Tanah and on both sides of the border, were, they say, the very first people on earth. Their race was founded by two brothers, who lived together happily until the elder one decided to go out and find some water. He fed his dog some dried food and followed it until it led him to an underground river. He went down into the river, believing that it would lead him to the secrets of the rest of the world and the key to prosperity. His younger brother waited in the Muyu for him to return, when he would emerge from nowhere, bleached white by so long underwater, bringing the wisdom he'd gleaned from other lands.

When the first white missionaries turned up, their arrival was greeted matter-of-factly. When they knew something of the language they realised that people were asking them for "the key". When they mouthed back some Christian platitude it was accepted without thanks, for the Muyu reckoned it was their older brother's duty to instruct them. The Muyu, characteristically strong-headed and independent, settled down well under the Dutch, largely because of the origin story. The colonials served them reasonably enough, building a rubber-processing factory and thereby satisfying one of the ambitions of the most businesslike tribe in West Papua. There was, however, no place in the origin story for yellow people. When the Dutch had gone and the first Indonesians arrived, they were taken to be devils. Something of their treatment of the Muyu bore that out. A very bad batch of soldiers had been posted in Mindip Tanah, with no training or schooling. They killed a few of the men and raped a lot of the women. Rebels in the area shot three of the armed devils and there was a violent retaliation, though there are no firm figures for numbers killed. The government began checking the area out for transmigration. Those things, we had heard, caused a massive flight across the border in 1984, and again the next year and the next, until in the seven hundred square miles between the Kao River and Papua New Guinea there were less than three thousand people.

There were three things we wanted to do in Mindip Tanah. We wanted to meet the rebels, to find out more about the flight, and to investigate a massacre rumoured to have taken place a few months before: dissidents in Merauké had told us that three hundred people were killed by soldiers attacking a village in the underpopulated zone. I felt like a goat tied to a rope, confined as we were to Mindip Tanah, but we would stretch the leash as far as it would go.

We had been given a week in Mindip Tanah, and it was all we were likely to need, if we couldn't get out of the place. Ideas had whizzed through my mind, like stuffing our beds and pretending to be ill and running for the border or, in wilder moments, setting fire to the army post then making a dash for it; but apart from anything else, we owed the pastors more than that. Though they knew nothing about us, and wouldn't have wanted to had they done so, they had put us up comfortably and were feeding us stupendously well, which looked like being one of the few benefits that Mindip Tanah had to offer. Both were old, experienced men, who walked for days to see their parishioners and doubtless knew all the gossip of the region, had we been brash enough to quiz them. We weren't, so we decided to seek our answers elsewhere.

The path was overbearingly hot. After just half an hour of walking my handkerchief stank of the traces of ammonia found in sweat. Damp patches on the path yielded leeches, that slipped in through the holes in our boots. Lucas, the guide we'd found, said that the track, now sedgy and overgrown, had once been a busy passage for villagers going back and forth to Mindip to sell food. It bore the marks of its better days. In places it cut through rubber plantations, the grey trees smothered by vines, the knife-wounds on the bark quite healed over. A tangle of scrub had once been a cemetery. For an hour we saw no one, and just became thirsty and frustrated ploughing through the heat, moving in and out of shade. Then, rounding a bend, we saw a family sitting on a log.

The child dangling from the father's chest was almost dead. Her skin had turned the same yellow as dead grass, and her body had shrivelled down as if something inside had sucked it dry. She had a bald head with yellow scabs, and protruding eyes. Her parents said she couldn't eat or drink. The other child, breastfeeding, was almost the same faded colour, and thin, and lolled around weakly, missing the pap. The family had come down from the village we were walking to to look for sago, and had given up for an hour or so in the heat.

Walking on we heard hacking on the path ahead of us, and soon caught up with another family, a grandmother, mother and daughter, all overladen with sago or the forest plants they had picked. The old woman, in just a straggly grass skirt, had stopped before we reached them, and she was sitting on the grass, coughing. With each cough the puckered skin and muscles of her stomach knotted up and her tongue shot out: she had tuberculosis, and she too was soon going to die. Adrian took her bag of plants to carry to the village. It was light but it had doubled her over like a rock.

An hour later we saw the first signs of Amuan, the village. There was a broken-down rubber station standing above a stream. Lucas said that before the flight it had processed Amuan's rubber; now that it had stopped it wouldn't work again. Further on there were the remains of houses, most simply patches of scrub a little less dense than the rest, others marked out by blackened poles. They had been burnt, but Lucas didn't know who had done it, or why. Only the path, blasted red and dry, stood out; the rest was sedges and thornbush, with the odd scrub cuckoo screeching from behind it.

Two buildings had remained in Amuan since the flight: the tin-roofed church and the schoolroom, and the returning fugitives had lived in those while they rebuilt their own houses. One hundred and thirty had come back from PNG, and now there were a dozen rickety thatch-and-stick dwellings. We were invited into one for water and sago, and rested while the villagers pressed in around us. Flies sped through the hut and droned out the other side. My head felt loose on my shoulders and I sat down, feeling strange and drugged. I felt better in a while and looked around the circle of quiet faces watching us. The people were short, shorter even than the Dani, but slim and well made, with close ears and broad noses. None of them was well. Among them were pot-bellied children with skin diseases: flaking ringworm, or regular stipples like inflamed scales. Most had red tips to their hair, which meant protein deficiency, and all were classically snotty-nosed, though whether that meant anything but handkerchief deficiency I didn't know. A breast-feeding mother, staring at us listlessly, had a body like an empty sack, and her baby struggled feebly with her breast. No one said anything till I spoke to them.

Life in the refugee camp had been horrendous. For the first week or two there had been nothing at all to eat; it was only as they began to spread out into the forest in Papua New Guinea that they found sago, and they lived on that alone for three months. Most of the Papuans on the other side were of the same tribe as them—the Muya—so were welcoming at first, letting them settle close to existing villages. They had a little of the tribal language in common, though no one from West Papua could speak Pidgin. The Indonesian government had claimed that there was nothing untoward, just people visiting their relatives across the border, but the United Nations got wind of the flight, and sent food and medicine to the squatters' camp. Despite that, life became worse and worse. Outbreaks of malaria, then of cholera, then tuberculosis, shot through the camps and, on poor diets, many people died (three hundred just in the first four weeks of the flight). They began to rely exclusively on the UN handouts—which were infrequent and often wanting—as the Papuan neighbours began to resent sharing their resources with a doubled population. Still, however, the villagers wouldn't return, as they believed that the Indonesian soldiers would kill them when they recrossed the border. They chose a gradual death in preference to a sudden one.

There was no schooling, and for three years the children who hadn't died slid back into illiteracy. The adults weren't allowed to work, so they too became bored, and remained as poor as they had been just after the flight. The exodus had been sudden, a series of panics that followed the killing of some soldiers by the OPM, then a blinding turmoil, oppression, the burning of houses, threats. In parties of five or six families they had dropped everything and gone, with nothing but the clothes they wore. Their money was useless in PNG, and without work they had nothing but charity to fall back on.

Ten months before we met them, despite their continuing fears, the first villagers had returned to Amuan. They found nothing but the church and the empty school there. Their livestock had fled and the gardens were overgrown, with the thick sword grass that takes several burnings and uprootings to get rid of. Nothing but scrub remained of their houses and all they had to eat was sago, which explained the protein deficiency the children suffered. They found that the biggest loss was their resolve. After three years of sitting about idly they had lost the urge to get themselves back together again. No one had opened up a garden or tried to tame a wild pig. The mission had helped them with tools and clothes,

185

but couldn't repair their motivation; to think about rebuilding their old lives was to think about the losses. When we got to Amuan, two hundred of the villagers, with eight thousand others from around Mindip Tanah, were still across the border. The Amuan people had sent messages to the remainder to tell them it was safe to return: the army hadn't murdered them. The remaining refugees didn't trust them, and stayed in the camps with their angry neighbours and declining food supplies.

On the way back Lucas heard a whistle from the bushes, and we stopped while his schoolfriend Pius emerged on to the path to join us. Like Lucas he was about nineteen, thin and a little shy. He shook hands with us a bit awkwardly and fell into step one pace behind. As we went on, however, Lucas, not very subtly, told us that his friend had been with the OPM. Pius bashfully owned up to it and began to tell us something of what had happened.

In late 1984 he, with most of his tribe, had been convinced that there was going to be a revolution. The brutality of soldiers up the Kao River had greatly boosted the independence movement in the area, and there was no one who didn't want to break away. Like many others, some as young as fourteen, Pius left school and took to the bush. The OPM had a roving camp close to the border run by Gerhardus Tomi, a little, wiry, energetic man, who was the commander of all the southern forces. Tomi—Pius had met him two or three times—moved from camp to camp planning the big strike. There was at the time a massive excitement among the Muyu. Something very big was going to happen, perhaps assisted by the ancestors, that would be triggered off by an armed revolution, but wouldn't depend on arms alone.

The OPM camp possessed only one or two old rifles—everyone else carried bows and arrows—but training was intensive, and the men learnt to survive on minimum subsistence. The camp would put up under sago thatch for a couple of weeks, with no tree clearance or raised structures that would give the position away, and people could eat only what they found or caught. Once a helicopter went over and they felt they'd been rumbled, so the whole camp dispersed into the woods, and reassembled elsewhere a few days later. Pius had left after several months, ill from sleeping on wet ground and disillusioned with the prospects for successful revolution. He had gone quietly back to school in Mindip Tanah, leaving Gerhardus Tomi to exhort his troops to the impossible.

186

We had walked on a little while when Lucas noticed we were being followed. We turned a corner and hid in the bushes beside the path. Soon two men came sneaking along, lifting their feet high so as not to make any noise, glancing furtively about them, like ridiculous comic sleuths. I stepped out of the bushes and one of them almost jumped into the other's arms.

"What are you doing?" I asked with some reason.

"*Bapak, tuan,* friend. We're returning to Mindip Tanah."

"Yes, yes, Mindip Tanah. We were taking a walk in the jungle."

They were grinning wildly, bobbing their heads. We let them go and they scurried away down the path ahead of us.

Back at the mission house two men had just finished talking to the pastors, and they were fingering their bags in the hallway, waiting for coffee they'd felt obliged to accept. They were both thin, with big noses sticking out of their wrinkled faces. The tall one had a bushy beard that seemed to have fallen a little way off his face, and sticking-out ears. They sat down awkwardly with us, and the pastors left the room to get on with business.

Both men were the heads of villages that no longer existed, and they were trying to persuade their people to get together and return to their broken-up homes. They had come from over the border a few weeks before, and were hoping for some help from the missionaries. One of the chiefs had lost two daughters in the camps and his other two were growing up illiterate and uncared for. Nearly all their people were still across the border, and some of them were close to starvation. The mission house unsettled them, but I pressed them a little on the details.

"Why," I asked, "why exactly did you leave in the first place?"

"They would have killed us if we hadn't gone."

"The soldiers?"

"No, no, the OPM."

It was only then that something of the real story began to come through. I patched it together over the next couple of days with accounts from other villagers.

In the beginning, when the Indonesian soldiers had come to Mindip Tanah for the first time, they were a careless and undisciplined bunch. Some of the Muyu women were raped and houses and gardens were looted, and dissenting villagers punished cruelly often just for fun. There are some specific stories of extreme brutality, like that of the boy caught hunting by soldiers and assumed to be OPM, who was shot in the thigh to cripple him and left in the jungle to die. By 1982 and '83 discontent had risen until it engulfed everyone, and Mindip Tanah had become a focal point for the OPM. In 1984 government consultants started surveying the land just south of Mindip Tanah for transmigration. For the Mindip people and the OPM it was the last straw. Gerhardus Tomi, the rebel leader, attacked an army post in Woropko, about twenty kilometres north of Mindip Tanah. No one was killed, but the people there feared a big retaliation by the soldiers. Woropko emptied, and the whole population fled across the border. In Mindip Tanah, a month or two later, two fifteen-year-olds ambushed a party of soldiers, having hidden beside the path to the airstrip. They shot three of them dead with metal-headed arrows, and people thought the revolution had begun. It hadn't, but suspected rebels started being rounded up, and they were killed by the army. People from Mindip Tanah began to flee too, but in trickles, not streams.

The OPM saw its chance. Tepenal, its armed wing, whipped up stories of a violent revolution to come, and started persuading people to flee to Papua New Guinea. It was at first a voluntary protest movement, in which people could register their displeasure at the soldiers and escape the consequences at the same time. As the fighters saw that people were doing as they said, however, they began to push harder, and started harassing the Muyu into leaving, possibly threatening them with death. As stories of an impending cataclysmic war began to spread, people panicked and fled across the border, dropping everything. The army, fearing an uprising, started stamping hard on subversion, which added to the panic, and to the membership of the OPM. While many fled from fear, others believed, as did the OPM, that flight to PNG would force other countries to see what was going on, and so build up some support for an independence movement. Others too thought their land was destined for transmigrants, and there was no point in staying.

The Muyu people, fleeing the OPM, the army, the war and the transmigrants, left behind an empty quarter, the ten-kilometre zone along the border, about thirty kilometres from Mindip Tanah. There the OPM holed up, aware that they knew the jungle and the army didn't. The soldiers were quite happy to leave it that way, and for the most part kept to the remaining villages, rather than the dangerous territory they neither understood nor cared for. While some people, in 1986 and '87 had been returning to their old villages, others had still been fleeing, partly because they feared the OPM, partly because they'd heard tales of returning refugees being tortured; it was true that soldiers had been working selected people over, even returning fugitives who had nothing to do with the OPM. Tepenal carried out the odd fruitless raid, but for the most part ran up and down the border recruiting from the refugee camps and keeping the stories of army killings boiling, to stop people from returning. It was either the OPM who burnt down the houses to keep people away, or the soldiers who did it to give the OPM no settling point, or the returning villagers destroying them as a health hazard: such is the nature of tales from many sources.

By 1988 support for the OPM around the southern half of the border had fallen away. Gerhardus Tomi, identified, had fled through PNG, and been granted asylum in Ghana. Though it had little idea about what was going on, and was unable to enter the Indonesian half of the island, the United Nations started urging the fugitives to return home. The majority, however, remained suspicious, of either the OPM or the army, and stayed put. When we arrived they had just been given an ultimatum by the Papua New Guinean government: either they move a hundred miles further into PNG, to a designated refugee camp and out of the trouble zone, or they return home. People seemed happy to do neither. If they went deeper into PNG it reduced their chances of ever returning and, despite the troubles the rebels had caused them, there was still substantial OPM support in the camps, which could be best mobilised close to the border. One thing puzzled me. The UN had been putting two million dollars a year into the refugee camps, and eighty thousand into repatriation in West Papua. Spread across eleven thousand fugitives (there were three thousand in the north as well) those were generous terms, yet people on both sides of the border were close to starvation. Someone, somewhere, had decided that his need was greater than theirs.

The night after we'd met the two chiefs the two old dogs that the pastors owned started howling and baying while I was reading in my room. I stood up and heard the sound of someone slipping away from the bushes at the window behind my chair. I shut it tight and locked the door.

Now that we were secure in Mindip Tanah, and clearly not going to be locked up, we became a little bolder, and I marched off to see the head of police again. I told him that my father's golfing partner the Chief of Immigration Police would be very angry if he knew we were being forced to sleep in Mindip Tanah. We should be allowed to walk off where we wanted. The chief of police said that there were dangerous people in the jungle—what if we met them?—and suggested I go and speak to the district officer, who might be able to give us permission. The district officer was a fat little Papuan man who had not got to his post, a rare one for a Papuan, through forthrightness. He hedged and ducked, rubbing his little hands down his trousers, grinning greasily. He suggested I go and ask the head of police. And, if we walked out of the village again, we should report to him, the DO, first. I wasn't going to hear him, and that day we wandered up the northern track to see villages that had been emptied and never repopulated.

On the path we met a party of schoolboys, who said they'd take us along to see, and they ran ahead of us through the rubber plantations, making big popping noises by exploding a leaf inside a hollow fist. We came out among the sticks of ruined houses, rather beautiful in filtered jungle light, tangled up in creepers. Among them were three still standing: hidden behind the dense secondary growth. The first of those was a church, a grand hall of planks and corrugated iron. Only a couple of panels had fallen from the walls; it was otherwise intact. Inside it looked as if an untidy congregation had just left, taking with it the smaller movable pieces. Apart from a bonfire in front of the altar and the remains of someone's lunch, it looked just as it might always have done, the raw benches in place, a cross upon the wall, the altar solid and unmoved. We all sat down in the pews for a moment and looked towards the altar.

The next house was the old police post, and that had fared less well. The front door had been violently kicked in: the lock was thrown across the room. Someone had taken pleasure in making a bonfire of the furniture inside, and writing, though inoffensive, had been scrawled in charcoal on the walls. Most of what could be broken had been, and even I felt a stab of vindictive revenge. Beyond the old police house, in a scrubby hollow of its own, stood the school. There was a gap between the wall and the roof, so we pulled ourselves through and jumped down into the classrooms.

There was the strange impression that school had finished for ever in the middle of a lesson. The desks, with their inkwells and chairs, stood in neat rows. The door of a school cupboard had opened, and books and chalk had slumped on to the floor, where they were mulching down into an erudite humus. All the blackboards still had their lessons written up; one, ironically, had taught the principles of government to an empty row of desks for three unchanging years. It looked either as if there had been a sudden alarm and everyone had fled, just locking doors behind them, or as if they had all expected to come back shortly, and pick up where they had left off. School was out, if not for ever then for a very long time.

Adrian had gone back ahead of me, and as I returned to Mindip Tanah alone, someone stepped out of the district officer's building and asked me to come inside. The little fat man was standing behind his desk and had blown himself up to look like a pufferfish. I looked around the room and saw the two spies sitting by their typewriters. They ducked behind piles of paper to avoid my glare.

"I told you," said the district officer, "that you had to report to me before you left the village. So, where have you been? Did you have my permission?"

I counted to five, then I leant towards him across the desk, opened my mouth, and burst into a violent mock rage. If he didn't leave us alone, I yelled, he'd be hanging from his ankles in the Jakarta police office with my godfather the colonel beating him round the head with a rifle butt. Who did he think we were? Ordinary tourists? We were most favoured visitors in his nasty little country, and a fine example he was setting. He could tell his amateur detectives—I pointed at the two men eyeing us with fascination from behind the paperstacks—that I'd have them boiled alive if they came near us again.

The district officer sat down sharply in his chair, eyes bulging at me like a toad before a boot. "Yes, *tuan*," he tried, "sorry, *tuan, tuan*, I didn't know."

"And you can keep your spies out of the flowerbeds as well. If there's anyone out there at night again I'll chop him up."

The district officer opened his mouth to deny it, but wiped his rubbery cheek instead and wound his fingers in knots around each other. I stormed out, keeping up the huff until I was out of sight.

He was, I hoped, off our backs for a couple of days, and we could afford to be a little freer moving around and asking questions.

I still had the massacre to find out about, and I had an idea where to go. The slaughter we'd heard about in Merauké had supposedly taken place at an OPM civilian camp close to the border. Indonesian troops had been led through the forest by disenchanted rebel followers, had burst into the camp and shot dead three hundred men, women and children. Pius, the man we had met on the path, had told us that friends of his had recently returned from the rebel camps. When I found him again he said that they perhaps knew people who had been in the camp at the time, but that they'd not be happy to talk about it. I gave him some money and asked him to find out a bit more. Pius came back a day later, having found someone who had been in the camp. He would talk to me if it was utterly secret, and he could be sure that no one would follow me to his house. For that reason only one of us could go. A friend of Pius's would take me to the house that night.

There was no moon. The last of the fruit bats had passed over the River Kao an hour before, and the forest was silent again. Pius's friend and I walked through the rubber plantations, out of even the shadow of the stars. I could see nothing and kept bumping into the man, which made him jump. We came—the man pointed them out—to a row of thatched houses, humped shapes I could pick out only where they blocked off the stars. He moved forwards slowly. I stepped ahead as if in black cotton wool: the darkness seemed to have muffled all my senses. A man suddenly stood up from beside the path. He held a long machete. He and Pius's friend whispered for a moment, then the guard moved down a trail through the bushes behind the huts. We waited, listening to the insects. The guard came back and Pius's friend followed him, me behind, into more darkness, until we came to the back steps of one of the row of huts. The machete man whispered into an invisible opening, and there was a hoarse whisper back.

The man I was due to meet sat behind a lantern made from an old margarine tin. He was nervous, and clicked his knuckles, watching the grain of the table. I tried to make smalltalk, but it wasn't much good. He burst out suddenly and started rattling away about the massacre, in a way that was hard to follow: I had to keep asking him to stop and start again. Not only had he been in the camp at the time, he also knew well one of the ex–OPM men that the soldiers had used to guide them there. He bore him no grudge; he too was now disillusioned with the OPM and simply wanted to keep out of trouble. The guide and three others had been co-opted into helping the soldiers in return for a clean record. They had led a small platoon for a week through the forest, back towards the camp they had recently run from. The soldiers had told them they simply wanted to make contact, perhaps negotiate a truce. The scouts knew otherwise but were too frightened to demur.

The OPM had been divided into eight battalions, each of a hundred and forty-four men. The camp the scouts were leading the soldiers to was composed of three battalions, living with their wives and families, housed on the marshy banks of the Fly River. There had been no action for several months, and the men had built stilted *bivaks* to live in, confident that they'd been forgotten about long ago. It was a bit like the refugee camps over the border, except that, being in an uninhabited zone, there was plenty of sago and hunting. There were no guns there, though all the men had bows and arrows. The soldiers got to the camp in the afternoon and hid near the entrance. At a signal they ran in, shouting at people to surrender. There was panic in the camp and people started fleeing in all directions, running blindly into the jungle. The soldiers opened fire.

"So," I said, convinced I was onto the big one, "how many dead?"

The man hesitated a moment then looked up frankly. "Four, and some wounded. The rest of the camp all fled."

"Four?! What about women and children?"

"None, the four were all men."

The camp had reconvened a few days later at another place and, when the people had calmed down, life went on very much as before, only without the stilted *bivaks*. It had been a normal military incursion with no civilian deaths, and a warning to beware of tall tales.

Having found out some of what we wanted, but seeing that there was no chance of getting to the rebels without getting everyone, not least ourselves, into substantial trouble, we began to look around for things with which to fill the time before the aeroplane came. Down on the banks of the River Kao was a dug-out canoe pulled on to a muddy beach. No one seemed to be using it, and I was all for sneaking down to the river at night, filling it up with our kit and disappearing off towards the sea, especially as I had just been reading *Huckleberry Finn,* which had the disastrous effect on me that Adrian had predicted. The idea was that we could drift by nights to Getentiri, at the junction of two big rivers. Then we could maybe get a bigger canoe or hitch a lift on a steamboat, and make our way down to Bade, where we could join a ship carrying out logs. Adrian, ever the voice of reason, talked me out of it.

Instead we went swimming in the river, which was excellent, labouring up against the strong current, then letting go and sliding down past the muddy bank to grab a branch before we were taken too far. On the other side of the river was the Mandobo land, that we went to see one morning. Unlike the Muyu it was fully populated, as almost no one had fled to Papua New Guinea. Their steadfastness was due to the work of one woman, who had saved her whole tribe from the dreadful exodus. The OPM had spread word through the Mandobo that they had a huge cache of weapons in the jungle, with which they were going to defeat the soldiers in the bloody revolution soon to come. There wasn't the popular support the OPM had made use of in the Muyu, so they had to rely on persuasion rather than threats. The Mandobo were all for it, for they too would have been only too delighted to push the soldiers off, once they and the Muyu had formed an army on the other side of the border. The one woman, however, insisted that she be taken to see the great store of arms, over the Kao River, across the forest and over the Muyu River to where the OPM had hidden it. It was a dangerous journey for a single woman, in a place where wife-stealing probably still went on, and among a tribe whose language she didn't speak. She got her way though, and when she reached the hut that contained the famous weapons she found two pre-war rifles and several hundred books that, as they were all broadly pro-revolutionary, the OPM had assumed would turn into guns at their command. Her report to the Mandobo elders kept them where they were.

Cargo cults and black magic were not the preserve of the OPM. One thing we felt we *could* ask the pastors about was religion, and they, like the other Catholics we'd met, were frank. Almost everyone in the area was nominally Christian, though that didn't stand for very much. As Brother Kase said, converting the Muyu souls was rather like lending them an outboard motor: Christianity was great fun at first but the excitement soon wore off, especially when there was a hitch. Everyone, Christian or no, still couldn't help but believe in the old spirits, even if the belief wasn't expressed. I got the impression that in times of trouble it was the old ways they ran to, rather than the Christian God they could be less certain of. Certainly black magic still had a power among them. A few years before we arrived an old man in the village had taken a shine to somebody else's young wife. When that became clear, the somebody else sent the wife to Merauké, to be away from the lecher. After five or six years it was felt that the old man would have forgotten his crush, and the woman was sneaked back into the Muyu to be with her husband again. The old man hadn't forgotten, however, and the day she arrived he put a special curse on her, using some old tribal words that had a great significance. Some kind heart heard the words and repeated them to the young woman, who at that moment fell ill, soon progressing into a coma, and thence to death.

Adrian asked the pastors how they could have kept going for so long, with those beliefs to contend with, and the awful troubles of the place, and being so far away from home for the rest of their lives. The answer would have been insincere had it come from anyone else, but from those dry and rather severe old sticks it could only have been true, "It's very simple," said Brother Kase. "I love those people."

Better still than swimming was volleyball, and it took place in the afternoons in front of the girls' school. I had been happily tripping down to the river for a swim when I was pounced on by an ambush of senior schoolgirls. They dragged me, giggling wildly, to the volleyball pitch where they were short of a player. There I was stuffed into the middle, while everyone, an audience of schoolgirls and matrons, jeered me from the sidelines and shouted encouragement. I was quite hopeless. Even when I hit the ball I fouled every shot, or knocked it sideways so conclusively that no one could reclaim it. I was taken charge of by a bossy and maternal woman of about sixteen, who kept slapping my hand when I got it wrong and exhorting me to pull myself together and get a move on, much to everyone's hilarity. In one volley, when I didn't know it had begun, everyone was shouting at me, and I couldn't see why, when the ball sailed over and landed on top of my head. The schoolgirls were crawling about on the ground as if mortally wounded, cackling their lungs out. Just in the nick of time, like the cavalry, Adrian came along, propelled with one arm twisted up behind his back by another mob of screeching women. He was shoved on to the pitch and made to play. I was glad to see that, though he was better than me, the girls thought it was just as funny when he got it right as when he got it wrong. They were in full cry, and I was having my hand slapped for the hundredth time by the bossy team captain and being propelled to the position I should have been in for the volley before, when the Javanese postman, standing on the boundary, caught my attention. "You're very good," he said, "very good indeed," and smiled his most charming smile. I was suddenly stopped short, struck by the gulf between those different people, each with their different charms: the Muyu extrovert, upfront, hilarious, the Javanese trying to please, with a well-intended, insincere compliment. These people, I felt could never share the same country without fighting.

After the volleyball, we were surrounded by women, all jeering and tugging our sweaty shirts. A hand, an anonymous hand, came through the crowd and pinched me hard and everyone giggled. There was another pinch, and another, and soon I felt I was being pulled apart. We both knew what it meant, and it was just too much to handle, so we fled, pursued by a plague of virgins. That night I was sitting quietly writing, with the window behind me tightly shut, when there was a gentle knock on the door. I took it to be one of the fathers, so I opened it incautiously, and before I knew it there were twenty women in my room. They all stood around my desk giggling, and I didn't know where to put myself. I stood up, sat down, and said, "How nice of you to drop in," or something like that. The crowd of bright eyes clustered round closer. "Er, can I teach you some English?" They giggled and I turned on my radio, trying to find the World Service, a voice of reason. One of the girls bashfully brought out a string bag she had woven and shoved it on to my desk, then hid behind the others. It was very nice and I thanked her for it, then all the other string bags came out. Everyone had brought one, and in a moment the desk looked like a marine chandler's. I nodded round at them with a fixed grin. Then the pinching began. Hands descended on me from all over, grabbing and tugging: it was getting to crisis point. Suddenly one of the girls gasped and remembered they should all be tucked up asleep, and the matron was coming round soon. In a flash they had gone, leaving just a mountain of string bags. Adrian got the same treatment the next night, but escaped dramatically when a pastor came in to see him.

A woman I fancied was the one who took us fishing. It was the final remedy for boredom while we waited for the plane, and perhaps the best, for we trooped down to the river with a couple of handlines and a tin pot of little crayfish that were to be bait. It was a lovely glowing afternoon, with a light breeze from the river, and the woman who took us was tall and strong-looking, with a dry humour and easy style. She had borrowed my machete and she cut down towards the river bank with neat strokes, telling us where to tread as we stumbled down the bank. At the bottom she made us sit down and organised our fishing lines, then sat beside Adrian with her knees drawn up. We caught some horrid ghostly pale crayfish, almost a foot long, that had eaten our little crayfish, and Adrian caught a strange elongated fish, that I could have bet him was likely to be new to science. Across the river little children were splashing about in canoes, or running down a mudbank and straight into the river, in curls of spray caught by the evening light. It was, for all the troubles of the adults, a great place to grow up in.

There was one more reminder that the OPM were not the romantic warriors I had wanted them to be. Lucas came to see us one day and asked if we'd like to meet a Muyu man who had made enemies of them. We followed him down a dry path to one of the far extensions of the village, where a couple of houses had been rebuilt. The man knew we were coming and came out on to the track to meet us. It wasn't until I shook hands with him that I noticed first that he was missing some of his fingers, then that he was missing his ears. We went up into his house, where his wife and child and some friends were waiting for us. He had been accused of passing information about the rebels to the police, though everyone in the house agreed he had never been an informer, but was rather the end of the line in an old family feud with one of the rebel leaders.

One day in 1984, just before the big migrations, he was sitting in his hut with his family. He didn't know that a mob of fifty or more rebels had already burst into the homes of five other men, all accused of being informers, and worked them over. When the OPM broke in, swinging sticks and machetes, he nearly died of fright. He was held down and his fingers were hacked off with a machete, while someone else sliced off both his ears with a knife. A baby suckling his wife was beaten to death with sticks, while the woman's joints were broken and her son was knocked unconscious. They were hauled off and thrown into a cage in the jungle for several days without any medical treatment. Then the family was released and they fled across the border, returning three months before we met them. The man's problems persisted, for work with few fingers was difficult, and he could never get the thought of what the rebels had done to leave his head.

We had run out of things to do and the plane was late. We had heard on the mission radio that the engine had broken down while it was taking off from somewhere remote, and it was holed up, waiting for a mechanic to come out and rescue it. Pastor Cor said not to expect anything until the plane was on the runway, and perhaps that would be weeks. I began to get very bored. We had been in West Papua too long and there was still much more to do. I kept thinking about home and my girlfriend, and was panicked into sudden desperation at night, sweating, convinced that we would never get out. After two days we heard the plane was coming and, with the whole village in procession, we trooped down to the airstrip, past the fateful spot where the three soldiers had been shot by the fifteen-year-olds. I still didn't expect to see the aeroplane but there it was: as yet a tiny mosquito against the clouds, the strange face of our saviour. It buzzed down low across the forest, touched down nicely on the grass strip, turned sharply and threw the front tyre off. We were stuck.

Brother Kase, who had been watching the landing with us, stared at the wheel a moment and shook his stringy head. "*Nej*, it will not go." He strode off sadly to the mission house to get his motorbike repair kit. Someone sauntered up to us and said that even if they did fix the plane it wouldn't take any passengers, and we'd have to wait till whenever another one decided to turn up, which might be months. The police chief was there too, and I'm sure I saw a glint of malice on his crooked teeth. On the airstrip the pilot and the engineer sat around the useless wheel and bickered. Some soldiers and a policeman pointed their guns at it and a crowd of villagers ebbed and swelled around the stricken plane. Eventually someone stirred into action and got a few villagers to hang on to the tail to pull the nose up, then jacked it up with a lump of wood. The engineer brought out his tool kit and puzzled over which one to use. He had a spanner and screwdriver. Brother Kase returned with a couple of spoons and they began to lever the tyre back on. The fire service—an old man with a battered extinguisher—stood by, and all the cardboard boxes, plastic bags, live birds and bundles of vegetables due to be loaded sweltered on the grass strip. Somehow it seemed to come together, and the cry went up that we could go to Merauké after all. We threw in our luggage and hurried after it. The propellers turned, the fire service stood ready and, shakily, with grunts and rattlings, we lifted into the turgid air.

Chapter 12

We hadn't met the rebels, so our trip to Mindip Tanah had mostly been a failure. I was left with the grim alternative that had been hanging over me for the five months of the trip. Sealed into the back cover of a guidebook was a letter from an exiled rebel I'd met in Amsterdam, soon before we left for Indonesia. It commended me to one of the OPM's six main coordinators in West Papua, who could arrange for us to enter a rebel camp and follow the fighters into the forest. I was worried about such a direct approach, as it was the perfect chance to give ourselves or the coordinator away, but more immediately because the only address I had for him was inside the government office where he worked. It was with foreboding that we boarded a plane to a town I'll call Kopko.

We booked into a guesthouse and I went off through the town to see if I could find the office, carrying the guidebook with the letter glued up inside it. I couldn't see it, and when I went into another office and asked the receptionist I was told it was on the other side of town, so I had to trudge back through all those streets, feeling that everyone was staring at me, with the guide-book burning in my hand. I had no idea what I was going to do. I couldn't just ask for Celsius Nipsan: the man didn't know I was coming and if I messed it up once I couldn't go back in for another try without people watching me very curiously.

A platoon of soldiers on drill marched past the front of the office, proud, with rifles on their shoulders. I began to feel small. Inside there were scores of people, typing, shuffling papers, being vaguely and unproductively bureaucratic, one sweeping the floor, another man taking round some fruit. Most of them were Javanese or from Sulawesi, though there were four or five Papuans in lowly attitudes. I couldn't just single them out and ask, "Which one of you is Celsius Nipsan?" A Javanese woman came up and asked me what I wanted.

"Ahh, I, yes, am a bit confused and—can I sit down? thank you—I was wondering if somebody here could tell me about hiring a truck."

"What truck?"

"Any truck. Not really any truck, but a very good one—does anyone perhaps know anybody with a very good truck? You know, a four-wheeled one, I mean a proper one that you can put things in?"

By then everyone was staring at me.

"Why did you come here to ask for a truck?" asked the Javanese woman waspishly. The other staff nodded at the soundness of the question.

"I, I was just passing by, and I needed some help, as it's so hard to know where to start. Is there anyone perhaps—er my Indonesian isn't very good—is there anyone who speaks English?"

A Papuan man caught my eye, a shifty-looking clerk with a thin beard. It could be him—he looked the sort—in fact he seemed to wink, as if he knew . . .

"You'd better go in there," said the woman, and pointed me at the door of the boss's office. The very thing I didn't want to do was to go into the boss's office. I was convinced that the clerk, staring hard at me like all the rest, was the one, yet how would I get to speak to him? There was no choice, however, beneath those curious glares, so I tapped nervously on the glass door and walked in. The four important men inside were having a meeting. None of them looked very happy to be disturbed. Above the table was a huge picture of the President, staring at me quizzically. What was I doing?

Hello, hello, I grinned, trying to deflect the curiosity my intrusion had brought on. To ask them for a truck was going to look very silly. They were all high-powered and very likely ran the town. I grabbed the hand of the man nearest me, a severe-looking Sulawesi man with swept-back hair.

"I'm George. George Monbiot, how do you do?"

"Akmal," he answered briskly.

The next man was Javanese, small, bespectacled, relaxed. "Sundardi."

Beside him was a local man, taller than most, hard and stringy, with thick grey sideburns. He fixed me with unmoving eyes. "Celsius," he said as he shook my hand.

I smiled quickly and moved to the next man, feeling foolish as I introduced myself again. "It's a truck; I've come about a truck. Can any of you help? I—"

"Do you speak English?" asked Celsius, and I saw I'd been saved by great luck. I told him all about the sort of truck I had in mind, trying, though the others were obviously impatient to get on with their meeting, to show how grateful I was that he should help me over such a trifling thing. Celsius, humouring the idiot Englishman, gave me some useless advice about getting a strong truck because of the bumpy road, and that maybe if I saw someone driving one I should ask to hire it from him. He was obviously keen to get rid of me and carry on with his meeting.

"It's extremely, extremely kind of you to let me know all that," I said. "Very few people would have gone so far out of their way, we, we must keep in touch. Do you think I could have your address?"

Celsius looked at me as if I was soft in the head, then resignedly took out a pad and wrote on it. I took the sheet. It was Celsius Nipsan all right, and there were unlikely to be two.

"Here, let me give you mine," I said. The others were shifting impatiently on their chairs: this intrusion was becoming a nonsense. I grabbed the pad and held it close, looking as if I was trying to remember my address. Then I wrote: "I am friend of Vinzen Araré's. Meet me in the Golden Horse Restaurant at seven o'clock." Celsius took the sheet and glanced at it, about to fold it and put it in his pocket. He glanced again. His firm features twisted a little then regained themselves. "Yes, yes, thank you very much," he said, and I made for the glass door before the stares of the men behind me bored into my back.

In the Golden Horse Restaurant, at seven o'clock, I was sitting on a plastic chair and trying to read the guidebook. Twice the Papuan woman serving had come to ask what I would eat, and I had sent her away without a decision. There was no one else in the restaurant, though whether that was a good or a bad thing I didn't know. I was sure he wouldn't come, or that I'd walked into an elaborate trap, sprung by a subtle agent of the Indonesians who had posed as OPM in Amsterdam, and was looking to lure journalists into compromising encounters. The door opened and I tried not to look. I caught grey sideburns out of the corner of my eye. I had been going to stand up and say "These seats are free" but in an empty restaurant it seemed a little silly. Celsius came and sat down beside me, with two huge men who settled at the ends of the table, that he introduced as his brothers. He was sweating a little, and had lost some of the authority he'd had in the office. He signalled to the woman, who went forward and locked the door from the inside. I had clearly chosen the right place, and I was amazed at how his role was acknowledged by the waitress. Celsius ordered some beers and said something about tourism—had I been in the forest yet? The wildlife was very good. But he was just as uneasy as I was.

I took out a knife and cut open the back cover of the guide-book, and gave him the letter that was glued there. Celsius opened it and began to read. There was a tap on the door and he shoved the letter under the table. I swung round to stare nonchalantly at a calendar. I was hardly being the undercover journalist I had styled myself. Eyes and a black fuzz of hair came over the half-cur-tained windows. Celsius waved at the waitress and she unbolted the door to let in another of his brothers.

He finished the letter and grunted, then knocked back his beer in one and ordered five more. I spluttered failingly at mine. It had the fluorescent tinge of methyl orange and tasted of sweetened polymer. Beer froth and sweat mingled on my chin. "I think per-haps I can help you," said Celsius, and knocked back his second beer.

Adrian was waiting up when I got back very late that night. "So what did he say?" he asked anxiously.

"I'm not entirely sure," I said, "but I think it's on." Then I grabbed my mouth and was sick in the next room.

Celsius had given me the name of a man in Jayapura who ran a guerrilla unit operating down the border near Arso. I had sug-gested the name of a hotel we might stay in, and he said someone would be sent to pick us up and get us to the leader's house in four days' time. We repaired to Jayapura. The town had all the tin-selly glitz of a place populated quickly for no particular purpose. Stuck at the top of the scarcely peopled forest land it was a little blip of overcrowding and pollution, unconnected to anywhere else but by an airstrip and a couple of shaky roads to nearby towns. Round and round on those tracks swarmed minibus taxis, each Indonesian driver striving to be the tackiest, with the help of

Rambo stickers, plastic dolls, false LED displays, and the consistent beat of pirated popsongs. It was an Indonesian town without the subtlety of Indonesia, and the tack was held up like a holy relic against the savage hinterland.

When we arrived in Jayapura we stepped into the still heat of an early afternoon, and the streets were empty. We walked down past the big mosque and a Protestant church, to a square of scorched grass. There stood, in the hyper-expressionist style of post-revolution everywhere, a statue of one of the island's liberators: Commodore Jos Sudarso, killed in the abortive attempt to take West Papua by force before the United Nations handed it over. Beneath him a frieze showed tribal Papuans in full paint and feathers being relieved of their colonial oppressors. Even on the frieze they didn't look very happy about it. As we admired the bronze Frankenstein the empty square was suddenly filled by the screams of a mass torture, reverberating against the shuttered walls. There was a frightful beating noise, then gurgling, as of blood and guts sucking through the plughole, then a hideous cackle, that went on, and on, and on. *The Fury of the Exterminator* was playing to all Jayapura, from the loudspeakers on the outside of the cinema.

The hotel I'd chosen randomly was the most expensive we had stayed in, seven pounds a night for two, and our money was running out. I wasn't by then averse to a little comfort, however, and a quiet room, with breakfast laid out in the morning, was a luxury which once acquired was hard to kick. The place was run by a fat Chinese man, with white skin, greased-down hair, and a wide amphibian mouth that quite unnerved me. He would paddle round in the mid-day gloom, his arms flopping feebly, emerging from corridors like a sinister swamp creature. We had been in the hotel for a couple of days when we realised he was running an army operation. The Chinaman had some sort of shady business going, that required more than straightforward financial help. Every so often an army jeep would pull up outside, and a high-ranking soldier would pace swiftly through the lobby and straight to the back of the building, where the Chinaman lived. After half an hour he would emerge, often holding a briefcase he hadn't had before, and, without any acknowledgement to the fat man waddling behind him, plunge straight into the jeep and roar off. It was intriguing, as well as slightly worrying.

At the hour our contact was due to meet us we were waiting

in the lobby, having told a gossipy cleaner that we were going birdwatching with a friend. The time for the meeting came, and with it another of those army jeeps. That would blow it, I was certain. The rebel would see it, assume the worst of us, and we would have forfeited our only chance of getting to where the action was. Just a few minutes later, however, a second jeep, a civilian one, drew up, and in it was a Papuan man in reflector glasses and a baseball hat. I realised we had made our contact, unsubtle as he was. We walked out, casual and stiff, and sat in the jeep beside him: I was convinced the fat Chinaman was watching us from somewhere in the shadows. Jojo, who hardly said a word, drove us down the seafront to a shantylike sprawl of streets leading up from the water. Washing flapped from sagging balconies, and chickens chased each other for scraps in the hot dust. Outside one of the doorways a man was bashing more dents into the ruptured side of a truck with a hammer. He nodded at us as we passed inside: tall, long-chinned and lean.

Four rebels were waiting for us inside. Three were by appearances small fish, but in the middle was an imposing man, with strong straight features and hair more wavy than curly: he looked a bit like a Pakistani. We were sat down and he started asking us questions. He wanted a guarantee that we were what we claimed, and said he would have to get in contact with our employers—the publishers—to check us out. I knew that was impossible, not least because of his lack of English, but he was just sizing us out. He deliberated a bit, then said he could give us some data and perhaps some photographs, but he didn't want to take us into the jungle. There was half an hour of discussion and long pauses, then he agreed to see what he could do for us. We would keep in touch with Frankie, a slightly weedy-looking man who sat against the back wall, and if the Pakistaniman decided we could move he would let Frankie know and the trip would be arranged for us. Jojo dropped us close to the hotel. As we walked in the Chinaman followed us with his axolotl's stare, and I felt we were already making mistakes.

We met Frankie twice, once in a bar and once in another hotel. The second time he was extremely nervous. Someone had told him he was being followed and had possibly been seen with us. We had to buy him several beers before he calmed down. What was wrong with being seen with us anyway? We were just a pair of idle tourists holed up in town. Frankie had imagined we'd been telling people all about him, that word had spread, and that soon the whole army would be banging on his door, and he'd be taken away and shot. With his skinny shoulders and nervous twitches he hardly seemed the stuff of bloody revolution. We spent a long time with him, trying to make friends and share his pathetic jokes. He assured us that he was really going to help, and offered to dig out a secret book he had, all about the OPM. He was disappointed when I told him we'd already read it.

That there was perhaps some basis for Frankie's fear we found out later the same day. The Chinaman had been loitering about in the lobby, watching us as we sat at the big table reading and writing. Then he slipped away, into the depths, and in his place emerged a tall Moluccan man, his head shaved at the sides. He sauntered over and sat at the table with arrogant calm, watching us. He started up a conversation brusquely, demanding to know where we came from, and where we were going. Neither of us was in the mood for talking, so we grunted replies and got on with what we were doing. He tried again. He came from Ambon. He was over in Jayapura looking for labouring work. Had we ever been to Ambon? It was a little tiresome. I put down my pen and it rolled off the table onto the floor. I bent to pick it up and saw, unmistakable beneath his civilian trousers, the boots of a military policeman. The man didn't know any English, so I told Adrian to ignore him and I'd explain later. I got on a little stiffly with my writing. The military policeman, impatient, barked out another question. What were our names? What we were doing in Irian Jaya? I told him that his way of breaking in was rude in our culture and we'd be glad if he could leave us alone. He stood up and left proudly, his boots clicking on the plastic floor. Quite what he wanted, or what he might have seen, we didn't know, but it was a crude reminder that we should move with care.

Next time we saw Frankie he was a little more relaxed. With him were two other friends in the OPM, who had come to tell us why they were fighting the Indonesians. Henkie had lost an uncle, three schoolfriends and a teacher to the army. All had been vaguely, if not actively, involved with the OPM. The uncle had fled into the forest in 1970, after an informer had given his name to the police. He was found in a small village by an Indonesian loyalist and shot when he was handed over to the soldiers. The three schoolfriends had been killed together in 1982, when they too had fled into the woods, straight into an army trap. The teacher was shot when escaping from jail, which Henkie said meant he had died under torture and later had bullets put through him. Henkie's brother was in prison. He had visited him a couple of times and seen lashmarks on his back. The other man, Mayor, had tales of friends being tortured with electric shocks and cells full of water, and others dying beneath the massed bodies of political prisoners piled into a tiny room. I believed some of it.

Frankie had relaxed more because the Pakistaniman had checked us out—clearly he hadn't—and found us sound. We had the go-ahead. Frankie would get us to the rebel headquarters, in the jungle somewhere close to Arso, and introduce us to the OPM's most senior field commander, who would take us out on a patrol. Frankie's enthusiasm and haziness were not reassuring. To buck up our hopes he brought out some photos of the rebels in the jungle. Why at that stage I still expected to see fierce black men stalking troops with bows and poisoned arrows I don't know: I guess I was still reluctant to abandon my romantic fantasy. There instead were the marks of unfulfilled intentions everywhere: red bandannas and Che Guevara moustaches, berets and reflector sunglasses. Among them were two submachine carbines and a few bolt-action rifles. They were a better equipped bunch than the rebels around Mindip Tanah, but they still didn't look like the Indonesian's nemesis.

Frankie was sure we could be out and into the forest in a couple of days, so we hung around the troop-infested hotel, waiting for the word. There was precious little to do in Jayapura and I was becoming bored and worried. I had little confidence in Frankie and was quite sure we could wait a month in that town without getting anywhere. If he did get us into the jungle he was likely to chicken out at the critical moment, or the rebels wouldn't want to know us, or we'd be kidnapped like a Swiss pilot was a couple of years before, and held until people at home—all primed by me to deny our existence if suspicious-sounding people with foreign accents rang up—acknowledged us and paid our ransom. I kept counting up our remaining money: it had gone down fast and I reckoned we'd be pressed to stay in West Papua for another three weeks. There was also the small matter of being caught by the police. If Frankie was right and they were interested in us, we could find ourselves being led into one of the traps the secret service was said to specialise in, and, ever sensitive to spies, they could keep us for a very long time at their pleasure.

Adrian and I went down to Hamadi beach on a Sunday. General MacArthur had left his landing vehicles there after fighting off the Japanese, and they still stood there, pointing out to sea, washed by the waves at high tide. It was a nightmare of armour plating flaking off in layers. Aluminium sumps remained shiny, and there was black rubber clinging to some of the rollers, but for the most part the machines had been rendered safe and rocklike. An artillery gun was choked solid with rust. We had the beach to ourselves in the morning, but it began to fill up at noon, and soon was covered in slick young Javanese, kicking up sand by revving their motorbikes on the strip, in tight jeans and shades. The Jayapura taxis turned up and unloaded families of picnickers, large Javanese men and their pretty wives, with picnic sets and Sunday clothes. They were the ones who had won the war of West Papua. They or their parents had had a bite at the pickings left by the Dutch, or the good civil service jobs to be had, or the gold in the hills beyond Jayapura. Unlike the transmigrants who had stayed on their sites, or the Papuans, they had flourished.

We were still bored, and the next day, when Frankie hadn't appeared, we took a taxi a few miles down the road to take a walk in the woods. The forest there was broken up by little farmed plots and an occasional stilted house. Soon Adrian found a municipal rubbish dump and he disappeared into the scrap iron to take artistic photos. We agreed to meet back at the hotel, and I wandered away down a slope towards a glittering stream.

It was hot, and I stopped by the river a moment to take off my shirt, then I crossed over and started to climb the other bank. Halfway up I brushed against a rotting stump, left after someone had burnt a few trees. I took another step and I was attacked. Hornets were all over my body, black and furious, and they were the giant jungle ones that could kill you with just three stings. I was horrified, but I stood stock still, as I knew they'd fly away if I didn't panic. For ten seconds I managed not to twitch, though I could feel them stuck in my hair, and crawling up towards the inside of my shorts. The buzzing was becoming louder, as reinforcements came and joined their friends from the stump. Suddenly I couldn't bear it, and I launched myself up the slope, shouting and beating at them wildly with my shirt. They began to sting, jabbing my head and my back. With every jab I panicked more, and tried to beat all parts of my body at once, yelling with pain and fright. I stopped suddenly: I was being stung to death. Still there were hornets trapped in my hair, and their heavy bodies were battering furiously, looking for a place to sting. I panicked a second more and hit them, and two of them stung me, then disentangled themselves and flew off. I counted the stings. There were eight: I was a dead man.

I stumbled across the rough fields, shouting for help, being suddenly overtaken by bouts of panic, falling into the furrows. In a clump of trees I saw a rickety house on stilts, with a ladder leading up to the platform, and I moved over to that and clung to the steps, shouting up at the entrance. No one came out, so I climbed up and looked in. Inside was a terrified family of five: a man, his young wife, two children and an old granny, staring out in horror at the fearsome sight before them. I remembered my shirt was off, my eyes were rolling with shock, my whole body was trembling. "Hello, hello." I had to reassure them. "It's all right, I'm George." I stepped forward to shake hands with the man, hit my head on the lintel and fell sprawling on top of his wife. She screamed and the children began to cry. I picked myself up, babbling apologies. I would have to get them to trust me. I spoke slowly. "It's very important you understand me. I have just been attacked by hundreds of insects." The man's mouth fell open; he didn't seem to believe what I said. "A swarm of insects. They came out of a tree and started flying round my head. Then eight of them bit me."

Only instead of "*serangga*"—which means insects—in my panic I had said "*semangka*"; or watermelons. The old granny was backing away from me, shaking her head and feeling for the back door, the children were almost choking to death. I wasn't getting through. I sat down beside the man and tried to explain it carefully. "I need help. I was walking in your field when I was attacked. Eight of them bit me, eight watermelons."

He stared at me, unable to move, his eyes getting bigger and rounder as I nodded assurances at him. He was obviously very stupid.

"Look—" I began again, and I saw that the young woman was whimpering with terror.

Then, however, a smile of relief spread across the husband's stricken face. "Ahh, *serangga!*" He stood up. "You stay there, I have some medicine for you."

I sighed with thankfulness, I was going to be saved. He'd have some old homegrown cure, evolved over many years to deal with hornets, most likely far more effective than the modern drugs. I lay down and the man came back and began to rub something into my back. It had a warm and soothing effect, and even as he rubbed, the pain began to ease away. I relaxed, and I turned round to see what he was using. The jar in his hand was eucalyptus chest rub, from a chemist in Jayapura. "No, no! I'm going to die!" I cried, and leapt from the room, forgetting it was ten feet off the ground. I crashed into the undergrowth below, then picked myself up and ran. A backwards glance showed the man in his doorway, a little round jar in one hand, my shirt in the other, staring in perplexity as I ran panicking over his gardens.

I ran through a cluster of huts, scattering pigs and chickens, people fleeing for their houses, then I found the road. A minibus was grinding up the hill, snorting and backfiring as it came towards me. I waved it to a stop and leapt in, squeezing between a couple of startled women. They looked at me as if I'd come from out of the ground, so I tried to reassure them by starting a con-versation. I could still feel the panic surging away inside me, but it seemed to be ebbing a little, and perhaps I'd be all right after all. The women relaxed as we got talking, and one of them, as I asked polite questions, started to tell me about her family. She had just got to her daughters when I convulsed. My whole body began to shudder and I drooled down my chest. I tried to speak but it came out as a gurgle. The woman, horrified, made to climb over into the back seat, so I grabbed her arm to reassure her and she let out a scream. The bus swerved and everyone was staring at me and wrapping their arms round their children. I wanted to tell them it was all right, I was just having some poison convulsions, but I made a lecherous grunting sound instead and started bubbling at the mouth. People were tapping the driver on the shoulder trying to get him to stop. By then he'd reached the bus station and every-one scrambled out, staring back and pointing me out to the other people in the terminal.

I managed to say "malaria" as it was the simplest explanation I could think of, and someone realised I was in trouble and helped me to get out. I stumbled away up the road, under the stares of the whole town, shuddering and sobbing, feeling as if I was being shaken by someone terribly strong. I had to keep grabbing things to stay upright. I fell through the door of the hotel and into our room, where, thankfully, Adrian was sitting on his bed. He started up: "God you look awful," but I fell face down on to my bed and started shivering violently. He got some antihistamines down me and very soon the fit began to subside. He made to fetch a doctor, but in just a few moments I was asleep. When I woke up twelve hours later I felt as if I'd just been through some big emotional disturbance, as if I'd been crying for a long time: I felt cleaned out and rather strange.

Revolution was all over the town, for black and white eyes only to see. A man came up to me one day and asked, "You like West Papua?"

"Well, yes."

"It has been destroyed." He raised his thumb in the air and saluted with the other hand. "To sovereignty."

Another time I saw a drunken Papuan man weeping and raging and trying to pull a soldier off his motorbike. His friends held him back. I asked a bystander what was going on. "They don't shoot you if you're drunk," he replied, then wandered off to look for something more interesting. It was extraordinary to see how widespread the discontent and revolutionary spirit was. There was the strong tacit feeling that whites were on the side of the Papuans, and soon after the formalities at the front of a conversation we'd be hearing about the coming revolt, and the terrible things the army and policemen had done to people in the town. There were more allegations of torture, political imprisonments and murder by the army. Everyone claimed to have lost a relative or a friend, and perhaps it was true. I heard some stories of heavy-handed lawmaking, like the man beaten to death by police for eating an expatriate's dog.

A Papuan policeman collared me in a bar one day. "It's coming to all of Melanesia," he said. "There's already a revolution in Fiji, and soon it'll get to New Caledonia. After that what's to stop it in Papua?" He was studying the principles of government in evening classes to become an administrator for the new regime. Everyone wanted independence, it seemed—all the Papuans that is—but in the face of the troops who ran with rifles up and down the main streets once a week, and the armoured cars that would parade around the square then go back to barracks, they had no power. There were four thousand soldiers in West Papua: enough, with their sophisticated weaponry, to keep the discontented population down.

It seemed that the OPM had smartened up a little since the last reports I'd read, in Britain before I left. They certainly had several hundred part-time fighters in the north, and at least three small camps of regulars who moved from place to place near the border or along the north coast. They were just beginning to arm themselves more effectively. The OPM had always had a few rifles that were left behind during the handover, and had taken others from their infrequent killings of soldiers on patrol. The main source, however, had been impoverished policemen and soldiers selling their weapons to the rebels: that's where they got carbines from, and a few M-16s and revolvers. As we arrived they were beginning to tap other sources. The five hundred regulars and part-timers in the area around Jayapura were soon to be fully armed, following a successful raid on an Indonesian arms dump. More important however was the Libyan connection.

Colonel Gaddafi had long ago noticed that the superpowers were all interested in the South Pacific. To be a superpower therefore he had to be interested in the South Pacific. To that end he had flown several OPM leaders out via Vanuato to Libya for training, and sent them back, a month before we turned up, with strategies for world revolution. They were followed by four cases of AK 47s, smuggled from a ship on to Biak Island by OPM members in dugout canoes. Just as they'd been loaded on to a truck, however, to be driven off and hidden in the middle of the island, the lorry was hijacked by a rival rebel faction and the guns were taken to west Biak, from whence it seems they never returned. For all that there was no way in which the OPM posed a genuine threat to Indonesia's hold on West Papua. There was no international back-up that could be taken seriously: asylum in Ghana and Vanuato, and help from a few fringe governmental sources in PNG, otherwise nothing. In West Papua they were helped a little by local people mucking in with bows and arrows when they got the chance. The well-drilled tribal army that had sprung up for a few months in the western highlands had fallen apart in 1983.

Frankie's friends in the forest shot a policeman during our first week in Jayapura. He was unarmed and cycling down to a shop to buy rice. The rebels came off badly in direct confrontations, and bow-and-arrow ambushes on armed patrols often resulted in more OPM dead than army. Picking off the odd soldier or military policeman was about all they could do. It would do little for the cause but satisfy old grievances. If the rebels did anything for the people it was to focus discontent, but the harsh reprisals suffered seemed infinitely to undo any good done to their side.

The next time we met Frankie I was convinced that we weren't going to get any action out of him. He seemed to have forgotten that he'd promised an excursion to the forest and, having overcome his fear, was much more intent on showing his new friends the tourists to the town. He slunk into our room one night and suggested very shyly that we go for a beer. I was laid out with food poisoning, but he followed Adrian to the Hawaii Bar. Two beers unloosed him, and he was soon telling Adrian about his many women.

"Why don't we go and get some?" The idea suddenly hit him.

"Where, Frankie?"

"Well, perhaps if we . . . In fact, if . . . We might see some outside?" He trailed off.

Frankie was not for real, and he wasn't going to get us to the rebel headquarters.

I went back to the Pakistaniman, and found him in full camouflage, sweeping the kitchen floor. He looked a little embarrassed and went and put a teeshirt on. I sat down. I knew it was going to be difficult.

"It's not easy," he said when he came back in. "You never know who might be following. You're very conspicuous you know, you and your friend."

I went through the old arguments, how a bit of publicity could only help the cause, how we were so discreet—Celsius had told him about the first meeting?—how we would pull out immediately if we thought we would cause them trouble. On the wall was a team photo of some of the indigenous administration under the Dutch, senior men. All of them were now abroad, promoting the rebel cause. The Pakistaniman came round slowly.

It was time, he decided, we got in touch directly with the fighters. He didn't want to expose them but he was obviously keen to delegate. It just happened that a unit commander was in town at the time, taking a break from the forest. He was one of their most closely guarded secrets, and he would want to check us out for himself before he decided to help. The Pakistani man would send him to make contact with us by five-thirty that afternoon. We would be sitting on the balcony of our hotel and keeping watch on the market square. The man would walk past, look up and raise his thumb in the air. We would then go down and follow him into a foodstall.

"How will we know it's him?" I asked.

"You'll know him by his beard."

Below us in the market square the lottery men were pinning up the evening's stakes on their stalls. The fruit stands were vividly coloured in the afternoon sun and the fish barbecue was shimmering as the coals warmed up. Hens scratched beneath the card tables and a couple of Chinese children span round and round on bicycles. The square was still mostly deserted. A fat man with a thick round beard wandered across the road, twice, then stopped in front of the quack's plastic skeleton and scratched his beard with his thumb. But it wasn't him: he strode off down the road without looking up, away from the foodstalls. A couple of Ambonese or Sulawesi men had wandered over from their taxis to flick through the magazines laid out on the table beneath us: issues bought in Jakarta three months before. One hiked up his shirt and scratched his thin belly. Soon there would be big crowds coming in to eat or gamble, then we couldn't be sure of seeing the sign, if it came. The quack was testing his microphone, "*Slamat soré, slamat datang*". He had laid bottles of coloured water out in front of the skeleton. I assumed he would use it to point out the parts the panacea would cure, rather than to effect a remarkable recovery. I turned away to talk to Adrian for a moment then I looked down. A man with a long and filthy beard was standing between the hotel and the fishgrill. He looked up deliberately, held my stare and nodded purposefully. I nodded back and waited for the sign. He slopped off, a drunk, treading on the backs of his shoes. Now the fish steaks were being laid out on the grill and the stallholders were hanging up paraffin lamps. It was five-fifteen.

At five-thirty precisely he came. There was no mistaking the man even before he made the sign. His beard was extraordinary. It hung almost down to his belly and was combed out into points. Two strands were plaited and hung with beads. He looked up a second, raised his thumb very casually, then sauntered off to the foodstalls. We stumbled off down the stairs after him. I gave him a minute to settle down, then, trying to be matter-of-fact, we strolled in and sat beside him, ordering some food before we noticed he was there. He looked about him tiredly and went on eating his black-rice pudding. I introduced myself tentatively, a bored Englishman making friends. He looked up, nodded, grunted a name we weren't supposed to catch, then got back to eating, pushing his beard out of the way to avoid dribbling down it. It was finespun, like steel wool. We arranged, when he had finished eating, to meet in our hotel room the next day. He got up and strolled away, back into the mystery he'd come from.

The Chinaman was worrying me. I was convinced we were being watched. He would paddle out of the pond-like gloom with puppyish movements of his arms, gulp at us for a moment then slop away on his unbuckled sandals. Any attempts to talk to him led to a slow turning away of his head, an awkward movement of his flippers, then retreat to the back room, his fat neck bent round to watch us as he went. Perhaps he was spying for the army.

The Beardman came to our room a little late, with a soft tap on the door, which opened and closed behind him in a single movement. He sat down on Adrian's bed, among the crumpled shirts, books and bottles of mosquito repellent. His eyes snapped with excitement, and when he turned the points of his beard shimmered in the light. He spoke with a hiss, rolling the words, chopping gently one hand on the other to illustrate an execution or a strategy. We had to lean forward to catch his words, which enhanced the resonance of what he told us.

His father had been one of the first revolutionaries, fighting in the Arfak Mountains revolt a couple of years before the Act of Free Choice. The Beardman had been brought up to fight almost before he had learnt anything else. By the age of fourteen he had petrol-bombed an army landing-stage, delaying part of an offensive sent to destroy the rebels. Since then he had gained increasing leverage within the OPM, and was soon commanding small jungle forays against the Indonesians. From Jayapura he moved up and down the border, or sometimes went a little west, often with just a group of five guerrillas, occasionally commanding successful attacks. The year before, 1987, he had machine-gunned an army launch and killed an officer.

The Beardman pulled out our map of the border area and told us what he could do for us. In three days' time we could leave Jayapura at night in a motorised canoe. We'd be covered up in nets in case we met a night patrol boat, when the Papuans could claim they were fishermen. He moved his finger slowly round the coastline, an inch, two inches. It crossed the border with Papua New Guinea.

"Can we do that?" asked Adrian.

"We," the Beardman hissed, "can do anything."

The assassin's fingers came down through the pale blue and landed among the coves and rocky beaches on the far side of the border. "We land there, then go over the rocks, slowly, and into the forest whilst it's still night." He flashed his eyes at each of us and grinned a second. Blue and purple lights caught the strands of his beard. "Then we move, on down"—a straight line down the border, to three inches below where we sat, south of Arso. "That is two"—he looked at our pale bodies—"three days down, and then"—his finger slid across the border, into a white triangle, "Relief Data Incomplete"—"we cross to the camp." We were set to go. The Beardman would come back to our room to tell us the details in two days' time; he would have fixed a boat and warned the camp we were coming. I was excited and a bit scared.

The Chinaman caught me as I came in from the market the next day. He stared at me with his amphibian eyes and put a flipper to his greasy hair. I glared back, angry about him and his fearful business. The broad mouth opened, I could see the denunciation coming. "A-are you, are you having a nice stay?" he asked, then ducked bashfully and turned his head away. He paddled off, nodding back at me as he went. It seemed to me that he wasn't a spy, he was just terribly shy. We spun out the two days listlessly. Adrian went to the cinema. The film was Ramboesque—*Grapple with Death,* or *Hellcamp 1999*—with guerrillas in an Asian rainforest fighting the forces of a despotic government. They wore berets and reflector sunglasses, and flaunted submachineguns. Before the film there were trailers for five or six others, all with interchangeable plots about honourable guerrillas using their Guevara moustaches to defeat an evil empire. There was so much jungle warfare, so many explosions, that Adrian reckoned film-making must be one of the greatest causes of deforestation. The audience was mostly Javanese and Sulawesi men, several in cut-off Rambo waistcoats, flash, conservative and young, the very people the indigenous guerrillas resented most.

An hour before he was due, the Beardman pushed into our room without knocking. His eyes and hair buzzed static.

"It's off," he hissed. "I'm going to the forest and I won't be back for several weeks." He tried to leave.

"What the hell's happening?" We had waited two weeks, I wasn't going to be foiled like that.

The Beardman shrugged nervously. "It wasn't anything to do with us, believe me. It's not how we work."

I caught his arm as he tried to go.

"Come back in a month," he said, "and I promise you, I promise I'll take you to the forest. But if I spend another hour here I'll die, OK?" He snatched his sleeve away and slipped through the door. By the time I was up and had looked out after him he'd disappeared.

That afternoon a troopship came into the harbour, huge, threatening and gun-blue. The town, insensitive and brash at other times, was buzzing. In the market I heard someone talking about a massacre, but I couldn't obtain any details. Convoys of army trucks sped off down the broken roads, without their customary circular tour of town. No one could tell us anything. We even plucked up courage to go to the police station, pretending to have some query about the length of our visas, and trying to draw the sergeant there into a conversation. He knew nothing, or he wasn't going to tell us, so we went back to the market, from stall to stall, twitching with curiosity and a little fear. But there were only rumours, that flared up, lit a chain of people, then died away without coming to anything. As we lay on our beds at night, and heard even the mosquitos whining their excitement, Adrian hit the solution obvious to anyone not pondering the problem too hard. "If there has been a massacre," he mused, "surely the place to find out about it is the hospital."

We were up there in the early morning and immediately there were signs that something had indeed gone wrong. Taxis were throbbing outside and several soldiers paced up and down twitchily. Two loads of Indonesian civilians, mostly women, were driven up, and they moved off quickly towards the big wards, with nervous feet. A soldier and a medical worker blocked our way. Adrian had his hand on his ear. "It aches terribly," I said, "so bad he can't even speak." We were let through and we moved towards the outpatients, away from the wards that the women were heading to. We slipped around a blocking wall. Across a yard full of cats and mouldering fruit was a door we figured led into a staff corridor, that led to the end of the outpatients' building, then into an external passageway that reached the complex of big wards. We moved across the yard quickly. The soldier might have seen us from the corner of his eye. The door was unlocked and we slipped quickly in, marching straight off towards the big wards. A voice behind us called out, but we ignored it, and opened and shut the end door as if the hospital belonged to us.

It was easy to see where the fuss was concentrated. Thirty or forty women and a few men, mostly from Sulawesi, had taken off their shoes and were queuing to enter one of the long ward buildings. Some were carrying flowers or presents. A few covered their noses with a hand from time to time, as if holding down a shock. We took off our shoes and joined the queue. The crowd filed slowly in, and I could smell lint and disinfectant, a quickening, guilty smell. There were only low sounds in the ward: the slow chop of the fans, quiet talk, a couple of rhythmic voices—people saying prayers. The bare feet shuffled in, the new visitors were quiet.

We were stopped inside the door by an orderly. Did we have a relative there? I moved in on him gradually, saying how we were mission health workers who needed to assess the situation, dropping impressive-sounding evangelical names, the medical supplies that the hospital would need, authorisation from the Ministry of Health. Adrian slipped past with the crowd and was in among the beds. As I hedged and stopped the orderly from going for the phone—this was an urgent survey, didn't he understand?—I could see in glances to the side wounded people lying in bandages and shock. A man on drips was dying: his whole torso was bandaged up and he lay utterly still, his wife weeping on a chair beside him. A child, by his bloodless look and the way the bandages were laid, had almost lost his arm at the shoulder, and turned and blinked his huge round eyes in shock. A soldier was coming down from the far end of the ward towards us. I raised my voice with the orderly, as if I was having an argument. The soldier turned his oncoming gaze from Adrian towards me. Adrian slipped his small camera out of a pocket and, without focusing, took some shots from the waist.

All the while he was questioning, in a quiet way, a male visitor, a Sulawesi man, who was shocked into stiffened, one-sentence answers by what he had to tell.

The soldier stood with his hands on his hips and started to question me sharply. He could see I was bluffing, but he didn't know why. What exactly was the name of the mission? Who was it in the ministry I'd spoken to? I saw Adrian slip the camera back into his pocket and say his condolences to the Sulawesi man, who stared ahead as if he hadn't noticed he'd been speaking. Beyond him were men with bandages around their heads, a couple with bandaged wounds to their arms or legs, one I saw with a stump. Shock held them in common silence. I made my apologies to the soldier. Perhaps we had made a mistake and come to the wrong ward. We'd go back to reception and check up there. He said he'd escort us and he took us to see some senior doctor, whom we utterly confused with a tangle of conflicting claims and bad Indonesian: we said we'd come back later when instructions from the mission were a little clearer.

Adrian had got the whole story. There had been a massacre at Arso. At three o'clock in the afternoon of the day before, local people had run into the transmigration area occupied by people from Sulawesi. The Sulawesi people, all spontaneous migrants, who had bought plots unfilled by the Javanese, had been asleep or relaxing in their houses. The local people had machetes, and they hit out at anyone they came across, running from house to house. Thirteen of the Sulawesi people had been killed, fifteen badly wounded—some would die—and many others injured more lightly. The visitor's immediate fears were for two young girls carried away by the attackers. He guessed they would be hidden in the jungle, and had no idea what would happen to them. The people were certainly not the OPM. They were all Arso men, farming the oilpalm estate up the road.

We had no more business in Jayapura. I was tired of the toing and froing, the tales of death on both sides, the unpleasantness. It was time to start tying up our story; it had almost come to an end. I wanted more than ever to go home.

Chapter 13

Before we tied the final knots in the story of West Papua I wanted to go back to those first transmigration sites, to see if life was really as miserable there as we'd first reckoned. We'd promised the people of Erom that we, the consultants, would be back some day and, almost at the end of the trip, we could go there without fearing deportation by the people in Merauké. As the roads had flooded and the river had risen, we took the boat to Erom. We found that life had become if anything worse for the transmigrants, at the end of their first wet season in West Papua.

All the crops they'd planted had died, including the cocoa and coffee plants they'd just been sent from Flores the time we'd seen them last. Their health had become worse, as the rains had brought on epidemic malaria: two people had died and most of the rest had been laid low by it. The nearest health post, despite the regular government promises, was still in Merauké and, with not a penny left on the site for a boat trip, the only way to get there was to walk for two days: which was how one of the smitten people had died. There was still no sewerage system, which was why all the children on the site were suffering a vomiting disease when we saw them. The head of the unit, the Sulawesi man who'd put the wind up us the last time we were there, had fled the site and gone to live with his wife in Merauké; no one else was allowed to leave. With nobody to represent them, some of the Erom people had been down to the town to ask a Catholic missionary to complain about their lot to the head of the Merauké transmigration department. He did so, and the head replied: "Those Flores people are dangerous; dangerous people. You give them an inch and they'll take a mile." The same man, on the salary of a minor civil servant, had just thrown for his daughter the biggest wedding Merauké had ever known, and he was building himself a second house; which served to explain why some of the transmigrants' supplies had not been getting through to them. The people at Erom, which

220

was not, we subsequently heard, the worst site round Merauké, believed they were likely to starve, as there were just three more months before their food subsidy ran out. We were still the only 'consultants' to have visited them.

In 1988, as I had learnt in Jakarta, the transmigration budget had increased by fifty-six per cent, and the governor of Flores was sending more of his people over to West Papua as a mark of good-will. That was why the Flores people were having their letters home intercepted and destroyed by the transmigration department in Merauké: so that word about the state of the sites there could-n't get back to their island. More Javanese were due to come, too: the government had announced its intention of getting a further one hundred and seventy thousand transmigrants into West Papua over the next five years. The Javanese site just to the north of Erom, called Jagebob, had, after three years, simply folded. The soil had run out, the pests had exploded, and the angry locals, deprived of their lands, had started shooting the transmigrants with arrows. Jagebob, which had mostly emptied out, was reckoned to have had more potential than the places chosen for the migrations still to come. We could confidently conclude that transmigration round Merauké was no better than we'd pictured it.

So we could start to stick it all together and see what we came up with. The questions—about why transmigration was happening in West Papua—were ready at last to be answered, and I found as I put all that I had heard and seen and read together, that my con-clusions had begun to emerge unbidden: the whole story could now be told. The government claim that transmigration to West Papua was for the good of the transmigrants wasn't for the most part worth considering. Though places in the north were certainly better than some of the sites round Merauké, they had nearly all been filled up long before. Those that remained, the red-soil sites, would be the end of many of the settlers who reached them. There wasn't a lot of credence to be given to the claim that transmigra-tion was good for the people of West Papua either. It had taken away their lands, taken away their jobs, caused conflict and misery wherever it was imposed and provoked them in some places to attack the new settlers. So what was it for?

The story of West Papua was a simple one. In 1963 it was taken over through hard negotiation and dirty tricks at the United Nations. The Indonesians wanted it because it was good for defence and full of natural resources. The Papuans didn't want them there and resisted their rule, so the Indonesians hit them as ruthlessly as they knew how. They fixed the referendum the United Nations had demanded and started digging out the resistance by its roots. As the roots were cultural the government tried to destroy the cultural differences between the Papuans and the Indonesians. They tried simple elimination, by bombing and strafing problem areas; they thought of removing all the children and re-educating them, they forced people to destroy their houses and wear Indonesian clothes. Some of these projects worked well, some less so, none of them involved the whole of West Papua. Transmigration was simply the latest, most universal and most permanent scheme for wiping out the differences between Java and West Papua. If ever it had had finer purposes they'd been perverted long before.

Transmigration would give "birth to a new generation of people without curly hair, sowing the seeds for greater beauty" said Izaac Hindom, the governor of West Papua.

"The different ethnic groups will in the long run disappear because of integration . . . and there will be one kind of man," said Mr Martono, the Minister for Transmigration. We could have saved ourselves the bother of six months in Indonesia and taken those words on trust.

Transmigration was the final solution, to the problem of resistance. Rather than relying on the Papuans to change, according to the various civilising programmes designed for them, the government could fill up the island with Javanese instead and the changes would come about automatically. The Javanese, when they became the majority, would overwhelm the indigenous people. It would be easy to do, when they, the transmigrants, owned all the lands of the Papuans, had destroyed their houses, had become, through force of numbers, the cultural norm, when the army backed them up in all their Indonesian-ness. When there were four million Javanese in West Papua and just one million Papuans, surrounded and divided by great swathes of settlers, there would be no ethnic problem in West Papua. The Papuans would become in time like the North American Indians, a dying, disenfranchised race confined to the tiniest reservations of what was once their own land.

In the Asmat, transmigration had been planned because the people were proud of their culture, independent and different to anyone else on earth. That was a threat to the Indonesian hegemony, so it had to go. Transmigration was the way to do it, alongside the 'acculturation' quoted as a purpose of the programme, next door in the Mappi. In Arso the local people had become rebellious, so they had to be put down. Transmigration was the way to do it, keeping them out of the forests that harboured them, surrounding them with loyal citizens. Wherever there were rebels there was transmigration. Wherever there was a strong culture with, until then, the blissful exception of the central highlands, there was transmigration. Wherever it happened spontaneous migrants came in too, and that was part of the plan. It didn't matter that they came not from the overcrowded central islands but from places that were themselves considered underpopulated by the government; what mattered was that as many non-Papuans as possible got into West Papua. Wherever there was transmigration the local people would be resettled: in Indonesian villages, where they could live like the transmigrants around them.

There was no thought of the cost of transmigration: the government had decided what it wanted to do in West Papua and, in common with its other plans, like the communist massacre in Java, or the invasion of East Timor, it would do it whatever the human or financial expense. It didn't matter much that transmigrants were suffering, that the method the government had chosen was one of the longest and most agonising ways of achieving what it wanted. It was effective, it would keep itself going, it could be done without an international outcry, so that was what counted.

There were other government interests that transmigration served. Commerce in West Papua was to be built around it. The Papuans didn't want to work on projects that destroyed their own homes, like the logging in the Asmat, or gold mining around Senggo. Transmigration would provide a Javanese labour force to do what the indigenous people didn't want to, or to put pressure on the indigenous people to do it. Those precious resources that the government had tried to extract since 1963, the timber and the minerals, could now be shifted without resistance, and the companies there could employ the people they wanted to: decent Indonesians, not hostile Papuans.

In that way defence was also a function of transmigration. Indonesia was sensitive about all its borders, especially its Melanesian border with a Melanesian country, Papua New

Guinea. There was no way the Papuans would defend their province against an incursion from the east; in fact they'd welcome it and join the invaders to fight their overlords and enemies. A few million loyal Javanese could be all the disincentive required to keep a foreign power from treading on Indonesia's foot in the Pacific.

That is the domestic version, and the least sinister side of what was happening—is still happening—in West Papua. The Indonesians were not the only people who wanted transmigration to flourish. When we were in Merauké we went to see the white consultants, the real ones. We'd been invited round to their club for drinks, and perhaps I shouldn't be so liberal with their story, but what we came across ought to be told. They were Europeans, Americans and Canadians, fifteen of them, and they worked for a Canadian company, that was brought in by the World Bank to assist the transmigration programme in Merauké. The World Bank was the group set up by mostly western nations to help countries with their reconstruction, development projects and economic management. It had added six hundred million dollars to the seven and a half billion that the government had spent on transmigration, and had sent out those consultants and others to survey and select the places for transmigrants to move into.

With two exceptions the consultants seemed not to be interested in the effects of what they were doing. The firm the World Bank had used before had packed up when half of its employees had resigned, disgusted by their work. The people we met, who had replaced them, were hardened and insouciant. On forty-five thousand dollars a year and all living expenses, they could afford to be, and to ignore the sight of ex-transmigrants filling that town with their pathetic attempts to keep themselves alive. Transmigration they said was just fine; the Papuans needed a kick up the pants because they were lazy and non-commercial; West Papua was a goldmine and it was in everyone's interests that it be exploited as quickly as possible.

Something they hadn't been allowed to ignore was the fuss that human rights groups had whipped up about the World Bank. In 1986 bodies like Survival International, Friends of the Earth and Tapol—the Indonesian human rights campaign—got together to show that the Bank was actively promoting one of the most destructive and inhumane projects that had ever been devised. The

Bank defended itself fiercely at first, then saw it was digging itself deeper into a hole, so it pulled itself out. It promised to rehabilitate some of the worst sites in West Papua and try to improve the lot of transmigrants approaching starvation. As the consultants knew all too well there was precious little they could do about the worst places, as there was simply nothing there to work on: no soil, no water, no weather, no infrastructure. It didn't help that they'd never been to quite a few of them, like Erom. Rehabilitation was what they'd been told to do, however, and in places with specific problems—like water contamination or insect attack—they could help to keep the settlers from the brink. At the same time, though, they would oversee the introduction of more and more transmigrants, to less and less suitable sites. But the big question we had researched—at home and in Jakarta and Jayapura—was why the World Bank had been funding transmigration in the first place.

The answer was that the Americans wanted it to happen, as it suited their interests in Indonesia. Those interests were substantial: the Straits of Malacca, between Sumatra and Singapore, were among the most strategic shipping lanes in the world, used by the US Seventh Fleet and a high proportion of America's freighters and supertankers. Indonesia, since the outbreak of the Vietnam War, had been either the greatest hope or the greatest threat in South East Asia, depending on whether the United States could persuade it to stay with them. It was a likely second site for the US Asian bases, if they got thrown out of the Philippines in 1991.

With powerful commercial interests in Indonesia as well—oil, gold, timber—it was very much in the United States's interest to maintain the status quo there. It is possible that the CIA assisted the attempted coup in 1965 that led eventually to the downfall of the left-leaning Sukarno, and the massacre of half a million communists in Java. There's no doubt that the next president, Suharto, came into power with the blessing of the US, and had stayed there with their help. He had been the Pentagon's ideal president: paranoid about communism, dependent on western finance and influential among other Asian leaders. The better Suharto strengthened his position and the more effectively his power was spread through the archipelago, the better it would be for the United States. Transmigration ensured that Suharto controlled West Papua in more than just name; that the resources of the province were extractable, and so available for allies like the United States; that the right-leaning government had influence spreading as far as the South Pacific.

The United States could make sure that the World Bank helped transmigration to happen because it had a twenty-per-cent stake in the Bank, far higher than that of any other country. The World Bank was based in Washington and run by a former Republican Congressman. It was effectively true that nothing the United States wanted the World Bank to do could be blocked. The other countries—Japan, Great Britain, West Germany, France—that subscribed to the Bank followed the States and ensured that transmigration was blessed and funded from abroad.

Other foreign interests had made the situation in Papua substantially worse. Indonesia was a huge arms market, and sophisticated weapons it had bought from the west had added tangibly to the miseries of the Papuans. The planes which bombed the Dani villages were American Bronco jets and the pilots who flew them were most probably trained by the British instructors in Java. The helicopters tribal leaders were dropped from, and which were used to strafe rebellious villages, were American, French and German; the vehicles and small arms the soldiers in Papua used came from Britain and America. The western countries argued that if they didn't supply the weaponry another country would, but they provided loans to help the Indonesians buy arms otherwise too expensive for them, and they served, by selling counter-insurgency weapons, to condone Indonesia's role in its provincial conflicts.

The United States gave Indonesia forty-two million dollars of military aid in 1985, which enabled it to buy its F-16 jets. To fix other arms deals the US had effectively given the country armoured cars, artillery pieces and boats. Australia had given patrol boats, and its airforce produced those maps of ours for the benefit of the Indonesian forces; European foreign aid donations such as prefabricated bridges and marine navigation equipment could, though designed for civilian use, free substantial military expenditure for other purposes. Britain was trying to sell light tanks and ground-attack aircraft: already British Aerospace's Hawk jets were flying in Indonesian squadrons. The armoured cars operating in Papua were re-equipped by the British company GKL, to make them more effective against rebels, or insurgents, or villagers. The planes used to carry transmigrants to West Papua were American

Lockheed Hercules. Doubtless transmigration, bombing, strafing and the torture of dissidents could carry on without western help; but it could be of no disadvantage to Indonesia to share the blame.

Other companies of course were taking resources out. The huge copper mine on Mount Ertsberg, in the western mountains, was run by the US Freeport Sulphur Company. The mine took up ten thousand hectares of tribal land and there was little compensation paid to the people who owned it. Because of that the people there rebelled, and with stolen dynamite blew up the pipeline carrying the copper ore to the coast. Villages were then strafed by the Indonesian army from helicopter gunships and bombed by Broncos; to intimidate the population girls were raped, then killed, slowly, by having sticks thrust up their backsides; soldiers took photographs of each other posing with their feet on the heads of the villagers they'd shot. American employees at the mine were well aware of what was happening, and seemed to regard it as entertainment. An Australian pilot wrote that he arrived at the mining town to be told "You're just in time to see a bunch of coons get their arses blown off". Indonesian jets were taking off for a strafing raid of the surrounding villages. They blitzed the homes of a thousand people; no one knew how many were killed. An American minerals company, as well as prospecting for oil in the Asmat, had been looking for a glue to make plywood from the timber being cut there. It was said to be experimenting with the pith of the sago palm, the staple food of the Asmat; who owned every tree that grew there.

From all I have heard the situation in West Papua is now as serious as it was when Adrian and I were there, and there are suggestions that in some respects it is worse. The motives of the Indonesian government, and of the western countries supporting transmigration there have shown no signs of changing: the evils of West Papua are persistent. The Papuans could be forgiven for thinking that all the world's learning, its technology and finance, had the single purpose of making their lives as terrible as possible.

As if we needed a reminder that those white consultants had misjudged the Papuans, we stumbled across, in the same Merauké region, an indigenous development project. A few miles up the river was a village of people who had lost their jobs in the town, when the transmigrants had displaced them. They had moved back

227

to their tribal lands but found there was nothing for them, as their forests, and therefore the sago and game, had mostly gone. With help from a qualified local man they'd found the one fertile patch of soil in their territory—a strip of about half a mile along the riverbank—and had started growing cash crops there. As they were close to the river they could keep them irrigated, and when we got there every garden had fruit trees growing, or coffee or cashew-nut plants. Several men ran a coconut plantation together, and rubber had just been put in. They were making money and everyone seemed excited about it. We were led round by a little man who kept shouting and jumping in the air and calling his friends over to see, and other people tried to drag us off to take a look at their gardens.

They found a gap in that impossibly crowded market, by growing crops that the transmigrants, on their infertile earth, could not. They'd widened it by getting to know the middlemen in Merauké and keeping them informed about what crops were coming and how much to expect. The man behind them was a genius called Bas Minggu. He was a Marind—an indigenous Merauké man—who, despite all that ran against him, had got a scholarship to study agriculture in a Javanese college. He'd returned to help pull his people out of their mess, and had persuaded the Canadian and New Zealand embassies to put up the money he needed. With thirty dollars for each family—one four-hundredth of the cost of resettling transmigrants—he had reversed the decline of three thousand Marind.

We met him in his workshop, where he was teaching people to undercut Merauké's imports. They were making chairs from local wood, solid ones that sold for a little under three pounds. One chair a day, with a minimal materials cost, was a good wage for a Merauké man, and still less than half the price of the chairs brought in from Jakarta. Outside were women preparing sago. Instead of the little adzes they normally used they were mashing it up with a huge grater, an invention of Bas's. It was strikingly simple: a plank with a handle at each end, and about a hundred nails sticking out of the middle. Two women pulled it back and forth, and found that it cut the time it took to process sago down to one third. That left them freer to get on with other things, like educating their children or helping the men to make money. Money had suddenly become essential to the Papuans, if they were to survive the assault of all that was happening to them. Without forests to feed them they would have to buy food, and they would have to learn to beat the migrants with their own stick.

It wasn't easy, Bas said, for the Marind to adjust to structured work. They still had a subsistence view of life, and found it hard to see the value of investment. Sometimes the projects misfired, and he would find that villagers were using their coconut plantations to make palm toddy, or letting some of their fruit trees go to rot when they were making enough money to live on. But on the whole the projects had brought back something that had been battered out of the people there. Pride was what we saw in the development village, and we hadn't come across it since the Dani, the one group of people who'd been able to stay the way they were. The effort, said Bas, was not to give them fish, but to give them fish hooks, and show them how to use them, so that the fish would be their own achievement. When people grasped what he was trying to do they went for it wildly, and they had mostly been successful. There were another eighteen hundred people round Merauké being helped by a group a Catholic missionary ran. It had similar objectives to Bas's, buying fruit trees for the villagers and helping them to market what they grew. With no government help, no technology and very little money, the two foundations had improved the lives of thirty per cent of the local Merauké people.

It was clearly not development itself that was blighting the Papuans; but development of the sort that favoured one group—the Indonesians—at the great and deliberate expense of the other. The Papuans could cope, despite all that was stacked against them by the government, with development that was sensitive and gradual, and designed to help them, not to destroy them. If the government had spent a fraction of its transmigration money, that seven and a half billion dollars, on assisting the gentle development of the Papuans, they might willingly have jumped at the chance to change.

In parts of West Papua where there weren't people like Bas and the Catholic missionary the inhabitants had chosen solutions of their own, which worked less well. The OPM was an extra problem for the Papuans, not a solution, and everything it did backfired on its own people. There was never a chance that Indonesia would relinquish West Papua, and attempts to pursue that as a solution all ended in tears. Something, we saw in 1988, needed to be done from the outside, however, quickly and effectively. The Papuans were running out of time. They were losing their livelihood and their identities, with nothing to replace them. Groups like Bas's were far between and underfunded, and reached just a tiny proportion of the people. A solution was needed that covered the whole of West Papua, before the indigenous people there became another colonial tragedy. I reckoned there was one place it could come from, and that was where the problem had started: the United Nations.

Indonesia was entirely dependent on foreign help. The thirteen developed countries which financed the nation supplied in 1988 half of its development budget, $5.7 billion for that year alone. Of that, $1.5 billion was special assistance, to get Indonesia out of the economic mess the oil prices and corruption had landed it in. Those countries, like Japan, the United States, Britain, Australia, Canada, Holland, France and West Germany, were, for long-term financial reasons, keeping Indonesia afloat. There was no need for them to do so unconditionally. The World Bank had already been imposing conditions on a loan it had made to help Indonesia restructure its economy. It demanded that, in return for the loan, Indonesia should start liberalising its big corrupt industries. There was no reason why similar, but humanitarian, conditions shouldn't be put on the money lent by those western countries. The conditions, I felt, should involve the repositioning of UN observers in West Papua.

They had been there before the Act of Free Choice in 1969, until which Indonesia theoretically had only partial rights to West Papua. That team had been entirely ineffective and had ensured, for its own purposes, that it saw nothing which might reflect badly on the Indonesians. There was good reason though to feel that a new team, with the backing of the countries that kept Indonesia solvent, would have teeth. The western countries could insist that they would make no further loans to Indonesia unless it allowed UN observers into Papua, and let them travel freely and report on what they saw. If the atrocities were still going on after the UN observers arrived, and the observers were constrained to report them, those benefactor countries could shut down some of the money they were giving, and that could cripple Indonesia. The Indonesian government would be forced to see that its own welfare depended on the welfare of the Papuans.

As well as stopping some of the things it was doing in West Papua, the government could be forced to put money into development for the genuine good of the Papuans. There were lots of possible industries that would give the people the choice of retaining their culture and making money at the same time. The sensitive management of tourism was one possibility; networks for selling forest products that could be harvested without destruction another; carvings, stone tools, bows and arrows could be made as ethnic ornaments for the West; cash crops could be developed on pockets of fertile land. While the Papuans could decide how they would like to be, to dress, to live, to eat, they would get the chance to compete with the rest of the world, on equal terms, not as inferior and disadvantaged citizens. All that would happen, quite simply, if enough people in the nations which gave money to Indonesia lobbied their governments and UN representatives.

As for troubles in Java, there were already some solutions to those, and none of them involved transmigration. The World Bank in its other role—as the reshaper of developing nations' economies—with some persuasive government ministers, was disbanding a few of the vast, corrupt monopolies that had crippled Indonesia's growth. The new labour pool in the Javanese countryside could be partly mopped up, and the migration to the cities stopped, by restructuring the island's economy. Giant industries in the cities, many of them controlled by government ministers or generals, which often lost millions through corruption and inefficiency, could be broken down and spread. Things the countryside produced could be processed in the villages—coffee beans turned into coffee, maize into flour—rather than exported raw and almost valueless. Local needs could be locally fulfilled. Already in Java, as we had seen, there were little tile-making sheds and brick-kilns, smithies for agricultural tools, furniture workshops, springing up in some parts of the countryside. They were beginning to supply the people of their regions with things they had imported from abroad, or from the big factories in the cities, which cost more money and employed fewer people.

In the countryside too people could produce more exports, as well as substituting imports. Pepper was one of the few commodities which had held a good price, and a quarter of a hectare could keep a family alive. Market gardening too, and fishponds, made far more money than rice did, and in tidal areas shrimps could thrust a peasant firmly into the merchant class with just half a hectare of ponds. Those things were happening in some places. They were too slow to help a lot of the unofficial people in Java, and they were held up by corrupt interests, but in that sort of economic restructuring lay the solutions to a great deal of Java's ills. There was a long way to go, a lot of training needed, but the principles were sound. Birth control, too, was gaining momentum: where the people were allowed to decide about it for themselves it was working well. Of all the solutions the government could choose, transmigration was the least appropriate and the least necessary. It did little to relieve the crowding in Java and, but for those in places like south Sumatra, caused nothing but trouble for the people who were moved.

Chapter 14

Back in Jayapura, before we went home, we found out what had happened to the two girls the Arso villagers had kidnapped during the massacre. The raiding party had fled with its hostages towards Papua New Guinea. They crossed the border just as a posse of soldiers caught up with them. As the soldiers had crossed the border without permission there was nearly a shoot-out between them and the Papuan army, which was averted when the Papuans persuaded the villagers to hand over the two girls, who went home with the soldiers. The Arso troubles didn't end there, however, for a local OPM faction had falsely claimed responsibility for the attack, and said it had killed one hundred and fifty of the Sulawesi migrants, a boast that corresponded badly to the fact that most of them were still walking around. In response the Indonesian government put pressure on the Papuans to empty the big refugee camps in the north of PNG, that were said to be rebel strongholds, and send the occupants to a resettlement site one hundred kilometres from the border.

The rebels had gone from Jayapura. There had been some arrests and the others had fled, and when we went round to the Pakistaniman's house we found it was empty. There was nothing more to be done in Papua, and it was time to go home. Our plane wasn't due for a few days, however, and we had just enough money to go back to the Baliem Valley, for our last look ever before we were blacklisted. We bought tickets to Wamena, and just before we went we called on an expatriate friend in town to say goodbye. We chatted about home and the relief of going back, but when we told him our immediate plans he mentioned the new directives that the government had issued. Transmigrants had been kept away from Papua's central mountains until then, but the Ministry had just announced that the first settlers were due to go. No one knew where they'd be put, but our friend guessed that the Baliem Valley was the only place big enough to suit the scale of transmigration. It didn't really sink in at the time.

The police didn't recognise us in Wamena, which was a relief, and a friendly sergeant we met put us up in some empty barracks for the night. We separated to wander round town, and as I went into the marketplace I met Suleman, leaning on the outside of a stall. We were delighted to see each other, and I bought him several beers in a stall by the road, as he seemed again to have forgotten he was a Muslim. He told me that the police had gone loopy in Wamena after we'd got out, and an officer had been sent over from Jayapura to give them a dressing down. Suleman himself, as no more than our hired man, wasn't troubled, and the fuss had mostly died away by the time he got back to the town. I tried not to believe Suleman when he told me that he and Arkilaus had run all the way from Mbua, and made it to Wamena in two days and a night.

Adrian and I each wanted to be alone for our last two days in Papua, as we had plenty to reflect on. He walked off east and I headed south, down the valley. Where, after a few rutted miles, the road ended, I set off along a sandy track, feeling a bit disoriented in the mountain air. The fields were full of wild gladioli, sticking out like pennants above the ranks of fallow grass. As I passed the beehive compounds villagers came to meet me, and took my hands, saying "*nayak, wa, wa, nayak*" or "*la-ok, la-ok*", and one old woman tugged my hair. I responded half-heartedly, for I wasn't all there. I found myself confused and, after a while, among those clear blue mountains, in the sharp air, I sat down beside the path to try to sort it out.

The trip was over, thank God and Allah and the ancestors. We had not been shot, or tortured or imprisoned, and I was going to see my girlfriend again. Yet, even through my relief, I felt no satisfaction over that. Though we had mostly got the story, and determined that there was something very wrong with transmigration, and something very wrong with West Papua, we had found that there were no easy answers, no edicts written on the sky in black. While much of what I'd seen was in all ways wrong, for other things there were many different truths: the government's truth, the transmigrant's truth, the local people's truth, my truth. Enlightenment had struck me down, and led me into darkness.

I'd seen too that there were no short answers to my own frustrations. My search for something more real than my job in London had led me round full circle to see that there were indeed no end points. I had ditched the troubles of regular work and taken on a whole fresh set, from which loneliness and anger would never be far removed. I was angry about myself, my inability, like the Papuans with their cargo cults to find the key, and I was angry about the issue, in a way I'd never been about something that wasn't my concern before. It was no longer the righteous indignation of the middle-class journalist at home, that was enlivening and satisfying to feel; but it was something dull and grinding and ineradicable, as if it was my life that those issues in Indonesia oppressed. There was, too, one more frustration, that I hadn't before been able to explain to myself. Indonesia had lost its enchantment, and become dark and inimical to me. I would never be allowed back, and I imagined then that I would never want to return. I lay back, among the yellow sedges and the wild gladioli; then I suddenly felt the pettiness of my own frustrations. The career dissatisfaction of a journalist: I held them up against the life or death of tribes, of people just as real, just as valid as Adrian and myself. I stood up again and began to walk.

War was brewing. Men around the gardens were getting ready for it, standing sentry with long spears and painted faces. It was likely to happen that day, for the alliance I was passing through had quarrelled with its neighbours and thrown them a challenge. I hung about but no one would tell me where the battle was to be, though I was sure they knew. There was a chance that even then the two sides were meeting in their finery, with head-dresses made from birds of paradise, tusks through their noses and wands of cockatoo feathers for taunting the enemy. Dani battles were about the only sort of serious warfare that seldom led to injury. The Dani were such hopeless shots that they could spend a whole day firing arrows at each other without hitting anyone. If someone was killed the battle would end, as the other side would run off to celebrate its feat. Normally, however, the warriors got bored of fighting halfway through and would start firing insults at each other instead. As the Dani were brilliant punners, a good jibe could get everyone laughing, and the whole thing could break down into a sort of armed party, with people crossing the battle-lines to meet old friends from the other war alliance. By all accounts such formal wars had less to do with winning than with putting on a show to please the ancestors. Like earthquakes, battles were said to be good for the sweet potatoes.

I missed the war but Adrian chanced upon it when it happened. He got to the battlezone just in time to see the combatants assembling, excited and dressed in the most stupendous costumes. They were just about to start when a platoon of armed police ran over the hill and broke them up with submachine guns. The Dani were solemnly escorted back to their villages. They were furious.

Before long my path reached a raw rocky gorge, cut by the Yetni River as it had broken down from the mountains to join the Baliem. I'd been told by the warriors that heavy rains had swelled the river and it was almost impossible to cross. From above it looked slight enough to jump, so I slid down the wall of the gorge to take a look. The Yetni was actually about ten yards wide, and fearsome. The grey water spat, flinging gravel up against the rocks. I tried to step into it in several places, but my legs were lifted off and I couldn't reach the boulders in the middle. I paced up and down looking for a route, then I heard a whistle from the farther cliff. A man was running down towards me with a digging stick. He was old and grey, but he pole-vaulted from his bank on to a rock in midstream. Then he set the stick against another boulder, and bounced across until he could reach my arm. He gave me a ferocious yank, and landed me on the rock beside him. Then, bracing himself with the pole, he shoved me hard at the other bank, so that I flew over and hit the boulder in midstream, from which I could wade and jump across. On the bank the old man cadged a cigarette, then wandered back on to his path. Later I heard that someone else had tried to cross the Yetni in the morning. A boulder had knocked his legs from under him and he was swept into the Baliem and drowned.

In the afternoon, when it began to rain, I walked down to a compound beside the big river. It was a cluster of round huts and two long haystack houses, ringed with a drystone wall and reached by different hurdles and passages, to keep people or pigs or spirits variously in or out. Two young men were training their vegetables on trellises, wearing seed headbands and necklaces of beads and pigs' bristles. One of them spoke Indonesian, and he seemed delighted when I asked if I could stop there for the night. He fussed around me in the men's hut, drawing up bundles of grass to make a bed and stoking the homely fire. Hanging from the pillars around the fireplace were several marsupial skulls. They were just old hunting trophies; though in some places, I'd heard, marsupial jawbones were used to magic back runaway wives. I sat in the hut while the men got back to their gardening. It felt like Christmas, with the fire glowing while the air became cold outside.

Other men came into the hut, and *wa-wa*ed in astonishment when they saw me. Two old ones kept hugging me, either as the warmest welcome or to be certain that I was real. I felt a great assurance sitting there, as if, in that smoky hut beside the Baliem River, I was home already. When everyone had turned up and the sweet potatoes had been cooked, a couple of men each produced a little bamboo mouth harp. They grasped the twangy bits with their teeth, and tugged a string to make them vibrate. The harps had a scale of two notes each, a repetitive 'dwang, dwong'; but the Dani were entranced. They started to sway from side to side, and an old man began to murmur, deep and prayer-like over the twanging of the harps. Two youths added their voices and lifted them slowly up in counterpoint, until they struck out into a full and fluent descant. Then everyone else joined in, and it was precise and resonant, each man working along his own level. It stopped dead, on the beat, then the old man jumped suddenly into another tune, a dance song, harsh and rapid, getting faster and more exciting as the others joined in, conducting fiercely with their hands. There must have been some signal from the leader that I didn't see, for they fell dead quiet at an arbitrary point, an impressive and unsettling effect. They started again, and they were still at it when I fell asleep.

In the morning two men were having an argument. I took them to be father and son, and the young one kept taking different penis gourds down from where they hung in the back of the hut and trying them on. The old man kept shaking his head and putting them back. He seemed mortified by the young man's taste: curly gourds were obviously indecent, and he couldn't allow his son to be seen in public with one. Before I left, the man who spoke Indonesian removed the bracelets—of woven grasses and orchid roots—he had worn round his upper arm. He put them on my own arms, then filled my bag with sweet potatoes, hugging me

237

with warmth before I walked out into the mist. The sun had just risen on my last day in West Papua, and I suddenly felt sad, and sick at the thought of going home. I set out to return to Wamena by a different route, over a hill that jutted out from the mountain wall. I climbed up slowly, then, halfway to the top, I sat down sharply in the grass, overcome by a sadness I couldn't quite place. An old woman waddled past me, peering up from under an enormous bag of leaves.

I could see, from my seat in the long grass of the hillside, most of the Baliem Valley. Far away Wamena glittered in the rising sun. Just beneath me, on the lower slopes of the hill, was a Dani compound, surrounded by the long tin roofs of a police post and a school. It seemed to me like all of West Papua. I had been sitting there for half an hour when I noticed there was someone standing beside me. He was about fourteen, a strange-looking, dirty boy, with a net bag on his shoulder and torn shorts. He was on his way to the school beneath us, but he sat down in the grass and asked for a cigarette. Without prompting he began to talk about the Indonesians, and the troubles they were causing in the valley. His father had been bullied by Javanese traders, but he couldn't fight back as he'd be beaten by the police. The boy's friend had been tied up and thrown by soldiers into the Baliem River: there was no profit in causing a fuss. It was, he said, past time for independence. Only then did I realise what was coming to him instead.

Transmigration was coming to the mountains. It would pull the people apart. Already the highland valleys had become overcrowded, as land was taken by spontaneous migrants, and more of the Dani children were surviving. There were no resources to share with new settlers, so the Dani would have to go. Their compounds would be burnt and their pigs despatched, and the people would either fight and be eliminated, or yield and become the listless and blasted people I had seen elsewhere. Transmigration would be their end.

I had become involved. I couldn't go back and imagine I had seen some distant issue that was not my own concern. It hurt me too. I turned to the boy to speak but he had gone. I could see him tripping slowly down the hillside to the school, in grubby shorts, with a cigarette, the last Dani I would ever meet. The sun touched the roof of the police post and glinted back at me. Something would have to be done.